US-China Rivalry and Taiwan's Mainland Policy

Dean P. Chen

US-China Rivalry and Taiwan's Mainland Policy

Security, Nationalism, and the 1992 Consensus

Dean P. Chen
Political Science
Ramapo College of New Jersey
Mahwah, New Jersey, USA

ISBN 978-3-319-83778-9   ISBN 978-3-319-47599-8 (eBook)
DOI 10.1007/978-3-319-47599-8

© The Editor(s) (if applicable) and The Author(s) 2017
Softcover reprint of the hardcover 1st edition 2017
This work is subject to copyright. All rights are solely and exclusively licensed by the Publisher, whether the whole or part of the material is concerned, specifically the rights of translation, reprinting, reuse of illustrations, recitation, broadcasting, reproduction on microfilms or in any other physical way, and transmission or information storage and retrieval, electronic adaptation, computer software, or by similar or dissimilar methodology now known or hereafter developed.
The use of general descriptive names, registered names, trademarks, service marks, etc. in this publication does not imply, even in the absence of a specific statement, that such names are exempt from the relevant protective laws and regulations and therefore free for general use.
The publisher, the authors and the editors are safe to assume that the advice and information in this book are believed to be true and accurate at the date of publication. Neither the publisher nor the authors or the editors give a warranty, express or implied, with respect to the material contained herein or for any errors or omissions that may have been made. The publisher remains neutral with regard to jurisdictional claims in published maps and institutional affiliations.

Cover illustration: © Jeremy Woodhouse / DigitalVision, Getty

Printed on acid-free paper

This Palgrave Macmillan imprint is published by Springer Nature
The registered company is Springer International Publishing AG
The registered company address is: Gewerbestrasse 11, 6330 Cham, Switzerland

PREFACE

Notwithstanding its close economic interdependence with Taiwan (also known as the Republic of China or ROC), the People's Republic of China (PRC) has posed serious security challenges to the former. Indeed, while proclaiming "peaceful unification" as its objective in dealing with Taiwan since January 1979,[1] the PRC has never renounced the use of military force to prevent the island's independence or coerce unification. Beijing has "drawn on its burgeoning economic resources to invest in its military capabilities, deploying advanced fighters and medium range ballistic missiles, more than a thousand of which are aimed at Taiwan."[2] Hence, my central query in this book is why the Kuomintang (KMT) administration under the former ROC president Ma Ying-jeou, from 2008 to 2016, pursued an under-balancing strategy toward the PRC, even sometimes alienating the United States.

---

[1] Nancy Tucker, *Strait Talk* (Cambridge, MA: Harvard University Press, 2009), pp. 139–140; Shelley Rigger, "Taiwan in U.S.-China Relations," in David Shambaugh, ed., *Tangled Titans* (Lanham, MD: Rowman & Littlefield, 2013), p. 294.

[2] Shirley Lin, *Taiwan's China Dilemma* (Stanford, CA: Stanford University Press, 2016), p. 1.

THE QUESTION

The obvious reasons seem to be the increasing reliance of Taiwan's economic well-being on trade with and investments in mainland China,[3] as well as the latter's greater diplomatic, economic, and military clout in international relations.[4] For neorealists like Kenneth Waltz and Stephen Walt, a state will balance against or bandwagon with the external threat based on the international systemic constraints it faces[5] or the perceived intention, offensive military capabilities, and proximity of that foreign power.[6] Therefore, in light of Taiwan's relatively weaker international position vis-à-vis the PRC, the KMT's accommodation toward Beijing may be the correct course of action. Vulnerable states, in order to reap security and economic gains, may choose to "under-balance" the stronger side, which may include mechanisms such as buck-passing, distancing, binding engagement, appeasement, bandwagoning, and other half or mixed measures.[7] However, there are two pitfalls to this observation. First, the growth of Taiwan's economic attachments to China began in the early 1990s and even accelerated during the years of the Democratic Progressive Party (DPP) president Chen Shui-bian from 2000 to 2008. Shirley Lin posits,

> Economic interdependence with China has become unavoidable if Taiwan wishes to continue to reap the benefit of a growing global economy. China's economic opening has restructured the regional and global economies; it has become the "factory of the world" and, importantly, one of the world's largest consumer markets. China has become an integral part of the global supply chain and the most important economic engine for Asia and the world. Therefore, Taiwan has very few alternatives if it wishes to diversify its outbound investments and trade flows away from China in order to hedge against economic and political risks. Taiwan's main competitors, from

---

[3] Lowell Dittmer, "Taiwan's Narrowing Strait," in Peter Chow ed., *The U.S. Strategic Pivot to Asia and Cross-Strait Relations* (New York: Palgrave Macmillan, 2014), pp. 15–16; Shirley Lin, pp. 4–10.

[4] Thomas Christensen, *The China Challenge* (New York: W. W. Norton, 2015), Chapter 1.

[5] Kenneth Waltz, *The Theory of International Politics* (New York: McGraw Hill, 1979), pp. 124–128.

[6] Stephen Walt, *The Origins of Alliances* (Ithaca, NY: Cornell University Press, 1987), pp. 28–33.

[7] Randall Schweller, "Managing the Rise of Great Powers," in Alastair Johnston and Robert Ross, eds., *Engaging China* (New York: Routledge, 1999), pp. 10–17.

Korea and Japan to Thailand and Indonesia, have all become dependent on investment in and trading with China. As an economy dependent on trade, which represents more than 100 percent of its GDP, Taiwan cannot be an exception.[8]

However, Chen took up a more restrictive and unfriendly policy toward Beijing.[9] While continuing to advocate for economic cooperation with mainland China, the current DPP president Tsai Ing-wen, who was inaugurated as the ROC's 14th president on May 20, 2016, has pushed for a cooler cross-strait policy stance than her KMT predecessor. Thus, striving for intimate commercial ties with the PRC does not consistently lead to amicable cross-strait political relationships. Second, although it has had no formal diplomatic relations with Taipei since its recognition of Beijing in 1979, in accordance with the "one-China" policy, the United States has committed to Taiwan's security, freedom, and democracy, as enshrined by Washington's Taiwan Relations Act (TRA) and President Ronald Reagan's "Six Assurances."[10] Consequently, though unsupportive of Taiwan's independence, America also seeks to deter the PRC's military aggression against the island and insists that cross-strait impasse must be resolved peacefully and with the consent of the Taiwanese people.[11] One scholar aptly describes Taiwan's importance to America's liberal ethos: "The U.S. would not risk its own security in the protection of any small islands a third of the way around the world, but it does so for one which constitutes an extension of democratic American identity on the doorstep of a large communist neighbour."[12] Moreover, as Washington has promoted its "rebalance to Asia" to check against Beijing's rising power, America's continued support for the ROC is a bellwether for US commitment to the Asia-Pacific region. Taiwan, in other words, is not "left out alone" in its strategic dealing with China, and, as a result, Ma's underbalancing is not an inevitable solution.

---

[8] Shirley Lin 2016, p. 8.
[9] Ibid., 160. See also Scott Kastner, *Political Conflict and Economic Interdependence across the Taiwan Strait and Beyond* (Stanford, CA: Stanford University Press, 2009), pp. 35–36.
[10] Alan Romberg, *Rein In at the Brink of the Precipice* (Washington, DC: Henry Stimson Center, 2003); Richard Bush, *At Cross Purposes* (Armonk, NY: M.E. Sharpe 2004).
[11] Wang Chi, *Obama's Challenge to China* (Burlington, VT: Ashgate, 2015), pp. 198–199.
[12] Oliver Turner, "The U.S. and China: Obama's Cautious Engagement," in Michelle Bentley and Jack Holland eds., *The Obama Doctrine* (New York: Routledge, 2017), p. 184.

The Theoretical Arguments

This work aims to make the following arguments. A neoclassical realist theory not only looks at the overarching distribution of power among states, which serves as the permissive/restrictive perimeter on how each individual state can behave, but also takes into consideration the "intervening" or "filtering effect" of unit-level variables (or *Innenpolitik*)—state–society relations, regime types, domestic institutions, leaders' perceptions, and strategic culture—that ultimately shape the contours and attributes of the chosen policy.[13] Taiwan's external systemic circumstances (i.e., security dependency on Washington) certainly limit its choice of alignment policy with respect to mainland China. On the one hand, through its strategic ambiguity policy, the United States merely acknowledges Beijing's "one-China" principle but refrains from recognizing it and insists that cross-strait differences must be resolved peacefully and consensually, hence allowing Washington's unofficial ties with Taipei to remain intact. On the other hand, America also deters Taiwan from declaring de jure independence, lest such a move would unnecessarily provoke the mainland and plunge the region into catastrophic military confrontation. US officials noted that the TRA did not automatically guarantee America's involvement in a cross-strait contention, especially one that was unilaterally triggered by Taipei. A free, democratic, and moderate Taiwan is essential to cross-strait peace and stability and, therefore, amenable to American national interests.[14] Consequently, both Presidents Ma and Tsai have assured Washington, respectively, that their administrations would seek to maintain "cross-strait status quo" and not to unilaterally jeopardize peaceful relations with Beijing.

However, there are also distinctive variations between Ma's and Tsai's "status quo." President Ma's cross-strait position was predicated upon the clear acceptance of the "1992 consensus," stipulating that both Taiwan and the mainland belong to a "one China" even though each side has retained different interpretations of what that China means. The KMT has dubbed this arrangement as "one China, respective interpretations". For the Chinese Communist Party (CCP), "one China" means the PRC, whereas the KMT has defined it as the ROC, founded in 1912, whose

---

[13] Norrin Ripsman et al., *Neoclassical Realist Theory of International Politics* (New York: Oxford University Press, 2016), pp. 141–143.
[14] Christensen, 2015, pp. 214–215.

legitimacy as China's central government has never ceased to exist in spite of its retreat to Taiwan after 1949. On the contrary, President Tsai Ing-wen, though acknowledging the "historical fact of the 1992 talks," has refrained from recognizing the "1992 consensus" and its underlying "one-China" principle, to the chagrin of Beijing leadership. While not embracing confrontation with the PRC, Tsai seems to uphold a mild or "soft balancing" approach to resist Beijing's pressure. This discrepancy and, in particular, Ma's policy stance are better explained by the elite or partisan fragmentation within Taiwan, which is manifested in the polarized national visions of the KMT and DPP. Though the KMT subscribes to a Chinese nationalistic identity, the DPP sees Taiwan as separate and different from mainland China.[15] Because Ma's two predecessors—Lee Teng-hui and Chen Shui-bian—championed a series of Taiwanization or nativization (*bentuhua*) and de-Sinification (*qu zhongguo hua*) campaigns to weaken the historical, cultural, and political bonds between Taiwan and China, the KMT president aimed to rectify them through several nation-building initiatives to reconstruct the centrality of the ROC, the legitimate "one China," which has sovereignty over both Taiwan and mainland territories. As Chu Yunhan succinctly put it,

> Taiwanese nationalists advocate a separate Taiwanese national identity and seek permanent separation from China, while Chinese nationalists oppose movement toward Taiwan independence and favor eventual reunification with China. In the end, the state became the arena. The competing forces strove to gain control of the governing apparatus and use its power to steer cross-strait relations, erect a distinct cultural hegemony, and impose their own vision of nation-building, either in the direction of Taiwanization or Sinicization.[16]

Yet, where do these divergent national identities and orientations come from? Shelley Rigger has noted that "the origin of today's 'Taiwan problem' lies in the Chinese civil war … Taiwan's position in Sino-American relations has changed over the decades since the PRC was founded, but it has remained a central concern."[17] Hence, even though Taiwan's changing

---

[15] David Gitter and Robert Sutter, "Taiwan's Strong but Stifled Foundations of National Power," *The NBR Special Report* 54 (2016), p. 16.

[16] Chu Yunhan, "Taiwan's National Identity Politics and the Prospect of Cross-Strait Relations," *Asian Survey* 44, no. 4 (2004), pp. 498–499.

[17] Rigger 2013, pp. 293–294.

and contested national identity is domestically negotiated and processed,[18] it is also impacted by the policies of and interactions between Washington and Beijing. The second-image reversed theory, in turn, looks at how a state's internal affairs are shaped, in the first place, by the strategic interests of foreign great powers. In light of such an "outside in" approach, the PRC's long-standing quest for unification with Taiwan has prompted Beijing to interfere in the island's domestic politics through the establishment of a united front with its old civil war rival, the KMT, on the basis of the "1992 consensus." "Common commitment to Chinese nationalism and opposition to Taiwan independence [and the DPP] bridged the gap between the KMT and the CCP, an unthinkable pair of strange bedfellows."[19] Ma's Chinese nation building, therefore, was reinforced by Beijing's blessing. At the same time, the United States has also been pivotal in fostering Taiwan's political liberalization and democratization since the 1970s, providing opportunities for the DPP and its supporters to cultivate a distinctive Taiwanese identity. Moreover, America and its Asia-Pacific allies have, in recent years, become wary of Beijing's assertive island reclamations and militarization in the South China Sea. The KMT's near identical sovereign claims with the PRC on the South China Sea maritime territories, accordingly, generated wrinkles between the Ma administration and the United States.[20] "As the PRC bases its own territorial claims [the Nine-Dashed Line] on those [Eleven-Dashed Line] drawn in 1947 by the ROC government, Beijing and Taipei are natural allies, and the mainland has been asking Taiwan to jointly defend the sacred territories of the Chinese nation against foreign incursion."[21] The Obama administration's reserved attitude on the "1992 consensus," accordingly, illustrated Washington's apprehension that the KMT was overly eager in boxing Taiwan into the "one-China" framework without gaining sufficient popular backing from the Taiwanese people.[22] Due to President Ma's unrelenting

---

[18] Christopher Hughes, "Negotiating National Identity in Taiwan," in Robert Ash, John Garver, and Penelope Prime, eds., *Taiwan's Democracy* (New York: Routledge, 2011), pp. 1–21.

[19] Wu Yu-shan, "Heading towards Troubled Waters? The Impact of Taiwan's 2016 Elections on Cross-Strait Relations," *American Journal of Chinese Studies* 23, no. 1 (2016), p. 65.

[20] Dean Chen, "U.S.-China Rivalry and the Weakening of the KMT's '1992 Consensus' Policy," *Asian Survey* 56, no. 4 (2016), pp. 754–778.

[21] Wu 2016, p. 73.

[22] Shirley Lin 2016, p. 174.

pursuit of engagement and accommodation with Beijing, it seems that Taiwan's status quo is "eroding" and its "freedom of action is becoming constricted" in the face of the PRC's growing military, economic, and international leverage.[23] The absence of Washington's endorsement of the "1992 consensus" might be one of the reasons behind the KMT's crushing defeat in the 2016 election. Notwithstanding the heightened competition between the United States and PRC, Washington continues to accord high priority to the maintenance and deepening of constructive cooperation with Beijing to manage various global security and economic issues.[24] Thus, whereas a less China-friendly Taiwan may be in the interests of the United States to counter the PRC's growing assertiveness in the Asia-Pacific, it is highly unlikely that Washington would renounce its enduring strategic ambiguity policy and support Taiwan to overstep on Beijing's sensitivity on the "one-China" issue.

Indeed, despite suggesting he may upend America's four-decades-old "one-China" policy during his transitory months before formally swearing-in as the 45th US president on January 20, 2017 (see Chapter 6), Donald Trump affirmed on February 9, 2017, in a call with China's president Xi Jinping, that he would continue to "honor the US 'one China' policy." While the potential for heightening of security and economic tensions remains for both countries, the new president has reduced the possibility of overturning the foundational anchor underpinning US–China relations and Eastern Asia's regional stability.[25]

It is my hope that, in the chapters ahead, readers will learn how international strategic and domestic political circumstances are mutually reinforcing in driving Taiwan's relations with mainland China. The KMT's (and the DPP's) often suboptimal mainland strategy is the result of the island's deep-seated fragmentations among elites and their polarizing national visions. The interests of the United States and PRC toward Taiwan also affect the intensities of these domestic divisions.

---

[23] Robert Sutter, *U.S.-Chinese Relations* (Lanham, MD: Rowman & Littlefield, 2013), pp. 246–247.

[24] Jeffrey Bader, "A Framework for U.S. Policy toward China," Asia Working Group Paper No. 3 (Washington, DC: Brookings Institution, March 2016), pp. 1–13.

[25] "Trump Backs 'One China' Policy in First Presidential Call with Xi," *The Financial Times* (February 10, 2017), https://www.ft.com/content/40825e36-ef3f-11e6-930f-061b01e23655

Acknowledgments

This book owes its inception to generous funding by the 2014 Taiwan Fellowship from the Ministry of Foreign Affairs, the Republic of China (Taiwan), and the 2016 Faculty Development Fund from the Ramapo College of New Jersey. In the absence of these financial awards, this author could not have done his interviews and research in the United States and Taiwan between 2014 and 2016. In addition, I would like to express my gratitude to the interviewees identified in this volume, for without their insights and inputs this book would not have been able to connect the causal linkages between the various international and domestic dynamics that, together, have shaped Taiwan's mainland policy between 2008 and 2016. Due to their sensitive former or current government/partisan capacities, some interviewees have chosen to maintain their anonymity, and this author has strictly followed that protocol. My heartfelt appreciation also goes to Professors Robert Sutter and Christopher Twomey and two anonymous reviewers who have read and commented on either the full or parts of this manuscript. Their suggestions and critiques have raised my attention to focus on important issues and perspectives that were either underaddressed or entirely ignored in previous rounds of drafting. The support and assistance rendered by the editors and editorial assistants at Palgrave Macmillan, in particular Anca Pusca, Anne Schult, Chris Robinson, and Sara Doskow, have ben superb and instrumental to the acquisition, reviewing, copyediting, production, and publication of this manuscript. Any mistakes or wrongful interpretations contained in this volume are the sole responsibility of this author. Many thanks also go to my family and friends, as well as supportive colleagues and students at Ramapo. Finally, I would like to dedicate this book to my parents, aunt, and the memories of my grandparents and uncle.

Contents

1 The Xi–Ma Summit Meeting and US Interests Across the Taiwan Strait   1

2 Politics Beyond the Water's Edge: Neoclassical Realism   41

3 Defining "One China"   69

4 The KMT Rebuilds the ROC: Useful Foreign Foes and Enemies from Within   101

5 US Strategic Ambiguity, Rising China, and Taiwan's Security   137

6 Tsai Ing-wen and the Weakening of the "1992 Consensus"   173

Index   203

LIST OF FIGURES

Fig. 1.1	The USA–PRC Cold War and the KMT's authoritarianism and "one-China" legitimacy, 1949–79	27
Fig. 1.2	The USA–PRC normalization and the emergence of Taiwanese democracy	31
Fig. 2.1	Causal scheme of the KMT's pro-China policy, 2008–16	61
Fig. 2.2	A neoclassical realist model of Taiwan's mainland policy (2000–16)	61
Fig. 4.1	Changes in the Taiwanese/Chinese identity of Taiwanese as tracked in the surveys by the Election Study Center, NCCU (1992–2014.06)	125
Fig. 4.2	Changes in the unification—independence stances of Taiwanese as tracked in surveys by the Election Study Center, NCCU (1994–2014.06)	126

List of Tables

Table 4.1	The Taiwanese public's views on the pace of cross-strait exchanges	85
Table 6.1	The Taiwanese people's public views on Ma Ying-jeou's definition of "1992 Consensus" based on "one China, respective interpretations" in which "one China" is the ROC	176
Table 6.2	The Taiwanese people's public views on the statement of handling cross-strait relations on the basis of the "ROC constitutional framework"	177
Table 6.3	The Taiwanese people's public views on President Tsai Ing-wen's inauguration address on May 20, 2016, emphasizing "respecting the historical fact of the 1992 talks"	177
Table 6.4	The Taiwanese people's public views on President Tsai's inauguration address on May 20, 2016, stressing that she would handle cross-strait relations in "accordance to the Republic of China Constitution, Act Governing Relations Between the People of Taiwan Area and the Mainland Area, and other relevant legislation"	177
Table 6.5	The Taiwanese people's public views on President Tsai's inauguration address on May 20, 2016, stressing that she would also manage cross-strait relations based on the "democratic principle and prevalent will of the people of Taiwan"	178

CHAPTER 1

The Xi–Ma Summit Meeting and US Interests Across the Taiwan Strait

For the first time since 1949, presidents of the People's Republic of China (PRC), Xi Jinping, and the Republic of China (ROC) on Taiwan, Ma Ying-jeou, shook hands and discussed cross-strait peaceful development in a historic meeting on November 7, 2015 in Singapore. The two sides of the Taiwan Strait split and became archrivals after Chiang Kai-shek's Nationalist or Kuomintang (KMT) forces moved the seat of the ROC government to Taiwan after being routed by Mao Zedong's Chinese Communist Party (CCP) which then established the PRC on the Chinese mainland.[1] Despite the gradual thawing of hostility between Taipei and Beijing since the late 1980s and the deepening of socioeconomic interchanges after 2008, a summit between the two chief executives had been almost inconceivable given the intensity of political sensitivity involved.

---

[1] The last time Chiang Kai-shek and Mao Zedong met was in September 1945, in Chongqing, China, when both leaders, at the urging of the Harry S. Truman administration, sought to forge a coalition government for a united China. However, the deep-seated mistrust and animosity between the KMT and CCP prevented a lasting peace agreement, and an all-out civil war soon ensued that eventually drove out Chiang's government to Taiwan in 1949. See Richard Bernstein, *China 1945: Mao's Revolution and America's Fateful Choice* (New York: Vintage Books, 2014).

© The Author(s) 2017
D.P. Chen, *US-China Rivalry and Taiwan's Mainland Policy*,
DOI 10.1007/978-3-319-47599-8_1

1 THE KMT–CCP UNITED FRONT: COMMITTING TO "ONE CHINA"

From Beijing's perspective, Taiwan is a renegade province whose ultimate recovery has been a long-standing and unyielding objective of the Chinese Communist Party authority to finally vindicate the sovereign unification and territorial integrity of the Chinese nation. Moreover, the PRC has never renounced the use of military force to take back the island if it declares formal independence or procrastinates indefinitely on the issue of reunification. Hence, a Chinese president greeting his Taiwanese counterpart could incur the danger of potentially according legitimacy to an independent Taiwanese state or, at least, two separate Chinese governments.[2] Indeed, an *Economist* analyst observed that the "summit was perhaps the biggest concession on a 'core issue' of sovereignty any Chinese leader has made since the early 1980s when, under Deng Xiaoping, China offered Taiwan a 'one country, two systems' solution and agreed with Britain on a similar deal with Hong Kong."[3] At the same time, however, as a self-governed vibrant democracy, Taiwan has long rejected the Hong Kong model and any appellations that would subjugate its president to an inferior or subordinate status when meeting with the Chinese leader. The impasse was resolved as Xi and Ma met each other in their capacities as "leaders of two sides" and addressed each other as "mister."[4] The nomenclature, in the words of Richard Bush, created "some equivalence between the two sides of the Taiwan Strait [and] avoided the fraught issue of the

---

[2] Austin Ramzy, "When Leaders of Taiwan and China Meet, Even Tiny Gestures will be Parsed," *The New York Times* (November 5, 2015), accessible at: http://www.nytimes.com/2015/11/05/world/asia/china-taiwan-xi-jinping-ma-ying-jeou-protocol.html.

[3] Banyan, "The Emperor's Descendants: Smiles and Handshakes Usher in What will be a Rocky Period for China-Taiwan Relations," *The Economist* (November 14, 2015), accessible at: http://www.economist.com/news/asia/21678247-smiles-and-handshakes-usher-what-will-be-rocky-period-china-taiwan-relations-emperors.

[4] "Hey Mister, Meet Mister: The Problems of Titles in China-Taiwan Meeting," *The Wall Street Journal* (November 4, 2015), accessible at: http://blogs.wsj.com/chinarealtime/2015/11/04/hey-mister-meet-mister-the-problem-of-titles-in-china-taiwan-meeting/. In another reminiscence of history, Chiang and Mao also addressed each other as "*shensheng*" or "mister" in many of their telegrams and letters, showing respect for each. See "Leaders Join Hands across Taiwan Strait for the First Time in 66 Years," *The Xinhua News Agency* (November 7, 2015), accessible at: http://news.xinhuanet.com/english/2015-11/07/c_134793648.htm.

political and legal status of Taiwan and its government."[5] Zhang Zhijun, the head of the PRC's Taiwan Affairs Office, remarked that addressing each other as "mister" is "pragmatic" and "in line with the one-China principle [that] the two sides show the spirit of shelving differences while respecting for each other."[6] In his own words, President Ma stated, "I was striving to establish a model of equality and dignity for future interactions between the leaders from the two sides."[7]

Consolidating the "1992 Consensus" and Warning Against Taiwan's Independence

Notwithstanding the historic significance and euphoria, the Xi–Ma summit was announced merely a few days before, and, as a result, caught many by surprise, especially as it was arranged when President Ma's tenure would soon expire in May 2016 and his plummeting approval rating called into question even his legitimacy to represent the public will of Taiwan. Despite the Ma administration's reaffirmation that there was "zero surprise"[8] in USA–Taiwan relations and that Taipei had informed Washington of his meeting with Xi in advance, there were suggestions

---

[5] Richard Bush, "Two Chinese Leaders Walk into a Room: The Singapore Meeting between Ma Ying-jeou and Xi Jinping," Brookings Institution (November 4, 2015), accessible at: http://www.brookings.edu/blogs/order-from-chaos/posts/2015/11/04-ma-xi-taiwan-china-meeting-bush.

[6] "Xi, Ma to Salute Each Other "Mister" in Historic Meeting," *The Xinhua News Agency* (November 4, 2015), accessible at: http://news.xinhuanet.com/english/2015-11/04/c_134782057.htm.

[7] Ma Ying-jeou, "When I said 'Mr. Xi': Ma Ying-jeou," *USA Today* (November 22, 2015), accessible at: http://www.usatoday.com/story/opinion/2015/11/22/taiwan-china-xi-jinping-ma-ying-jeou-1992-consensus-column/76215872/.

[8] Taiwan's *Liberty Times* published an exclusive story that cited a "credible source" as saying that the Ma administration had only notified the US government through theAIT on November 3, 2015, merely a day before the news broke out and four days before the summit. However, President Ma refuted against this report, commenting that his administration "would never let the U.S. learn about such a development from the media." See Stacey Hsu, "Ma Rebuffs Claims on U.S. Notice of Xi Meeting," *Taipei Times* (November 17, 2015), accessible at: http://www.taipeitimes.com/News/front/archives/2015/11/17/2003632643. See also "Ma Stresses 'Zero Surprise' Policy in Taiwan-U.S. Relations," *The Focus Taiwan News* (November 16, 2015), accessible at: http://focustaiwan.tw/news/aipl/201511160009.aspx.

about Ma's insufficient communication with America regarding the planning of the summit.[9]

The meeting also took place on the sidelines of President Xi's long-planned state visit to Singapore.[10] To be sure, the suddenness of its occurrence was not random as Taiwan's presidential election was only two months away, and most expected that Tsai Ing-wen (now president), the candidate and chairwoman of the Democratic Progressive Party (DPP), which supports Taiwanese independence and cooler relations with mainland China, would easily capture the presidency along with boosting her party toward winning a robust majority in the island's legislative branch, the Legislative Yuan.[11] Following its devastating electoral loss in November 2014, the KMT has "degenerated into a political organization wracked by internal squabbles and factionalism."[12] The party is in utter disarray[13]—tarnished by the Ma administration's poor handling of many socioeconomic issues, the loss of support among traditional KMT supporters and centrist voters, the rising anti-China sentiments among Taiwanese youths and civil societal forces fearing Taiwan's greater economic dependency on the PRC, and the inability of the party to decide on a presidential candidate until fairly late in the campaign season (i.e., the abrupt replacement of the initial

---

[9] In this author's interview on February 24, 2016 with Dr. Robert Sutter, professor of Practice of International Affairs at the Elliot School of International Affairs, the George Washington University, he noted that while it is understandable why the planning of such a meeting would be kept secret, the United States was "taken by surprise." In an interview with this author on February 25, 2016, Dr. Richard Bush, director for the Center for East Asia Policy Studies at the Brookings Institute, said that President Ma informed the U.S. "on a very short notice before the news went public." Bush served as the chairman of the Board and managing director of the AIT, from 1997 to 2002. The AIT is the United States' unofficial representative office or embassy in Taiwan.

[10] "Leaders of Taiwan and China Hold Historic Meeting: A Display of Amity Points to Tougher Times Ahead," *The Economist* (November 7, 2015), accessible at: http://www.economist.com/news/asia/21678115-display-amity-points-tougher-times-ahead-leaders-taiwan-and-china-hold-historic.

[11] J. Michael Cole, "China-Taiwan Summit: Empty Symbolism or Game Changer?" *The CNN* (November 5, 2015), accessible at: http://www.cnn.com/2015/11/05/opinions/china-taiwan-summit-no-game-changer/.

[12] Dennis Hickey and Emerson Niou, "Taiwan in 2015: A Turning Point?" *Asian Survey* 56, no. 1 (2016), p. 61.

[13] David Brown and Kevin Scott, "China-Taiwan Relations: KMT Disarray Shapes Campaign," *Comparative Connections* 17, no. 2 (September 2015), pp. 77–86, accessible at: http://csis.org/files/publication/1502qchina_taiwan.pdf.

KMT presidential candidate Hung Hsiu-chu by the then KMT chairman and mayor of New Taipei City, Eric Chu, on October 17, 2015).[14]

Consequently, to a great extent, Xi Jinping wanted to use the meeting with Ma to bolster the KMT's flimsy electoral chances by demonstrating that cross-strait ties would be more peaceful and stable under its government than the more independence-minded DPP.[15] A less friendly administration on Taiwan could further complicate Beijing's strategic interest, especially in light of massive waves of anti-China protests and occupying movements in both Taiwan and Hong Kong in 2014. In spite of Taiwan's deepening economic integration with mainland China after Ma came to office in 2008, only a minority of the Taiwanese public holds favorable views toward China, and an increasingly substantial proportion even identifies themselves as Taiwanese only and Taiwan as a completely separate state from China. The failure to resuscitate the KMT and stem the tide of Taiwanese independence, therefore, could seriously compromise Xi's political authority and credibility both domestically and internationally.[16]

While no formal agreements or joint statements were issued from their talks, Xi and Ma reaffirmed their mutual commitment to sustain and consolidate cross-strait peaceful relations on the foundation of the "1992 consensus"—a tacit political formula reached by representatives from each side of the Taiwan Strait at Hong Kong in November 1992 that agreed to orally express the "one-China" principle with their different or respective definitions of what that China means.[17] In accordance

---

[14] This author's interview with Chih-wei Chou on July 28, 2016. Chou was chairperson of the Kuomintang's Culture and Communications Committee from April 2016 to October 2016.

[15] Simon Denyer, "China, Taiwan Leaders Pledge Peaceful Ties at Historic Encounter," *The Washington Post* (November 7, 2015), accessible at: https://www.washingtonpost.com/world/china-taiwan-leaders-shake-hands-smile-before-historic-encounter/2015/11/07/1b2ee572-84c5-11e5-8bd2-680fff868306_story.html.

[16] Te-Ping Chen, "China-Taiwan Summit: A High Stakes Gamble for Xi Jinping, Ma Ying-jeou," *The Wall Street Journal* (November 4, 2015), accessible at: http://www.wsj.com/articles/china-taiwan-summit-a-high-stakes-gamble-for-xi-jinping-ma-ying-jeou-1446645837. See also Austin Ramzy, "Meeting with Taiwan Reflects Limits of China's Checkbook," *The New York Times* (November 6, 2015), accessible at: http://www.nytimes.com/2015/11/07/world/asia/china-taiwan-meeting-economy-protests-singapore.html?action=click&contentCollection=Asia%20Pacific&module=RelatedCoverage&region=Marginalia&pgtype=article.

[17] "President Ma, Mainland Chinese Leader Xi Meet in Singapore, Agree to Jointly Consolidate Cross-Strait Peace and Prosperity," *The Mainland Affairs Council, Republic of*

with this "one China, respective interpretations" (OCRI) rubric, the KMT has designated China as the ROC whereas the CCP refers to it as the PRC. Thus, "from the very beginning, Taiwan's emphasis was on the 'respective ways,' while the mainland was more interested in the 'one China' principle, but there was no denying that the official position of the KMT government was 'one China.'"[18] Chapter 3 will elaborate on the origins of and evolvement of the "1992 consensus" as well as Beijing's changing construction of the "one-China" principle. Ma posited that if his successor could persist in promoting the "1992 consensus," he is confident that "the status quo will be able to be maintained and continue to move forward."[19] In a similar vein, Xi noted that without sticking to the "common ground of the 1992 consensus," the "boat of peaceful development will encounter terrifying waves or even capsize."[20] Intending to convey this message to the DPP, the Chinese leader also stressed: "No matter which party or organization, and no matter what they stood for in the past, as long as the 1992 consensus and its core values are acknowledged, we stand ready to have contact… Any actions separating the country will never be allowed by the people across the Strait."[21] On that basis, he recognized Taiwan's desire for greater international participation and invited the island to join China's "One Road, One Belt" initiative, the Asian Infrastructure Investment Bank (AIIB), and the Regional Comprehensive Economic Partnership (RCEP) in an appropriate manner.[22]

To sum up, Xi Jinping's objectives were to underscore the effectiveness of the KMT government's approach to cross-strait relationship after 2008 and to warn the then presidential candidate, Tsai Ing-wen, and the rest of Taiwan against deviating from that trajectory. Ma Ying-jeou, on the other hand, wished to defend his record and persuade the Taiwanese people that the KMT's policy stance represents the most responsible choice

China (Taiwan) Press Release No. 062 (November 7, 2015), accessible at: http://www.mac.gov.tw/public/Attachment/511811162758.pdf.

[18] Wu, "Heading towards Troubled Water"? p. 64.

[19] "Historic Ma-Xi Meeting Focuses on '1992 Consensus,'" *The Focus Taiwan News* (November 7, 2015), accessible at: http://focustaiwan.tw/news/acs/201511070043.aspx.

[20] "China Focus: Xi Calls for Adhering to One-China Principle in Meeting with Ma," *The Xinhua News Agency* (November 7, 2015), accessible at: http://news.xinhuanet.com/english/2015-11/07/c_134793533.htm.

[21] Ibid.

[22] Ibid.

for stabilizing cross-strait ties.[23] "Without the bit-by-bit accumulation of goodwill over seven years of rapprochement, Mr. Xi and I may not have trusted each other enough to meet in Singapore," writes Ma. "This mutual trust is precious—but vulnerable. It is founded on the 1992 consensus: 'one China, respective interpretations.' Some have called that a 'masterpiece of ambiguity.' Ambiguity or not, it works well and is now the master plan for peace in the Taiwan Strait."[24] During his visit to the USA in late 2015, Eric Chu, noted that Ma's cross-strait policy was the "right thing, and we should insist on that." Our party (the KMT) "thinks the 1992 consensus is a very important foundation for the past seven and a half years of cross-strait relations… If I'm elected president for the next four to eight years, I would not only open the door for the two sides, we would cooperate together economically or in international spaces together."[25]

Stressing on Common Chinese Heritage

President Ma, according to the official press release by Taiwan's Mainland Affairs Council (MAC), made some unprecedented inroads in the closed-door meeting with Xi. He elaborated, in greater length, on Taiwan's democratic system, its desire for more meaningful international engagement, the people's fear about Chinese military and missile threats,[26] and the content of the "1992 consensus" based on "one China, respective interpretations."[27] The president emphasized the centrality of the ROC

---

[23] Shannon Tiezzi, "China and Taiwan Leaders Emphasize Kinship, 1992 Consensus in Historic Talk," *The Diplomat* (November 7, 2015), accessible at: http://thediplomat.com/2015/11/china-and-taiwan-leaders-emphasize-kinship-1992-consensus-in-historic-talks/.

[24] Ma Ying-jeou, "When I said 'Mr. Xi': Ma Ying-jeou."

[25] William Wan, "Ahead of Taiwan Elections, Presidential Candidate Defends Outreach to China," *The Washington Post* (November 17, 2015), accessible at: https://www.washingtonpost.com/news/worldviews/wp/2015/11/17/taiwans-ruling-party-now-the-underdog-a-q-a-with-its-presidential-candidate/.

[26] Ma mentioned Taiwan's concerns about China's military threats, especially its missiles, to Xi, who only responded that these were "not aimed at Taiwan." President Ma revealed that he wasn't satisfied by Xi's reply. See Stacy Hsu, "Ma Defends Significance of Meeting with Xi," *Taipei Times* (November 9, 2015), accessible at: http://www.taipeitimes.com/News/front/archives/2015/11/09/2003632021. See also "Taiwanese Concerned about China's Military Threat, Ma Told Xi," *The Focus Taiwan News* (November 7, 2015), accessible at: http://focustaiwan.tw/news/acs/201511070033.aspx.

[27] To be sure, the DPP and many critics challenged that Ma did not firm up when meeting with Xi, as the president failed to fully address Taiwan's democracy and freedom to choose

and that the ROC Constitution does not allow for "two Chinas," "one China, one Taiwan," and "Taiwan independence."[28] In addition to urging the further deepening of cross-strait economic cooperation, Ma suggested that a "hot line" be established between senior Taiwanese and Chinese officials handling cross-strait affairs in order to fend off misunderstandings and reduce tensions.

Furthermore, both Ma and Xi reiterated the notion that people on both sides of the strait are Chinese and should work toward the betterment and rejuvenation of the Chinese nation.[29] Xi maintained that "no matter how much ordeal the two sides have undergone and how long the two sides have been isolated from each other, they cannot be pulled apart... We are brothers who are still connected by our flesh even if our bones are broken."[30] The Chinese leader described the "compatriots" on both sides of the Taiwan Strait as "members of the Chinese nation" and urged them to "cooperate and jointly work for the great revival of the Chinese nation."[31] In line with Ma's China-centric national identity

---

its future and the existence of the ROC—at least these issues were absent in Ma's opening remarks. They further questioned whether the president even raised these topics in the closed-door meeting with Xi Jinping, noting that the PRC side only stressed on the "one-China" principle component of the "1992 consensus." See "DPP Presidential Candidate Bashes Ma's Advocacy of '1992 Consensus,'" *The Focus Taiwan News* (November 7, 2015), accessible at: http://focustaiwan.tw/news/aipl/201511070040.aspx. To dispel any doubts, the ROC's Mainland Affairs Council released the full transcript of Ma's remarks during the closed-door portion of the conference. See Austin Ramzy, "Taiwan Debates Its President's Meeting with Xi Jinping of China," *The New York Times* (November 9, 2015), accessible at: http://sinosphere.blogs.nytimes.com/2015/11/09/taiwan-china-xi-ma-meeting/?ref=world&_r=0. See also "MAC Head Seeks to Dispel Doubts about Ma's Remarks in Xi's Meeting," *The Focus Taiwan News* (November 9, 2015), accessible at: http://focustaiwan.tw/news/acs/201511090009.aspx.

[28] "Full Text of ROC President Ma Ying-jeou's Remarks in Meeting with Mainland Chinese Leader Xi Jinping," the Mainland Affairs Council, Republic of China (Taiwan) (November 7, 2015), accessible at: http://www.mac.gov.tw/public/Attachment/511923353567.pdf.

[29] Ibid. See also "China Focus: Xi Calls for Adhering to One-China Principle in Meeting with Ma," and Shannon Tiezzi, "China and Taiwan Leaders Emphasize Kinship, 1992 Consensus in Historic Talk."

[30] "Xi Tells Ma: No Force Can Pull Us Apart," *The Xinhua News Agency* (November 7, 2015), accessible at: http://news.xinhuanet.com/english/2015-11/07/c_134793106.htm.

[31] "Xi-Ma Meeting Turns Historic Page in Cross-Strait Relations: Official," *The Xinhua News Agency* (November 9, 2015), accessible at: http://news.xinhuanet.com/english/2015-11/09/c_134795583.htm.

and his administration's endeavors to rebuild the "one-China"/ROC ruling legitimacy on Taiwan after 2008,[32] the president echoed, "The people of both sides are Chinese, descendants of the emperors Yan and Huang. The two sides should cooperate to promote cross-strait prosperity."[33] Predicated on a strong Chinese nationalism, the Xi–Ma summit, therefore, produced a message to the international community in general and the USA in particular—that is, the Taiwan Strait issue remains China's internal affair. Xi said, "The two sides of the Taiwan Strait should prove with concrete moves to the world that the Chinese from both sides have the capabilities and wisdom to solve their own problems."[34]

However, although the Xi–Ma meeting solidified the "pan-Chinese" union between the KMT and CCP, it failed to pressure the DPP to accept the "1992 consensus" and to assuage the Taiwanese people's overarching anxiety about the PRC's aggressive intent toward the island. Meanwhile, the KMT remained inept and out of touch with Taiwan's rapidly changing demographics, as its "one-China" appeal has gained little attention from the younger Taiwanese generation.[35] On January 16, 2016, Eric Chu, receiving only 31 percent of the votes in a three-way race, lost hugely to the DPP's Tsai Ing-wen, who won 56 percent. Her party also got 68 of the 113 Legislative Yuan seats, compared with the KMT's 35 seats.[36] Despite having the lowest turnout rate since 1996,[37] the election results have, for the first time since Taiwan's democratization

---

[32] Jean-Pierre Cabestan, "Cross-Strait Integration and Taiwan's New Security Challenges," in Gunter Schubert ed., *Taiwan and the "China Impact"* (New York: Routledge, 2016), p. 283.

[33] "Opening Remarks by President Ma Ying-jeou at His Meeting with Mainland Chinese Leader Xi Jinping," the Mainland Affairs Council, Republic of China (Taiwan) (November 7, 2015), accessible at: http://www.mac.gov.tw/public/Attachment/511923294871.pdf.

[34] "Xi: Cross-Strait Chinese Have Capabilities, Wisdom to Solve Their Own Problems," *The Xinhua News Agency* (November 7, 2015), accessible at: http://news.xinhuanet.com/english/2015-11/07/c_134793175.htm.

[35] Zheng Wang, "The Real Reason the Xi-Ma Meeting Was Historic," *The Diplomat* (November 9, 2015), accessible at: http://thediplomat.com/2015/11/the-real-reason-the-ma-xi-meeting-was-historic/.

[36] "Taiwan's Political Landslide: Not Trying to Cause a Big Sensation," *The Economist* (January 23, 2016), accessible at: http://www.economist.com/news/asia/21688916-much-anything-victory-tsai-ing-wen-and-her-party-represents-generational-change-not.

[37] "Voter Turnout was Lowest since 1996," *Taipei Times* (January 18, 2016), accessible at: http://www.taipeitimes.com/News/taiwan/archives/2016/01/18/2003637469.

began in the mid-1990s, created a unified DPP-controlled majority in both branches of the central government and given rise to a less China-friendly administration on Taiwan. Douglas Paal observed that the DPP has the upper hand, and Taiwan is not going toward China's direction for the time being. The defeated KMT is also unlikely to continue Ma Ying-jeou's position that both the mainland and Taiwan share "common Chinese roots."[38]

2 Cross-Strait Rapprochement and Heightened USA–PRC Competition

Essentially, the Xi–Ma summit represented the culmination of cross-strait peaceful development under the KMT administration and fits nicely with the analysis of this book, which seeks to examine and explain President Ma Ying-jeou's rapprochement policy, from 2008 to 2016, toward the PRC and implications on the island's relationship with the USA.

US Interests Toward the Taiwan Strait: Democracy and Strategic Ambiguity

The impact of Ma's détente policy on USA–Taiwanese ties was manifested in two levels: ideational and strategic. First, as mainland China becomes more powerful and assertive in the second decade of the twenty-first century, the KMT government's close "leaning" toward Beijing, committing to the "1992 consensus," galvanized fervent domestic oppositions and heightened political tensions, generating instability and polarization on the island. The incongruity between the KMT's mainland policy and Taiwan's public preferences threatened an erosion of the island's democratic governance,[39] which is contrary to America's liberal normative commitment to Taiwan's democracy and freedom.[40]

---

[38] This author's interview with Douglas Paal on March 16, 2016. Paal is vice-president for Studies and director of the Asia Program at the Carnegie Endowment for International Peace. He previously served as the director of the AIT between 2002 and 2006.

[39] Christopher Hughes, "Revisiting Identity Politics under Ma Ying-jeou," in J-P Cabestan and Jacques deLisle, eds., *Political Changes in Taiwan under Ma Ying-jeou* (New York: Routledge, 2014), pp. 120–136.

[40] Shelley Rigger, *Why Taiwan Matters* (Lanham, MD: Rowman & Littlefield, 2011), Chapter 4.

Second, Washington has long predicated its Taiwan Strait policy on a strategic ambiguity framework[41] aiming to deter both Taipei and Beijing from unilaterally upsetting the cross-strait status quo as the USA commits to a vaguely defined "one China" while signaling its intolerance toward either the PRC's forceful reunification or Taiwan's unprovoked declaration of formal independence. It is a delicate dual-deterrence approach that requires both credible threats of punishment and credible assurances. Indeed,

> the major challenge in U.S. policy toward relations across the Taiwan Strait is to achieve two somewhat contradictory goals at once: on the one hand, Washington needs to maintain a strong enough regional military presence and support for Taiwan's defense to discourage the mainland from coercing or invading the island; on the other hand, the United States needs to reassure Beijing that the purpose of its arms sales and military presence is not to support the permanent legal separation of Taiwan from the Chinese nation.[42]

Paal commented, in his conversations with the author, that it is not in America's interests to "stir up" Taiwanese independence because it would negatively affect USA–China ties and Taiwan's own security.[43] Sutter, in a similar vein, noted that Taiwan has long been a "sensitive issue" for both Washington and Beijing, and, as a result, the USA's support for the island must be cautious in order not to provoke nationalist sentiments in mainland China and cause instability in Sino-American relations.[44]

Without stating clearly its policy response in the event of a crisis, Washington also intends to use its ambivalence to prevent both sides from taking reckless actions and demand all resolutions be reached through peaceful and consensual means. The process and pace of cross-strait interactions must be mutually agreed upon by the peoples across the Taiwan Strait. While serving as the chairman of the Board and managing director of the American Institute in Taiwan (AIT) from 1992 to 2002, Richard

---

[41] Nancy Tucker, *Strait Talk* (Cambridge, MA: Harvard University Press, 2009), Chapter 1. See also Dean P. Chen, *U.S. Taiwan Strait Policy: The Origins of Strategic Ambiguity* (Boulder, CO: Lynne Rienner Publishers/First Forum Press, 2012).

[42] Thomas Christensen, *The China Challenge: Shaping the Choice of a Rising Power* (New York: W.W. Norton, 2015), p. 190.

[43] This author's interview with Douglas Paal.

[44] This author's interview with Robert Sutter.

Bush confirmed that he made the initiative to convince the Bill Clinton administration to insist that the democratic preferences and aspirations of the Taiwanese people be taken as one of the prerequisites for a peaceful resolution of cross-strait differences.[45]

America's dual-deterrence or strategic ambiguity was demonstrated in the 1995–96 Taiwan Strait crisis,[46] when the PRC launched a series of dangerous military and missile exercises in the vicinity of the strait to counter Taiwan's president Lee Teng-hui (even though he was the KMT leader back then) who stressed on Taiwan's political independence during his speech at Cornell in May 1995 and who was running for reelection in the island's first-direct presidential race in March 1996. The Clinton administration deployed two aircraft carrier battle groups off of Taiwan to deter Beijing's aggressive moves.[47] Yet, although Lee won the election, Clinton, in his visit to Shanghai in 1998, reassured the Chinese leader Jiang Zemin by publicly giving the "three no's" statement, that is, the USA would not support Taiwan's independence; "two Chinas" or "one China, one Taiwan"; or Taiwan's membership in international organizations for which statehood is a requirement. Washington also distanced itself from Lee's "two-states theory" in July 1999 that described the relationship between Taiwan and China as "special state-to-state."[48] Despite President George W. Bush's strong commitment to defend Taiwan and its democracy, his administration voiced staunch opposition when the DPP president Chen Shui-bian set out a series of anti-China, or de-Sinification, policies to drive the island toward greater political separatism between 2000 and 2008.[49] Likewise, on the eve of Tsai Ing-wen's first bid for Taiwan's presidency in 2012, an Obama administration official used a reporting from the *Financial Times* to voice its qualms about her independence proclivity.[50] Such "indirect" expression of concern (or distrust) probably played an important part in her failure in that campaign.

---

[45] This author's interview with Richard Bush. Bush further elaborated that given the PRC's authoritarian system, the mainland Chinese people's preferences cannot be easily measured and accessible, but Taiwan's democracy has changed cross-strait relationship. The Taiwanese people should "have a seat at the table" to express their wishes.

[46] Robert Ross, "The 1995–96 Taiwan Strait Confrontation: Coercion, Credibility, and the Use of Force," *International Security* 25, no. 2 (Fall 2000), pp. 87–123.

[47] Thomas Christensen, *The China Challenge,* pp. 192–193.

[48] Ibid., p. 195.

[49] Ibid., pp. 209–216.

[50] "U.S. Concerned about Taiwan Candidate," *The Financial Times* (September 15, 2011), accessible at: http://www.ft.com/intl/cms/s/0/f926fd14-df93-11e0-845a-

In light of these premises, the KMT and Ma government's promotion for closer ties with Beijing, in the absence of strong popular support on Taiwan, raised concerns from Washington. In spite of their opposing stances on the question of Taiwan's relations vis-à-vis mainland China, the pro-independence Lee/Chen and pro-unification Ma share a common ground: changing the status quo unilaterally. While the former devoted their efforts to maximize the psychological, if not physical, difference between Taiwan and the mainland, the latter was paving the way for an eventual union through closer socioeconomic interdependence and integration. According to Jean-Pierre Cabestan, "Since Ma came to power in 2008, the KMT has revived, to some extent, its traditional and somewhat old-fashioned Chinese nationalism, a nationalism that once again places the unity, if not the unification of the Chinese nation/race, at the heart of its ideological discourse."[51] The KMT leader aimed at denouncing and deconstructing Chen's "de-Sinification" project and Lee's Taiwanization policy attempts. Shelley Rigger described the KMT's and Ma's position as follows:

> As inheritors of a tradition that stresses mainland recovery and Chinese nationalism, it is hard for today's KMT politicians to abandon unification as a goal. At the same time, however, they well know that unification has little appeal for Taiwanese voters—and the PRC's Communist system has been anathema to their party for decades. The way they square this circle is by holding out the hope that the two sides might someday sit down and negotiate to create a united, non-Communist Chinese nation attractive enough to win over Taiwan.... Ma himself has repeatedly said that [unification] will not happen while he is president, [but] he has set democratization of the mainland as a precondition for starting any kind of unification process.[52]

Yet, President Ma's mainland policy probably contributed toward the "weakening of Taiwan's statehood and international status...as well as towards forfeiting a domestic political consensus and endangering national security."[53] Hence, unless unification is the choice of the Taiwanese people, expressed through democratic process, the KMT's policy stance

00144feabdc0.html#axzz3bm75hK48.
[51] J-P Cabestan, "Cross-Strait Integration and Taiwan's New Security Challenges," p. 292.
[52] Shelley Rigger, *Why Taiwan Matters*, p. 7.
[53] J-P Cabestan, "Cross-Strait Integration and Taiwan's New Security Challenges," p. 293.

contradicted America's interests just as the DPP's position under Chen Shui-bian had undermined Washington.

Is the KMT Too Closely Tied with the PRC?

The USA has, since 2011, announced the "pivot" or "rebalance to Asia" policy to cope with the PRC's more belligerent foreign policy behavior by deepening America's security and economic ties with states across the Asia-Pacific. The KMT's similar "one-China" sovereign position with Beijing over the contested claims on the East and South China Seas' island and maritime territories, as a result, raised some alarms from America as well as regional states in Asia, including Japan, Vietnam, and the Philippines.[54] "Taiwan has adopted sometimes confrontational policies toward Japan and South China Sea disputants that exacerbate tensions and work against U.S. efforts to calm regional tensions."[55] The Xi–Ma meeting, in fact, occurred in the context of such rising contentions in the South China Sea. Unyielding to a series of American freedom of navigation operations in the South China Sea, conducted since late 2015 by US warships, and unrelenting to Washington's call for China to address its disputes with other claimants in accordance with the international law, Beijing has persisted and escalated its reclamation projects in the region to enlarge submerged reefs into islands capable of hosting military airstrips, equipment, and soldiers. Consequently, Xi Jinping's flexible overture to meet with Ma Ying-jeou might be orchestrated in order to generate a united front between Beijing and Taipei to counterbalance the USA and other disputants.[56] President Ma was probably more interested in making the summit one of his "political legacies" than in joining Xi in forging a united front; however,

---

[54] John Tkacik, "Pacific Pivot, Taiwan Fulcrum: Maritime Taiwan and Power Transition in Asia," in Peter Chow, ed., *The U.S. Strategic Pivot to Asia and Cross-Strait Relations* (New York: Palgrave Macmillan, 2014), pp. 227–261. In that same volume, also see Lowell Dittmer, "Taiwan's Narrowing Strait: A Triangular Analysis of Taiwan's Security since 2008," pp. 15–29. See also Cheng-yi Lin, "The Rise of China and Its Implications for U.S.-Taiwan Relations," in Gunter Schubert ed., *Taiwan and the "China Impact"* pp. 261–281.

[55] Robert Sutter, *The United States and Asia* (Lanham, MD: Rowman & Littlefield, 2015), p. 95.

[56] Simon Tisdall, "China Initiates Taiwan Meeting as South China Sea Tensions Rise," *The Guardian* (November 4, 2015), accessible at: http://www.theguardian.com/world/2015/nov/04/china-taiwan-meeting-south-china-sea-tensions.

their meeting probably provided the Chinese leader a "platform" to convey such an impression.[57]

Though Washington has refrained from explicitly and clearly voicing its position (whether endorsing or opposing) on the "1992 consensus," the KMT's common stance with the CCP on "one China" influenced other "side issues" which could inadvertently "complicate or destabilize U.S. interests."[58] China's territorial and maritime claims on the South China Sea would be a pertinent case in point since the PRC's so-called "Nine-Dashed Line" today is originated from the ROC's "Eleven-Dashed Line," created in 1947 when the latter was still ruling the Chinese mainland. The USA does not challenge the Chinese (ROC or PRC) sovereign claims on these maritime territories. The scope and substance of these claims, nonetheless, should be addressed peacefully with other claimants in accordance with international law. Thus, America does not condone any parties, while exerting their respective claims, taking actions that would inflame greater tensions or conflicts. That certainly applied to Taipei as well.[59] On January 28, 2016, for instance, the US State Department and the AIT registered an unusually harsh response when President Ma visited the Itu Aba (also known as the Taiping) Island in the Spratly of the South China Sea. The KMT leader sought to make his peaceful initiatives while reaffirming the island indisputably as an ROC sovereign territory. At the same time, Ma wanted to prove to the Permanent Court of Arbitration (PCA) in the Hague (to which the Philippines had filed a case to determine the legitimacy of China's claims over the South China Sea) that Taiping is an island capable of sustaining human habitation and economic life.[60] Thus, with regard to the Taiping, the ROC enjoys "full rights associated with territorial waters, a contiguous zone, an exclusive economic zone (EEZ), and continental shelf in accordance with UNCLOS [the United Nations Convention on the Law of the Seas]."[61] Washington, however, called Ma's visit "disappointing" and "unhelpful" to resolving the dispute in

---

[57] In their interviews with this author, Sutter, Bush, and Paal all expressed similar views on this matter.
[58] This author's interview with Richard Bush.
[59] Ibid.
[60] Ralph Jennings and Julie Makinen, "Taiwan President Makes Waves with South China Sea Visit," *The Los Angeles Times* (January 28, 2016), accessible at: http://www.latimes.com/world/asia/la-fg-taiwan-south-china-sea-20160128-story.html.
[61] "Taiping Island is an Island, Not a Rock," Press Release No. 023, The Ministry of Foreign Affairs, Republic of China (Taiwan) (January 23, 2016), accessible at: http://www.

the region.⁶² As Beijing was "militarizing"⁶³ some of the islands in the South China Sea by placing surface-to-air missiles and radar systems,⁶⁴ the USA was dismayed by any unnecessary provocations that could threaten to escalate confrontations.⁶⁵ As will be noted in Chaps. 5 and 6, on July 12, 2016, the PCA ruled against the PRC's "Nine-Dashed Line" claim over the South China Sea and also stipulated that the Taiwan-controlled Taiping Island merely a "rock," hence repudiating the latter's rights to a 200-nautical mile EEZ.

Ma's détente policy also renewed the debate in Washington over whether to revamp its Taiwan Strait policy or simply abandon Taiwan altogether as China becomes a more challenging global power. Though abandonment does not represent the mainstream view in America and the Obama administration has certainly ruled out such proposition,⁶⁶ Ma and the KMT's close attachment to the CCP and their shared interest on

mofa.gov.tw/en/News_Content.aspx?n=1EADDCFD4C6EC567&s=542A8C89D51D8739.

⁶² "U.S. 'Disappointed' over Ma's Taiping Island Visit," *The Focus Taiwan News* (January 28, 2016), accessible at: http://focustaiwan.tw/news/aipl/201601280007.aspx.

⁶³ On February 24, 2016, Admiral Harry Harris, the head of the U.S. Pacific Command, stated in a hearing before the Senate Armed Services Committee: "In my opinion, China is clearly militarizing the South China Sea; you'd have to believe in a flat earth to believe otherwise." See "Pacific Command Chief Urges New Capabilities as Tensions Mount with China," *Navy Times* (February 24, 2016), accessible at: http://www.navytimes.com/story/military/2016/02/23/pacom-harry-harris-china-militarizing-south-china-sea/80796756/.

⁶⁴ Shannon Tiezzi, "South China Sea Militarization: Not All Islands Are Created Equal," *The Diplomat* (March 1, 2016), accessible at: http://thediplomat.com/2016/03/south-china-sea-militarization-not-all-islands-are-created-equal/.

⁶⁵ Bush, in his interview with this author, commented that although President Ma made a long and good speech on Taiping, there was no reason why he couldn't make the same speech in Taiwan. While the ROC has established a permanent presence and administration on Taiping since 1956, the island was also claimed by the PRC, Vietnam, and the Philippines.

⁶⁶ On these abandonment arguments, see Bruce Gilley, "Not So Dire Straits," *Foreign Affairs* 89, no. 1 (Jan/Feb 2010), pp. 44–60; Charles Glaser, "Will China's Rise Lead to War?" *Foreign Affairs* 90, no. 2 (March/April 2011), pp. 80–91; John Mearsheimer, "Taiwan's Dire Strait," *National Interest* no. 130 (March/April 2014), pp. 29–39; and Charles Glaser, "A U.S.-China Grand Bargain?" *International Security* 39, no. 4 (Spring 2015), pp. 49–90. The rejoinder arguments are: Nancy Tucker and Bonnie Glaser, "Should the United States Abandon Taiwan?" *The Washington Quarterly* 34, no. 4 (2011), pp. 23–47; Richard Bush, "U.S.-Taiwan Relations since 2008," in Jean-P Cabestan and Jacques deLisle eds., *Political Changes in Taiwan under Ma Ying-jeou* (New York: Routledge, 2014), pp. 217–231.

maintaining the "one-China" framework have generated a greater note of caution. Thus, just when Xi Jinping was meeting with Ma Ying-jeou in Singapore, Ashton Carter, the US secretary of defense, revealed America's concern about China's land reclamations in the South China Sea and remarked that the USA is "changing fundamentally our operational plans and approaches to deter aggression, fulfill our statutory obligations to Taiwan, defend allies, and prepare for a wider range of contingencies in the region than we have traditionally."[67] The Obama White House expressed that "we would certainly welcome steps that are taken on both sides of the Taiwan Strait to try and reduce tensions.... But we will have to see what actually comes out of the [Xi-Ma] meeting."[68] Daniel Russel, America's assistant secretary of state for East Asia, said, "It's very hard to know whether [the Xi-Ma] meeting is going to have any effect on the [Taiwan] elections and if it did, what effect it would be.... But, everyone is waiting to see how the conversation goes and whether the discussions between the two leaders continue the positive momentum of the last several years that has seen the relaxation of tensions."[69]

Tsai Ing-wen's high popularity during the 2016 presidential race grew further in the wake of her successful visits to the USA and Japan in the summer and fall of 2015, respectively, during which she pledged that, if elected, her government would "strengthen [Taiwan's] partnerships" with Washington and Tokyo and to "maintain the status quo" in dealing with Beijing.[70] The DPP chairwoman further affirmed, in her speech at

[67] Cheryl Pellerin, "Carter: Responses to Russia, China Involves Innovation," The U.S. Department of Defense News (November 7, 2015), accessible at: http://www.defense.gov/News-Article-View/Article/628144/carter-response-to-russia-china-involves-innovation.

[68] "White House Cautions on Historic China-Taiwan Meeting," The AFP (November 3, 2015), accessible at: http://news.yahoo.com/white-house-cautious-historic-china-taiwan-meeting-200700481.html.

[69] David Brunnstrom, "U.S. Says Unclear if Taiwan-China Meeting will Influence Taiwan Elections," Reuters (November 4, 2015), accessible at: http://www.reuters.com/article/2015/11/05/us-taiwan-china-usa-idUSKCN0SU07920151105. See also "White House Cautions on Historic China-Taiwan Meeting," The AFP (November 3, 2015), accessible at: http://news.yahoo.com/white-house-cautious-historic-china-taiwan-meeting-200700481.html.

[70] Shannon Tiezzi, "Cross-Strait Relations: The DPP's Tightrope Walk," The Diplomat (June 5, 2015), accessible at: http://thediplomat.com/2015/06/cross-strait-relations-the-dpps-tightrope-walk/. Shannon Tiezzi, "What Taiwan-Japan Relations Might Look Like in 2016," The Diplomat (October 9, 2015), accessible at: http://thediplomat.com/2015/10/what-taiwan-japan-relations-might-look-like-in-2016/. See also Tsai's remarks, "Fostering

the Center for Strategic and International Studies (CSIS), that she would base her cross-strait policy on the "existing ROC constitutional order" and "the will of the Taiwanese people."[71] Tsai's greater moderation put the USA more at ease about her candidacy in 2016 than her first run in 2012.[72]

3   Main Argument

Hence, why the KMT administration under Ma Ying-jeou pursued a policy that risked alienating its chief security guarantor—the USA—and losing its political autonomy by under-reacting to or under-balancing against the PRC is my central query. My argument stresses that the ruling KMT elites' China-centric nationalism and its political objective to rejuvenate a "one-China"-dominant political discourse and legitimacy to supplant pro-independence political forces within Taiwan are the critical determinants behind Taipei's accommodationist policy toward Beijing, even at the expense of providing the mainland China with greater leverages over Taiwan and distancing Taipei from Washington. My goal here is to deepen the understanding on how elite politics and domestic political dissensus, as manifested in the KMT's and DPP's competing and opposing visions of nation-building projects, can derail Taiwan's national security.

The "Second-Image Reversed": External Powers and Domestic Politics

Essentially, the interrelationships between international balance of power and domestic or unit-level politics and how these two levels shape foreign policy decisions have been long-standing topics of interest in the field of international relations and security studies. Before examining how domestic political factors could exercise autonomous filtering functions to channel

---

Peace through Global Contributions: A Pragmatic and Sustainable Approach to Taiwan's Foreign Policy," (September 22, 2015), accessible at: http://english.dpp.org.tw/dpp-29th-anniversary/. And, "Taiwan Can Build on U.S. Ties," *The Wall Street Journal* (June 1, 2015), accessible at: http://www.wsj.com/articles/taiwan-can-build-on-u-s-ties-1433176635.

[71] Tsai Ing-wen, "Taiwan Meeting the Challenges: Crafting a Model of New Asian Value," Speech at the CSIS (June 4, 2015), accessible at: http://csis.org/files/attachments/150603_Tsai_Ing_wen_transcript.pdf.

[72] Wu, "Heading towards Troubled Waters"? p. 69.

the impact of international systemic constraints (the focus of Chap. 2), this section seeks to look at how external influences shape or constitute domestic interests and policy preferences in the first place. This "second-image reversed" theory, thus, concentrates on how international forces affect domestic politics, which, in turn, shape policy outcomes.[73] Though recognizing that domestic political and interest structures are crucial factors behind national policy decisions, Peter Gourevitch stresses that one "must explore the extent to which that structure itself derives from the exigencies of the international system."[74]

Indeed, two aspects of international system exert powerful impacts upon the character of domestic regimes and constitutions as well as patterns of socioeconomic interests: (1) the distribution of power among states and (2) the distribution of economic activity and wealth. Domestic politics, in short, is a product of "war and trade."[75] The anarchic nature of international system and changing distribution of power among states generate uncertainty and fear of insecurity. States are constantly living under the threat of being conquered, occupied, annihilated, or made subservient. As a result, the perennial struggles for power and survival among states induce them "to organize themselves internally so as to meet these external challenges." War is similar to a market: "it punishes some forms of organization and rewards others."[76] To be sure, the vulnerability of states to international pressures is not uniform since some countries occupy a more exposed position than others. For instance, the different external security environments for Great Britain and Germany in the late nineteenth century dictated their respective opposing domestic political arrangements, with the former being a liberal democracy whereas the latter an authoritarian militarist state. The greater susceptibility to foreign wars and security challenges led to the creation of absolutist and garrison states in Prussia/Germany.[77]

---

[73] Peter Gourevitch, "The Second-Image Reversed: The International Sources of Domestic Politics," *International Organization* 32, no. 4 (1978), pp. 881–912. See also Steven Lobell, "Second Image Reversed Politics: Britain's Choice of Freer Trade or Imperial Preferences, 1903–1906, 1917–1923, 1930–1932," *International Studies Quarterly* 43, no. 4 (1999), pp. 671–693; and Ayse Zarakol, "Revisiting Second Image Reversed: Lessons from Turkey and Thailand," *International Studies Quarterly* 57, no. 1 (2013), pp. 150–162.
[74] Peter Gourevitch, "The Second Image Reversed," p. 882.
[75] Ibid., p. 883.
[76] Ibid., p. 896.
[77] Ibid., pp. 896–897.

Furthermore, foreign security and economic contingencies could often empower or enervate the state, providing central policymaking elites with the autonomy and moral imperatives to supplant and overcome domestic oppositions, institutional barriers, and entrenched societal interests, or vice versa. Examining British foreign economic policy choices, Steven Lobell contends that the "commercial composition" of external contenders played a significant role. When the UK was surrounded by emerging contenders which adopted both imperialist and liberal economic policies, London rejected mercantilist policy preferences in 1906 and 1923. Nevertheless, by 1932, "when Britain confronted primarily imperial contenders who favored economic autarky and self-sufficiency, this shift in the commercial composition of contenders strengthened [domestic] economic nationalists over free traders, contributing to Britain's adoption of imperialist preferences."[78] Likewise, the emergence of liberal ideas and internationalist interests in the 1920s and 1930s inspired greater demands for commercial liberalization in America.[79] Since domestic protectionist interests had been firmly institutionalized and politically entrenched throughout the nineteenth century, economic liberalization was perceived by many Congressional members as tantamount to endangering their constituents' economic well-being and, thereby, harming their own electoral prospects. With the passage of the Trade Reciprocal Act of 1934, the delegation of Congressional trade policy authority to the executive branch made trade liberalization more probable. External events are also crucial by cultivating opportunities for leaders to remold domestic institutions and change interest articulations. In the words of Jeff Frieden, "The [Great] Depression and eventually World War II weakened the economic nationalists and allowed the state to reshape both policies and policy networks. By the late 1930s, economic nationalists were isolated or ignored, and most relevant decisions were placed within the purview of relatively internationalist bureaucracies."[80] The Franklin D. Roosevelt administration essentially construed America's national interests in terms of economic liberalization and multilateralism. Foreign crises in the 1930s and 1940s gave

[78] Steven Lobell, "Second Image Reversed Politics," p. 688.
[79] Jeff Frieden, "Sectoral Conflict and Foreign Economic Policy, 1914–1940," *International Organization* 42, no. 1 (1988), pp. 59–90. See also Judith Goldstein, *Ideas, Interests, and American Trade Policy* (Ithaca, NY: Cornell University Press, 1993).
[80] Jeff Frieden, "Sectoral Conflict and Foreign Economic Policy, 1914–1940," p. 88.

the president the room to maneuver and take initiatives to reformulate societal interests and political institutions. "The Depression and World War II removed many of the institutional, coalitional, and ideological ties that had bound policymakers in the 1920s. In the United States, the result was the defeat of economic nationalism, but of course the crisis had very different effects elsewhere."[81]

Ronald Rogowski, in *Commerce and Coalition*, has noted that political interests and regime outcome are the inherent consequences of international free trade and protectionism. The Stolper–Samuelson theorem, also known as the factor endowment theory, proposes the following:

> In almost any society, protection benefits (and liberalization of trade harms) owners of factors in which relative to the rest of the world, that society is poorly endowed, as well as producers who use that scarce factor intensely. Conversely, protection harms (and liberalization benefits) those factors that—again, relative to the rest of the world—the given society holds abundantly, and the producers who use those locally abundant factors intensively. Thus, in a society rich in labor but poor in capital, protection benefits capital and harms labor; and liberalization of trade benefits labor and harms capital.[82]

Hence, it should be obvious that the economic ramifications of international trade policy will engender domestic political cleavages. The beneficiaries of safer or cheaper trade will support yet greater liberalization, while gainers from higher trade barriers will lobby even greater self-sufficiency or protectionism. On the contrary, those who are harmed by freer trade will demand protection or imperialism, and victims of high tariffs will seek more openness. "The beneficiaries, potential or actual, of any such exogenous change will likely to be strengthened politically and the economic losers weakened politically."[83] Broadly speaking, increasing exposure to trade must entail in either urban–rural (labor and capitalists against landlords) or class (landlords and capitalists against labor) conflict.[84] For instance, in Great Britain, where labor and capital are abundant and land is scarce, liberal urban interests will pit against the protectionist

---

[81] Ibid., p. 89.
[82] Ronald Rogowski, *Commerce and Coalitions: How Trade Affects Domestic Political Alignments* (Princeton, NJ: Princeton University Press, 1989), p. 3.
[83] Ibid., p. 6.
[84] Ibid., p. 7.

countryside. Democracy is more likely to be observed in such a case. On the contrary, in pre-industrial economies, such as Japan and Germany in the late nineteenth century, where labor was bounteous and land and capital scarce, the reactionary coalition of capitalists and landed gentries was more likely to arise to counteract the pro-free trade labor forces. If the marriage between "iron and rye" were empowered politically, as a result of the declining world trade, the institutional outlook would become fascism.[85] Thus, the "fatal and malignant alliance" of land and capital had become detrimental to the principles of freedom and democracy.

Great Power Rivalry and Nation-Building Projects

By the same token, foreign policy dynamics or inter-state relationships also drive nation-building policy choices or visions within a polity. According to Harris Mylonas, "external support and sponsorship of [nation-building] movements in foreign states is a very old practice in the international system."[86] As Ernest Gellner maintained, the political principle of nationalism holds that the "political [state] and the national unit should be congruent."[87] The reality, however, depicts that the number of potential nations is much greater than that of possible viable states, and, as a result, "many of these nations live or, until recently have lived, not in compact territorial units but intermixed with each other in complex patterns." Not all nationalisms, in other words, can be satisfied at any rate at the same time, and the satisfaction of some inevitably "spells the frustration of others."[88] Hence, the collective initiative designed to "render the boundaries of the nation congruent with those of its governance unit [the state]" is a crucial component of nation building.[89] It is a "process of socio-political development, which ideally—usually over a longer historical time span—allows initially loosely linked communities to become

---

[85] Ibid., p. 33.
[86] Harris Mylonas, *The Politics of Nation-Building: Making Co-Nationals, Refugees, and Minorities* (New York: Cambridge University Press, 2012), p. 31.
[87] Ernest Gellner, *Nations and Nationalism* (Itaca, NY: Cornell University Press, 2006), p. 1.
[88] Ibid., p. 2.
[89] Wayne Norman, *Negotiating Nationalism: Nation-Building, Federalism, and Secession in the Multinational State* (New York: Oxford University Press, 2005), p. 25.

a common society with a nation-state corresponding to it."[90] In a sense, then, nation builders seek to constitute the so-called "imagined political community" as both inherently "territorially limited" and "sovereign."[91] Yet, at the same time, the nations to which they "give political expression always loom out of an immemorial past, and, still more important, glide into a limitless future."[92] Thus, the other essential aspect of nation building is the shaping or engineering of national identities based on a "mixture of [common, voluntarist] loyalty and identification and of extraneous incentives, positive or negative, on hopes and fears."[93] Indeed, nations and their identities can be defined "in terms both of will and of culture, and in terms of the convergence of them both with political units." In these conditions, wrote Gellner, "Men will to be politically united with all those, and only those, who share their culture. Polities then will to extend their boundaries to the limits of their cultures, and to protect and impose their culture with the boundaries of their power. The fusion of will, culture, and polity becomes the norms, and one not easily or frequently defied."[94] Though in most cases a national identity already exists, political actors try to configure or reconfigure it "qualitatively, and not just quantitatively, by addressing the values and beliefs that characterize the national identity in question, as well as the sentiments that bring it to life."[95] Consequently, these national beliefs, sentiments, and values can be instilled, eliminated, modified, strengthened, or weakened significantly from one generation to the next. For instance, on the question of the nation's homeland, Wayne Norman suggested that:

> Over a short period of time, members of the nation could come to hold a different conception of what its borders are or ought to be, of whether some other group also has a legitimate claim to the same territory as part of its homeland, of whether both groups can or cannot cohabit the territory in peaceful cooperation, and of how vital some particular chunk of the historical homeland really is to the nation and to the priorities and well-being of individual members of the nation.[96]

---

[90] Jochen Hippler, "Violent Conflicts, Conflict Prevention and Nation-Building—Terminology and Political Concepts," in Jochen Hippler ed., *Nation-Building: A Key Concept for Peaceful Conflict Transformation?* (London: Pluto Press, 2005), p. 6.
[91] Benedict Anderson, *Imagined Communities* (New York: Verson, 2006), pp. 6–7.
[92] Ibid., pp. 11–12.
[93] Ernest Gellner, *Nations and Nationalism*, p. 52.
[94] Ibid., p. 54.
[95] Wayne Norman, *Negotiating Nationalism*, p. 33.
[96] Ibid., p. 37.

Nationalism has its own "amnesia and selections which, even when they may be severely secular, can be profoundly distorting and deceptive."[97] In sum, a nation-building project is frequently employed by internal or external actors (or both) as an instrument to establish "a political and social system constituted under a nation-state where this appears to serve their interests, where it fulfils particular functional requirements to a greater degree than a previously existing arrangement, or where it strengthens their power or weakens that of their opponents."[98]

Mechanisms involved in nation building include having a unifying ideology, integration of society, and the creation of a functional centralized state, and they mainly rely on three policy types: accommodation, assimilation, and exclusion. Whereas accommodation stresses on the peaceful coexistence and mutual respect of the "differences" of multiple groups within a state through agreed upon legal, civic, and institutional norms and frameworks, assimilation and exclusion usually aim at the complete adoption of the dominant group's culture, identity, and way of life by the lesser core groups or total physical removal or annihilation of the latter.[99] It should be noted, however, that accommodation does not mean that the leading state actors are indifferent toward the "loyalty" of the non-core group members. The latter is still required to obey and swear allegiance to the central state apparatuses, and, on some occasions, may still be discriminated against by national policies and laws. Thus, even in a liberal democracy, where accommodation is usually observed by constitutional guarantees, central state elites cannot be entirely neutral about national identity issues as deliberate or implicit indoctrinations are enacted through, for instance, language, education, and military service policies.[100] Under the KMT's authoritarian rule from 1947 to 1987, for instance, the central leaders were clearly pushing for a strong assimilation policy to forcefully integrate the local Taiwanese population to speak, behave, and think like the Chinese. While vowing to defeat the CCP, the Chiang government also voiced its staunch opposition toward Taiwanese independence. Since democratization, however, the ROC has opted for accommodation to stress on protecting and respecting Taiwan's multi-ethnic and linguistic makeups. A clear "Taiwan-first" consciousness has

---

[97] Ernest Gellner, *Nations and Nationalism*, pp. 55–56.
[98] Jochen Hippler, "Violent Conflicts, Conflict Prevention and Nation-Building," pp. 6–7.
[99] Harris Mylonas, *The Politics of Nation-Building*, pp. 21–22.
[100] Wayne Norman, *Negotiating Nationalism*, pp. 54–55.

increasingly been consolidated into the island's mainstream identity and superseded the KMT's "China-first" orientations.[101] Yet, this new national or civic identity is inevitably "bent" to serve the interests of the prevailing political leadership, so that the DPP would place a much higher premium on the native Taiwanese ethnic origins, whereas the KMT would continue to stress on the common Chinese ancestry between the mainland and Taiwanese compatriots.

Nation building, therefore, may be peaceful, violent, or a hybrid of both. In extreme circumstances, there may be intensive upheavals and bloodshed (such as ethnic cleansing and genocide). The magnitude of contention and bargaining between the ruling or dominating political elites, known as the host state, and the "non-core groups," defined as "any aggregation of individuals that is perceived as an unassimilated ethnic group (the relevant marker can be linguistic, religious, physical, or cultural) by the ruling political elites of a country," is often contingent upon the balance of power among the external patrons supporting or opposing one of these local entities.[102] In other words, the choice of accommodation, assimilation, and exclusion may very well depend on the power configurations of great powers in the international arena and their strategic, ideological, and ethnic ties with the political actors within the state. Domestic actors may bargain more (or less) intransigently or opt for greater (or less) brutality if one of the parties to the conflict is backed by a strong (or weak) external power or "reference state." Sometimes, a host state may engage in violence against a minority group if the latter is assisted by adversarial foreign states or international third parties, as illustrated by NATO's involvement in the Kosovo crisis in 1999.[103] Due to strategic or cultural motivations or both, a foreign power may also be

---

[101] Shirley Lin 2016c, p. 211.

[102] Mylonas 2012, pp. 25–26. Also, the non-core groups and the ruling elites do not necessarily correspond, respectively, to the numerical minority and majority. The ruling state may comprise a minority group but, due to its greater military and/or economic capabilities as well as strong foreign support, is able to subdue and dominate the majority population.

[103] Many path-breaking studies have examined these relationships. See Erin Jenne, "A Bargaining Theory of Minority Demands: Explaining the Dog That Did Not Bite in 1990s Yugoslavia," *International Studies Quarterly* 48, no. 4 (December, 2004), pp. 729–754; Erin Jenne, *Ethnic Bargaining* (Ithaca, NY: Cornell University Press, 2007); Idean Salehyan, "Transnational Rebels: Neighboring States as Sanctuary for Rebel Groups," *World Politics* 59, no. 2 (January 2007), pp. 217–242; Arman Grigoryan, "Third-Party Intervention and the Escalation of State-Minority Conflicts," *International Studies Quarterly* 54, no. 4 (December 2010), pp. 1143–1174; and Harris Mylonas, *The Politics of Nation-Building*.

inclined to support its ethnic brethren in a civil conflict of another state in order to protect its safety or to deepen the animosity of the warring factions. The external power, taking advantage of the protracted conflict of the divided state, can strengthen its security, prestige, and wealth through such "divide and conquer" tactics.[104] In its conflict with Ukraine, Russia's forcible annexation of Crimea in March 2014, justified by Moscow on the grounds of defending Russian-speaking civilians there from attacks directed by Kiev, demonstrated President Vladimir Putin's strategic calculation to weaken Ukraine and prevent the latter's alliance with the West.[105]

USA–PRC Relations and Nation Building in Taiwan

In a similar vein, the emergence of the KMT–DPP political divide and nationalistic cleavages in Taiwan did not develop in a vacuum. Even though their partisan antagonism can be traced to the KMT's authoritarianism and its attempt to assimilate the Taiwanese population into Chinese, one cannot dismiss the impact of external forces. Indeed, their opposing policy articulations and nation-building perspectives regarding Taiwan's relations with mainland China are shaped, in part, by the prevailing and changing USA–PRC strategic relationship since the onset of the Cold War era.[106] Whereas the USA has played an important role in supporting, albeit unobtrusively, the native Taiwanese aspiration for self-determination and fostering the liberal party politics in Taiwan's democratization, the PRC has endeavored to use social and commercial exchanges to deepen cross-strait ties and, simultaneously, reach out to the KMT in Taiwan to jointly constrain the expansion of the DPP.

[104] Alexis Heraclides, "Secessionist Minorities and External Involvement," *International Organization* 44, no. 3 (Summer 1990), pp. 341–378; Pieter Van Houten, "The Role of a Minority's Reference State in Ethnic Relations," *European Journal of Sociology* 39, no. 1 (1998), pp. 110–146; Stephen Saidman, "Explaining the International Relations of Secessionist Conflicts: Vulnerability versus Ethnic Ties," *International Organization* 51, no. 4 (1997), pp. 721–753; David Davis and Will Moore, "Ethnicity Matters: Transnational Ethnic Alliances and Foreign Policy Behavior," *International Studies Quarterly* 41, no. 1 (March 1997), pp. 171–184; and Stephen Saidman, "Discrimination in International Relations: Analyzing External Support for Ethnic Groups," *Journal of Peace Research* 39, no. 1 (2002), pp. 27–50.

[105] Sidney Tarrow, *War, States, & Contention* (Ithaca, NY: Cornell University Press, 2015), pp. 3–4.

[106] John Copper, *The KMT's Return to Power* (Lanham, MD: Lexington Books, 2014), p. 18.

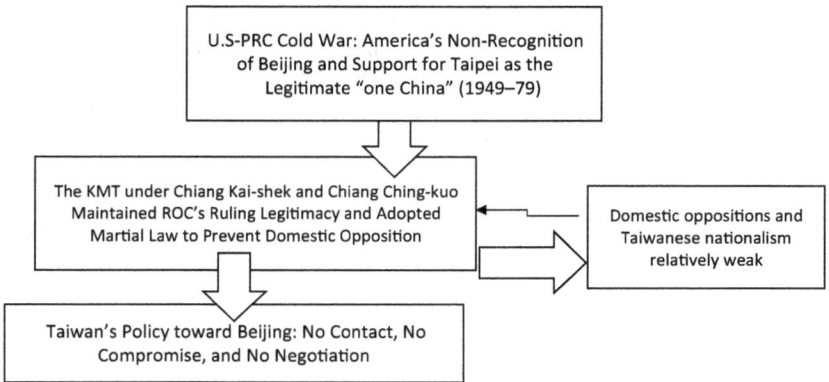

Fig. 1.1 The USA–PRC Cold War and the KMT's authoritarianism and "one-China" legitimacy, 1949–79

The USA and Taiwan
The KMT's "one-China" stance was buttressed by America's continued recognition of the ROC on Taiwan as the sole legitimate Chinese government between 1949 and 1979 (see Fig. 1.1). For the 30 years since the ROC retreated to Taiwan after 1949, American Cold War policy and its isolation of Beijing empowered Taipei's claim as the only legitimate Chinese government which was usurped by the insurgency of "Communist bandits" (*gongfei*).[107] The relocation to Taipei from Nanjing of the seat of the ROC's central government was conceived as only temporary. Taiwan represented "the last and only hope for the KMT to retake power on the mainland, and Taipei, the island's provincial capital, was designated the 'wartime provisional capital' (*zhanshi shoudu*) by the exiled regime."[108] To convey the image of the ROC as the true heir of Chinese traditional culture and ruling authority to its international counterparts and also to the overseas Chinese and the domestic audience, the KMT regime "took pains to assume the role of inheritor of traditional values as the direct descendant of Chinese political orthodoxy (*daotong*)."[109] The primary mission of the

---

[107] Chang Hui-chin and Richard Holt, *Language, Politics, and Identity in Taiwan* (New York: Routledge, 2015), pp. 20–21.
[108] Chang Bi-yu, *Place, Identity, and National Imagination in Postwar Taiwan* (New York: Routledge, 2015), p. 24.
[109] Ibid., p. 30.

KMT, in other words, was to "prepare itself for the day when legitimate authority—that of the Republic of China and its Nationalist Party-led regime—would be restored to the mainland."[110]

On Taiwan, Chiang Kai-shek not only deepened anti-communist sentiments among the Taiwanese people but also endeavored to foster "Chinese nationalism, cleanse the island of Japanese influence, and transform the former Japanese subjects into knowledgeable and patriotic Chinese citizens."[111] The narrative of nationhood propagated by the KMT leadership, through government propaganda, arts, media, and history and geography education, during its first 50-year rule of Taiwan (1949–2000) had always been "China-centric."[112] In short, the KMT had mostly identified China as the genuine "motherland," a glorious nation with a long history, magnificent civilization, and bountiful resources. Taiwan, in contrast, was marginalized as peripheral and secondary.[113]

But Washington had not been too enthusiastic about the KMT's retreat to Taiwan in the late 1940s.[114] Unimpressed by the KMT's inept and corrupt governance on the Chinese mainland, the USA aspired to create a free and autonomous Taiwan, where self-determination and liberal democracy could eventually take root. This liberal vision was articulated early on by the Harry Truman administration. While opposing America's further involvement in the Chinese Civil War and giving more aid to the KMT regime, Secretary of State Dean Acheson was very sympathetic to the plight of the native Taiwanese, persuading the president that it was important to give the Taiwanese "a chance to express their own desires for their own future."[115] He was receptive to the idea of creating an independent Taiwan, though the administration dropped that thought as soon as it was discovered that the independence movements on the island then were too weak to stage a successful bid.[116] In March 1949, Acheson

---

[110] Rigger 2013, p. 297.

[111] Chang Bi-yu, "So Close, Yet So Far Away: Imagining Chinese 'Homeland' in Taiwan's Geography Education," *Cultural Geographies* 18, no. 3 (2010), pp. 385–386.

[112] Chang 2015, p. 1.

[113] Chang 2010, p. 389.

[114] Lin Hsio-ting, *Accidental State: Chiang Kai-shek, the United States, and the Making of Taiwan* (Cambridge, MA: Harvard University Press, 2016).

[115] "Meeting in the President's Office with Senators Wherry and Bridges on China," April 28, 1949, Secretary of State Acheson's Memorandum March-May1949/Box8/RG59/250/49/5/6-7, National Archives, College Park, MD.

[116] Lin 2016b, 128–134.

warned that "it is a cardinal point in our thinking that if our present policy is to have any hope of success in Formosa, we must carefully conceal our wish to separate the island from mainland control."[117] As the special consultant to the State Department, John Foster Dulles posited, on April 21, 1950, that Taiwan would serve as "a concrete example [to mainland China] of a better way to economic improvement and national and individual freedom than through Communism."[118] Dean Rusk also wished to foster an autonomous Taiwan as a "showcase of liberal democracy."[119] The US government also thought about the feasibility of putting Taiwan under UN trusteeship. In any event, the outbreak of war on the Korean peninsula on June 25, 1950 firmly solidified America's determination to safeguard Taiwan from the PRC. [120] "No longer would the United States acquiesce in the Communist conquest of the island. Instead, a variety of schemes were resurrected to create an independent Formosa, preferably a liberal, democratic, Chiang [Kai-shek]-less Formosa," observed Warren Cohen.[121]

Later, even staunch realists like Richard Nixon and Henry Kissinger, though promising not to challenge Beijing's "one-China" principle, adamantly insisted on the defense of Taiwan's freedom and autonomy.[122] In the 1972 Shanghai Communiqué, for instance, the USA's statement on Taiwan was artful, subtle, and somewhat confused. "The United States acknowledges that all Chinese on either side of the Taiwan Strait maintain there is but one China and that Taiwan is a part of China. The United States government does not challenge that position."[123] In addition,

---

[117] "Statement by the Secretary of State (Acheson) at the 35th Meeting of the National Security Council on The Formosan Problem," March 3, 1949, PSF/NSC Meeting # 35/Truman Papers/Box 220, HST Library.

[118] "Memorandum on Formosa," April 21, 1950, John F. Dulles Papers, 1860–1988/China, People's Republic of, 1950/Box47, Seeley G. Mudd Manuscript Library, Princeton University.

[119] Warren Cohen, *Dean Rusk* (Totowa, NJ: Cooper Square Publishers, 1980), p. 46.

[120] Thomas Christensen, *Useful Adversaries* (Princeton, NJ: Princeton University Press, 1996), p. 130; Robert Accinelli, Crisis and Commitment (Chapel Hill, NC: University of North Carolina Press, 1996), p. 27.

[121] Warren Cohen, *America's Response to China* (New York: Columbia University Press, 2010), p. 187.

[122] Harry Harding, *A Fragile Relationship* (Washington DC: Brookings Institute, 1992), p. 44; William Burr ed., *The Kissinger Transcripts* (New York: The New Press, 1998), p. 66.

[123] The excerpts from the Shanghai Communiqué (formally entitled "The Joint Communiqué of the People's Republic of China and the United States of America," February

America reaffirmed "its interests in a peaceful settlement of the Taiwan question by the Chinese themselves." The verb "acknowledges" is used in place of "recognizes," indicating Washington's mere cognizance of, but not necessarily agreement with, Beijing's position.[124] Kissinger recalled: "If the United States recognized Taiwan as part of China, our saying we want a peaceful solution has no force. It is a Chinese territory.... For us to go to war with a recognized country...over a part of what we would recognize as their country would be preposterous."[125] It is also interesting to note that Taiwan is made merely a "part of China" instead of "province of China." If the USA had referred to Taiwan as a "province of China" and then later recognized the PRC as the sole legal government of China, then the island would effectively be treated as a province under Beijing's direct sovereign jurisdiction.[126] The phrase "does not challenge" can also be construed as merely "accepting" rather than agreeing to.[127] Interestingly, the notion of the "Chinese on either side of the Taiwan Strait" may also be antiquated in today's context, particularly as a substantial proportion of Taiwan's citizens do not perceive themselves as Chinese.[128]

As Washington normalized diplomatic ties with Beijing starting in the 1970s, the US support for the KMT government dwindled, and it has become more vocal in criticizing the KMT's repressive and undemocratic governance. The KMT government was pressured to loosen up its "one-China" myth and to shore up its ruling legitimacy through an alternative channel: allowing political liberalization and democratization on the island. For decades, writes Shelley Rigger, "Washington had overlooked its anti-Communist ally's human rights abuses, but by 1979, the United States had switched its allegiance to Beijing. Taipei had lost its privileged position and with it, protection against scrutiny."[129] The island's democratic transition, therefore, "gave it a powerful new claim on Americans'

27, 1972) are quoted from Bush 2004, 128–129. See also Romberg 2003, 233–234. See the full text of Shanghai Communiqué at: http://history.state.gov/historicaldocuments/frus1969-76v17/d203.

[124] Dennis Hickey, "America's Two-Point Policy and the Future of Taiwan," *Asian Survey* 28, no. 8 (1988), p. 883.

[125] Kissinger's quote is taken from Timothy Crawford, *Pivotal Deterrence* (Ithaca, NY: Cornell University Press, 2003), p. 190.

[126] Bush 2004, p. 129.
[127] Romberg 2003, p. 47.
[128] Rigger 2013, p. 295.
[129] Rigger 2011, p. 75.

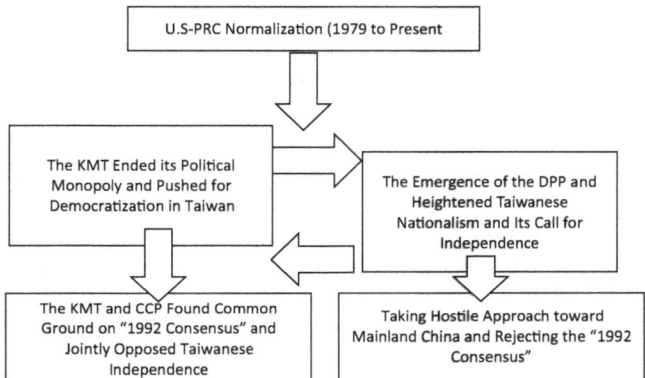

Fig. 1.2 The USA–PRC normalization and the emergence of Taiwanese democracy

affection and loyalty."[130] Political opposition and activities erupted more voraciously and different expressions of opinion were permitted to thrive in Taiwan's burgeoning free marketplace of ideas. The DPP was organized and established in such a context and seized upon the new political opportunity to challenge the beleaguered KMT and advocate for greater self-determination and Taiwanese independence. Ultimately, the DPP's Chen Shui-bian terminated the KMT's enduring one-party monopoly of political power by winning Taiwan's presidency in 2000 and 2004. The KMT, under Ma Ying-jeou, returned to power in 2008 and held on to it in 2012. Then, on January 16, 2016, the DPP won both the presidency and the Legislative Yuan majority (see Fig. 1.2).

Nevertheless, Taiwan's democratization saw the growth of not only a vibrant civil society, dynamic elections, and free market economy but also the antagonistic and polarizing contentions between the KMT and DPP, with the former aiming to defend and rebuild the ROC "one-China" centrality, whereas the latter sought to denigrate the ROC and its "one-China" claim whenever possible and, at the same time, prop up the prospect of creating a Republic of Taiwan. According to John Copper, the "KMT and the DPP took different positions on promoting democracy." The KMT pushed democratization to convince the world that the ROC deserves its support and its democracy as a model for a future united Chinese nation

---

[130] Rigger 2013, p. 297.

that includes both Taiwan and the mainland.[131] In contrast, the DPP advanced the idea that a democratic Taiwan is essentially different from mainland China and the two are inherently separate and incompatible.[132]

The PRC and Taiwan

Whereas the USA has played an important role in fostering the liberal party politics in Taiwan's democratization, the PRC has endeavored to use commercial exchanges to deepen cross-strait ties and, simultaneously, reach out to the pro-unification forces in Taiwan to constrain the expansion of the DPP and their supporters.[133] Seeing the rise of independence proclivities, fostered by Lee Teng-hui and Chen Shui-bian and the DPP's political ascendancy in Taiwan, Beijing sought to shape the island's internal politics to its advantage. Though remaining steadfast regarding the use of military coercion to prevent Taiwanese independence, the PRC has, since the mid-1990s, relaxed its interpretations of "one China" in order to more tacitly accommodate the KMT's OCRI within the "1992 consensus." As will be noted in Chap. 3, in its more expansive definition of "one China," the CCP leadership has eschewed its previously unequivocal position that China must be the PRC, thereby indirectly condoning the KMT's interpretation that China could also be the ROC.

Beijing's greater patience and flexibility on this issue reached its zenith under Hu Jintao and has been closely followed by Xi Jinping. Susan Shirk posits, "The [CCP] aimed to isolate politically Chen Shui-bian and the Democratic Progressive Party while encouraging other groups to block Chen's drive toward independence, as well as laying the groundwork for forward progress after 2008 when a new president will be elected."[134] Hence, in April and May 2005, the Hu Jintao administration reached out to the chairmen of the KMT and the People First Party (PFP), Lien Chan and James Soong, respectively, and invited them to visit the mainland. Both the KMT and PFP were in the "pan-blue" coalition that supported better relations with China on the basis of economic cooperation and the "1992 consensus." The Hu-Lien meeting represented the first ice-breaking between the top KMT and CCP leadership since 1949. Hu, in an

---

[131] Copper 2014, p. 20.
[132] Ibid.
[133] This author's interview with Richard Bush and Robert Sutter.
[134] Susan Shirk, *China: Fragile Superpower* (New York: Oxford University Press, 2008), p. 207.

unprecedented gesture, credited the KMT for its great sacrifice during the fight against Imperial Japan in the Second World War.[135] Beijing's overture helped to solidify the KMT–CCP united front and consolidated their mutual commitment to a united Chinese nation and to jointly oppose Taiwanese independence. After Ma came to power in 2008, cross-strait relations warmed up drastically, and Beijing never concealed its preference for the KMT to win in the 2012 and 2016 elections.[136]

Domestic Politics Filters International Systemic Influence: Neoclassical Realism

Once domestic beliefs and interest articulations have been established, by the combined forces of international and domestic factors, they begin to assume a "life of their own" or become "institutionalized." According to Judith Goldstein and Robert Keohane, as ideas are successfully incorporated into the terms of political debate and embedded in organizations, their influence "will be reflected in the incentives of those in the organization and those whose interests are served by it." They may also be prolonged for decades or even generations even though the original interests that promoted them have long faded.[137] At a later time, these institutionalized ideas continue to "exert an effect: it is no longer possible to understand [foreign] policy outcomes on the basis of contemporary configurations of interests and power alone."[138] In line with neoclassical realism, this research, therefore, also emphasizes the importance of elites' political interests and nation-building initiatives as they may dilute the effects of international structural constraints. In essence, foreign policy outcomes are not necessarily based on well-calibrated national interest considerations. Rather, they may result from domestic political contentions, inner conflicts, human emotions, and decision-makers' nationalistic perceptions—factors that could be irrational, parochial, and even dangerous from the vantage point of international community.[139] The discussion on neoclassical realism will be the main focus of Chap. 2.

---

[135] Ibid., p. 208.
[136] Copper 2014, p. 171.
[137] Goldstein and Keohane 1993, p. 20.
[138] Ibid., p. 21.
[139] Gideon Rose, "Neoclassical Realism and Theories of Foreign Policy," *World Politics* 51, no. 1 (1998), pp. 144-72. Randall Schweller, *Unanswered Threats: Political Constraints on the Balance of Power* (Princeton, NJ: Princeton University Press, 2006).

Notwithstanding the heightened rivalry between Washington and Beijing and China's unabated military threats toward Taiwan, however, the latter's highly polarized internal political identities and elite-societal divisions have led the KMT administration to "appease" or under-balance against a increasingly assertive China. In the words of a neoclassical realist, Randall Schweller, dangerous political divisions exist "when [leaders] and groups within society do not confer legitimacy on the institutions that structure it and, even more so, when a significant segment of the [political elites] and population intend to overthrow the state."[140] Thus, for a deeply fragmented polity, the presence of an external threat may actually widen intra-groups' or intra-elites' contradictions, leading a large part of the socio-political community to either actively collaborate with the foreign enemy or remain passive rather than resisting or counterbalancing the challenge. The external power may even assist the domestic interests and elites in their quest to propagate certain ideological or nation-building initiatives. Elites and societal forces, in other words, may find it imperative to ally with the "foreign foe" in order to combat the "traitorous enemies from within." This is reinforced by the fact that political elites and societal actors lack consensus on whether the revisionist power constitutes a genuine national security threat.

Between 2008 and 2016, the KMT president, Ma Ying-jeou, aimed to rectify the anti-China and ROC-delegitimizing policies established by the previous Chen Shui-bian administration of the DPP, which wished to construct an independent Taiwanese republic, freed from Chinese influence. Thus, the DPP and its supporters tend to view China (whether the ROC or PRC) as an imminent threat to Taiwan's freedom and democracy, whereas the KMT (despite its historical feud with the CCP) has found common ground with Beijing in opposing Taiwanese independence and maintaining cross-strait peace and economic cooperation on the basis of the "1992 consensus." The KMT government, then, has enacted the "one-China" political, economic, and ideational campaigns in numerous venues, through bilateral economic integration, political rhetoric, revisions of school textbooks, name rectifications in official proclamations and documents, and linking Taiwan–China's historical memory and cultural heritage and their common victimization by Imperial Japan in the first half of the twentieth century. The KMT government was pushing for these policies not only to consolidate cross-strait ties but also to supplant the

---

[140] Randall Schweller, *Unanswered Threats*, p. 51.

DPP's de-Sinification initiatives, even though there had been heightened public opposition in Taiwan to a closer China–Taiwan relationship. As already noted, the Xi–Ma meeting provided a forum for the CCP to voice its support of the KMT and the "1992 consensus" platform in the 2016 election, thus driving the wedge between the two parties and among the people of Taiwan.

In sum, this work aims to contribute to the neoclassical realist model of international relations by illustrating how interrelations between international structural constraints and domestic politics, particularly elite and societal dissensus, determine Taiwan's mainland policy and how incoherent national identities within Taiwan could undermine the island's security positions. Hence, a state, though facing an externally assertive power or threat, may not select a counterbalancing strategy. Rather, the choice of foreign security policy depends on the state's internal political environment, such as elite politics and elite-societal relations.

4   Plan of the Book

Chapter 2 examines the theory of neoclassical realism, reviews several notable works, and postulates how the paradigm could enrich our understanding of the Ma Ying-jeou administration's China policy in the midst of greater USA–China rivalry. Then, Chap. 3 traces the origins and development of the "1992 consensus" policy. Specifically, it also uses the neoclassical realist model to examine why, despite its growing power and influence vis-à-vis Taiwan, Beijing has allowed for greater latitude in the interpretations of "one China." As the power-politics explanation is inadequate in accounting for the PRC's behavior, this chapter proposes that one must not dismiss the role of ideational variables such as discourse and "argumentative persuasion" in shaping the interests, identity, and articulation of the policy elites responsible for cross-strait relations. This author seeks to show, through the policy statements and rhetoric expressed by officials from Taipei and Beijing, the changing construction of the "one-China" principle, and how the PRC has gradually come to terms with the continued existence of the ROC even though it remains unlikely to explicitly and formally recognize it. Nevertheless, in light of the rising political power of pro-independence forces on Taiwan, the CCP elites have opted for the "lesser of two evils" as the ROC and its Constitution, at least, stipulate both Taiwan and the mainland belonging to a one Chinese nation. Such tacit understanding has strengthened the KMT–CCP united front on the foundation of the "1992 consensus." In spite of Tsai's successful election in January 2016, the Xi Jinping administration has maintained its stance that the DPP must accept the "1992 consensus" and its core principle of "one China."

Chapter 4 delves into the cross-strait policy of President Ma Ying-jeou between 2008 and 2016. In essence, its emphasis is on the KMT's efforts to rehabilitate the ROC's centrality and ruling legitimacy after years of de-Sinification and Taiwanization campaigns pushed by Lee Teng-hui and Chen Shui-bian. This chapter aims to demonstrate that the Ma administration was engaging in a nation-(re)building project to integrate Taiwan and the mainland through (1) bilateral cross-strait economic integration; (2) revisions of school textbooks; (3) name rectifications in official proclamations and documents; and (4) linking Taiwan and China's shared historical memory and cultural heritage. These nation-building mechanisms constituted the Ma government's under-balancing approach toward the PRC. Strictly following the ROC Constitution promulgated on the Chinese mainland in 1947, Ma further underscored that the relations between both sides are, in fact, not state-to-state since Taiwan and the mainland are merely two regions, though currently separate due to the Chinese Civil War, that are waiting for reunification under the democratic ROC government. Such an assertion is identical to the reunification position of Chiang Kai-shek and Chiang Ching-kuo. The KMT leader stressed on the importance of not only adhering steadfastly to the "1992 consensus" as the bedrock for cross-strait peace but also focusing on connecting the Chinese national, historical, and cultural bonds between the compatriots on both sides of the strait. Between 2013 and 2015, Taipei held a high-profile commemoration of the ROC's struggle against imperialism and fascism in the Second World War and the KMT's strenuous efforts to defeat Japan and recover Taiwan back to the embrace of China. The Ma government's pro-China endeavors, however, led to growing discontent from the Taiwanese people, galvanizing mass demonstrations and ultimately leading to the KMT's declining electoral fortunes in 2014 and 2016.

Chapter 5 looks at the ramifications of President Ma's "1992 consensus" policy on Taiwan's relations with the USA. This chapter discusses America's strategic ambiguity policy and how the KMT's cross-strait policy has contradicted some of the major premises of Washington's long-standing national interests. The KMT–CCP rapprochement is then analyzed in light of intensification of USA–PRC rivalry since 2010, especially in the territorial and maritime contentions in the East and South China Seas. Finally, Chap. 6 will conclude this book by projecting how future USA–China–Taiwan relations will evolve under Tsai Ing-wen. Though the DPP administration is unlikely to put up an all-out challenge against Beijing's "one-China" principle, it will certainly promote a more hostile approach by placing Taiwan closer to the US–Japanese security and economic axis. Refraining from accepting the "1992 consensus," Tsai has been more receptive to the notion that both sides are two independent states having no particular historical and cultural linkages. The new president's task is definitely easier than her predecessors' since more and more Taiwanese people (especially youth) are embracing the Taiwan-based identity and consciousness. The USA may welcome greater distancing between the two sides as Taiwan could contribute more to America's rebalancing to Asia. Nonetheless, if history is any guide, Washington is also unlikely to change its course and tolerate any drastic or radical moves toward independence. In spite of increasing competition with the PRC, the USA's pursuit of strategic ambiguity in the Taiwan Strait will likely persist beyond Barack Obama's presidency into the Donald Trump administration that begins in January 2017 (see Chapter 6).

References

Accinelli, Robert. 1996. *Crisis and Commitment*. Chapel Hill: University of North Carolina Press.
Anderson, Benedict. 2006. *Imagined Communities*. New York: Verso.
Bernstein, Richard. 2014. *China 1945: Mao's Revolution and America's Fateful Choice*. New York: Vintage Books.
Burr, William. 1998. *The Kissinger Transcripts*. New York: The New Press.
Bush, Richard. 2004. *At Cross Purposes*. Armonk: M.E. Sharpe.
———. 2014. U.S.-Taiwan Relations Since 2008. In *Political Changes in Taiwan under Ma Ying-jeou*, ed. Jean-P Cabestan and Jacques deLisle, 217–231. New York: Routledge.
Cabestan, Jean-Pierre. 2016. Cross-Strait Integration and Taiwan's New Security Challenges. In *Taiwan and the "China Impact."*, ed. Gunter Schubert, 282–300. New York: Routledge.
Chang, Bi-yu. 2010. So Close, Yet So Far Away: Imaging Chinese 'Homeland' in Taiwan's Geography Education (1945–68). *Cultural Geographies* 18(3): 385–411.
———. 2015. *Place, Identity and National Imagination in Postwar Taiwan*. New York: Routledge.

Chang, Hui-Ching, and Richard Holt. 2015. *Language, Politics and Identity in Taiwan*. New York: Routledge.

Chen, Dean. 2012. *The U.S. Taiwan Strait Policy: The Origins of Strategic Ambiguity*. Boulder: Lynne Rienner Publishers.

Christensen, Thomas. 1996. *Useful Adversaries*. Princeton: Princeton University Press.

———. 2015. *The China Challenge*. New York: W.W. Norton.

Cohen, Warren. 1980. *Dean Rusk*. Totowa: Cooper Square Publishers.

———. 2010. *America's Response to China*. New York: Columbia University Press.

Copper, John. 2014. *The KMT Returns to Power*. Lanham: Lexington Books.

Crawford, Timothy. 2003. *Pivotal Deterrence*. Ithaca: Cornell University Press.

Davis, David, and Will Moore. 1997. Ethnicity Matters: Transnational Ethnic Alliances and Foreign Policy Behavior. *International Studies Quarterly* 41(1): 171–184.

Dittmer, Lowell. 2014. Taiwan's Narrowing Strait: A Triangular Analysis of Taiwan's Security Since 2008. In *The U.S. Strategic Pivot to Asia and Cross-Strait Relations*, ed. Peter Chow, 15–29. New York: Palgrave Macmillan.

Frieden, Jeff. 1988. Sectoral Conflict and Foreign Economic Policy, 1914–1940. *International Organization* 42(1): 59–90.

Gellner, Ernest. 2006. *Nations and Nationalism*. New York: Cornell University Press.

Gilley, Bruce. 2010. Not So Dire Straits. *Foreign Affairs* 89(1): 44–60.

Glaser, Charles. 2015. A U.S.-China Grand Bargain? *International Security* 39(4): 49–90.

Goldstein, Judith. 1993. *Ideas, Interests, and American Trade Policy*. Ithaca: Cornell University Press.

Goldstein, Judith, and Robert Keohane. 1993. Ideas and Foreign Policy: An Analytical Framework. In *Ideas & Foreign Policy*, ed. Judith Goldstein and Robert Keohane, 3–30. Ithaca: Cornell University Press.

Gourevitch, Peter. 1978. The Second-Image Reversed: The International Sources of Domestic Politics. *International Organization* 32(4): 881–912.

Grigoryan, Arman. 2010. Third-Party Intervention and the Escalation of State-Minority Conflicts. *International Studies Quarterly* 54(4): 1143–1174.

Harding, Harry. 1992. *A Fragile Relationship*. Washington: Brookings Institution Press.

Heraclides, Alexis. 1990. Secessionist Minorities and External Involvement. *International Organization* 44(3): 341–378.

Hickey, Dennis. 1988. America's Two-Point Policy and the Future of Taiwan. *Asian Survey* 28(8): 881–896.

Hickey, Dennis, and Emerson Niou. 2016. Taiwan in 2015: A Turning Point? *Asian Survey* 56(1): 57–67.

Hippler, Jochen. 2005. Violent Conflicts, Conflict Prevention and Nation-Building—Terminology and Political Concepts. In *Nation-Building*, ed. Jochen Hippler, 3–14. London: Pluto Press.

Houten, Pieter Van. 1998. The Role of a Minority's Reference State in Ethnic Relations. *European Journal of Sociology* 39(1): 110–146.

Hughes, Christopher. 2011. Negotiating National Identity in Taiwan: Between Nativization and De-Sinicization. In *Taiwan's Democracy*, ed. Robert Ash, John Garver, and Penelope Prime, 51–75. New York: Routledge.

———. 2014. Revisiting Identity Politics under Ma Ying-jeou. In *Political Changes in Taiwan under Ma Ying-jeou*, ed. Jean-Pierre Cabestan and Jacques deLisle, 120–136. New York: Routledge.

Jenne, Erin. 2007. *Ethnic Bargaining*. Ithaca: Cornell University Press.

Lin, Cheng-yi. 2016a. The Rise of China and Its Implications for U.S.-Taiwan Relations. In *Taiwan and the "China Impact."*, ed. Gunter Schubert, 261–281. New York: Routledge.

Lin, Hsiao-ting. 2016b. *Accidental State*. Cambridge: Harvard University Press.

Lin, Shirley. 2016c. *Taiwan's China Dilemma*. Stanford: Stanford University Press.

Lobell, Steven. 1999. Second Image Reversed Politics: Britain's Choice of Freer Trade or Imperial Preferences, 1903–1906, 1917–1923, 1930–1932. *International Studies Quarterly* 43(4): 671–693.

Mearsheimer, John. 2014. Taiwan's Dire Strait. *National Interest* 130: 29–39.

Mylonas, Harris. 2012. *The Politics of Nation-Building*. New York: Cambridge University Press.

Norman, Wayne. 2005. *Negotiating Nationalism*. New York: Oxford University Press.

Rigger, Shelley. 2011. *Why Taiwan Matters*. Lanham: Rowman & Littlefield.

———. 2013. Taiwan in U.S. China Relations. In *Tangled Titans*, ed. David Shambaugh, 293–311. Lanham: Rowman & Littlefield.

Rogowski, Ronald. 1989. *Commerce and Coalitions*. Princeton: Princeton University Press.

Romberg, Alan. 2003. *Rein In at the Brink of the Precipice*. Washington DC: The Henry L. Stimson Center.

Rose, Gideon. 1998. Neoclassical Realism and Theories of Foreign Policy. *World Politics* 51(1): 144–172.

Ross, Robert. 2000. The 1995–96 Taiwan Strait Confrontation: Coercion, Credibility, and the Use of Force. *International Security* 25(2): 87–123.

Saidman, Stephen. 1997. Explaining the International Relations of Secessionist Conflicts: Vulnerability Versus Ethnic Ties. *International Organization* 51(4): 721–753.

———. 2002. Discrimination in International Relations: Analyzing External Support for Ethnic Groups. *Journal of Peace Research* 39(1): 27–50.

Salehyan, Idean. 2007. Transnational Rebels: Neighboring States as Sanctuary for Rebel Groups. *World Politics* 59(2): 217–242.

Schweller, Randall. 2006. *Unanswered Threats.* Princeton: Princeton University Press.

Shirk, Susan. 2008. *China: Fragile Superpower.* New York: Oxford University Press.

Sutter, Robert. 2015. *The United States and Asia.* Lanham: Rowman & Littlefield.

Tarrow, Sidney. 2015. *War, States, & Contention.* Ithaca: Cornell University Press.

Tkacik, John. 2014. Pacific Pivot, Taiwan Fulcrum: Maritime Taiwan and Power Transition in Asia. In *The U.S. Strategic Pivot to Asia and Cross-Strait Relations*, ed. Peter Chow, 227–261. New York: Palgrave Macmillan.

Tucker, Nancy. 2009. *Strait Talk.* Cambridge: Harvard University Press.

Tucker, Nancy, and Bonnie Glaser. 2011. Should the United States Abandon Taiwan? *The Washington Quarterly* 34(4): 23–37.

Wu, Yu-shan. 2016. Heading towards Troubled Waters? The Impact of Taiwan's 2016 Elections on Cross-Strait Relations. *American Journal of Chinese Studies* 23(1): 59–76.

Zarakol, Ayse. 2013. Revisiting Second Image Reversed: Lessons from Turkey and Thailand. *International Studies Quarterly* 57(1): 150–162.

Author's Interviews

Interview with Robert Sutter, Professor of Practice of International Affairs at the Elliot School of International Affairs, George Washington University, February 24, 2016 in Washington, DC, USA.

Interview with Richard Bush, Director for the Center for East Asia Policy Studies at the Brookings Institute, February 25, 2016 in Washington, DC, USA. He was Chairman of the Board and Managing Director of the American Institute in Taiwan (AIT), from 1997 to 2002.

Interview with Douglas Paal, Vice-President for Studies and Director of the Asia Program at the Carnegie Endowment for International Peace, March 16, 2016 in Washington, DC, USA. He previously served as the Director of the AIT, from 2002 to 2006.

Interview with Chou Chih-wei, July 28, 2016, Taipei, Taiwan. Chou was Chairperson of the Kuomintang's Culture and Communications Committee from April 2016 to October 2016.

CHAPTER 2

Politics Beyond the Water's Edge: Neoclassical Realism

The theory of neoclassical realism examines how domestic political ideas and interests, once embedded and institutionalized, could constrain the central leaders' foreign policy decision-making. The foreign policy outcome, therefore, may be suboptimal and incompatible with the state's national security requirements. Indeed, "the greatest weakness to Taiwan's survival comes not from without, but instead lies in the deeply rooted political divide within."[1] "Because intense political competition has been viewed in zero-sum terms, neither the Democratic Progressive Party (DPP) government of Chen Shui-bian nor the Kuomintang (KMT) government of Ma Ying-jeou has been effective in reaching consensus about what should be done to strengthen Taiwan."[2] As a result of their irreconcilable ideological orientations and diverged national visions on the relationship between Taiwan and China, the DPP is prone to taking a hostile approach toward the mainland whereas the KMT is leaning more upon appeasement. Each party consistently opposes the other, irrespective of the merits of the policy issues.

For instance, the offensive aspects of Taiwan's defense plans during the Chen Shui-bian years galvanized fierce criticism from the KMT. The DPP president's ability to gain legislative approval for billions of dollars of offered US arms encountered protracted opposition from the KMT

---

[1] Gitter and Sutter 2016, p. 15.
[2] Ibid., p. 14.

and its political allies controlling the majority seats of Taiwan's Legislative Yuan. The Kuomintang contended that the DPP's defense agenda was "needlessly provocative and that a more accommodating policy could defuse the threat from China."[3] In contrast, despite his pledge to enhance Taiwan's security and defensive capabilities, President Ma Ying-jeou was unwilling to seek the minimum level of defense spending (three percent of GDP) that he had earlier stated would be required to effectively defend the island; instead, he deemphasized military preparedness in favor of economic cooperation and diplomatic engagement with China. The president's changes met with widespread disapproval from the DPP, which favored increasing military spending to strengthen Taiwan against the growing Chinese threat. In addition, the DPP tirelessly stressed that President Ma was too soft toward Beijing. The Ma administration also faced a huge political setback as the DPP sided with the Sunflower students' movement that occupied the Legislative Yuan in March 2014 to stymie the KMT's push for a deeper economic integration with China.[4] Burdened by such long-standing and deleterious divisions, "Taiwan is much weaker than it has to be since it cannot carry out needed reforms and effective policy in economic, social, and national security areas important to preserving and advancing national power in the face of China's threats."[5] Summing up the acrimonious KMT–DPP relationship, Gitter and Sutter have commented:

> The record of the DPP's struggle for power against a previously authoritarian KMT reaches back over 40 years and is full of twists and turns where one side or the other saw the opponent engaging in reprehensible practices. As a result, the level of trust between the two camps is low. Perhaps of more importance, the DPP stalwarts base their platform on an identity for Taiwan very different from the one China view of the KMT that is more acceptable to Beijing. Many of the older generations in the DPP identify with a Taiwan separate from China. They see Taiwan's interests as best served by avoiding entanglements with China that could diminish the island's autonomy and independence. These clashing identities and views of Taiwan's future…make calls for Taiwan's government to reach a consensus on how to approach the mainland in political talks extremely difficult to achieve.[6]

---

[3] Cal Clark and Alexander Tan, *Taiwan Political Economy* (Boulder, CO: Lynne Rienner Publishers, 2012), p. 138.
[4] Gitter and Sutter 2016, p. 14.
[5] This author's interview with Robert Sutter.
[6] Gitter and Sutter 2016, p. 16.

Portraying itself as the "saviour" of Taiwan, the DPP has accused the KMT of "selling Taiwan out to China" and further implied the latter as "destroyer of Taiwan and its statehood."[7] In sum, the ongoing polarized elite politics, national identity fragmentations, and partisan gridlock in Taiwan led to the implementation of unsound mainland policy and threatened to derail the island's security interests.

1 THE THEORETICAL FOUNDATIONS OF NEOCLASSICAL REALISM

Thus, the inability of a state to charter a coherent foreign security policy is frequently the result of its highly contentious and polarizing domestic politics. The neoclassical realist approach, in essence, has three core assumptions. First, it seeks to explain particular foreign policy behaviors and not simply broad international structural outcomes. Second, it takes the international system as the most crucial long-term cause of changes in any nation's foreign policy behavior. Finally, the theory layers domestic-level factors into their explanatory models in order to achieve greater predictive and empirical precision. Therefore, while power is essential to account for changes in any nation's foreign policy behavior, it is not sufficient because domestic-level politics, interests, regime types, institutional arrangements, cultural legacies, and intentions vary from state to state, and such domestic variables often have a dramatic impact upon foreign policy behavior, serving a "filtering" function between international conditions and strategic policy outcomes.[8]

Gideon Rose posits, "A theory of foreign policy limited to systemic factors alone is bound to be inaccurate much of the time.... To understand the way states interpret and respond to their external environment, one must analyze how systemic pressures are translated through unit-level intervening variables such as decision-makers' perceptions and domestic state structure."[9] In addition, Fareed Zakaria contended:

[7] Clark and Tan 2012, p. 138.
[8] Rose, "Neoclassical Realism and Theories of Foreign Policy," pp. 144–172. Other major neoclassical realists include William Wohlforth, *The Elusive Balance* (Ithaca, NY: Cornell University Press, 1993); Thomas Christensen, *Useful Adversaries* (Princeton, NJ: Princeton University Press, 1996); Fareed Zakaria, *From Wealth to Power* (Princeton, NJ: Princeton University Press, 1998); Christopher Layne, *The Peace of Illusions* (Ithaca, NY: Cornell University Press, 2006); and Colin Dueck, *Reluctant Crusaders* (Princeton, NJ: Princeton University Press, 2006).
[9] Rose, "Neoclassical Realism and Theories of Foreign Policy," p. 152.

> A theory of foreign policy must not ignore domestic politics, national culture, and individual decision-makers. But, from the standpoint of social science, a first-cut theory that generalizes across regimes, cultures, and peoples is more useful than a country-specific explanation, since it can be applied to a larger number of cases.... In order to achieve some balance between parsimony and accuracy, a first-cut theory can be narrowed in scope and layered successively with additional variables from different levels of analysis—regime types, bureaucratic politics, the psychological tendencies and personalities of statesmen... A good account of a nation's foreign policy will [therefore] point to the role played by systemic as well as other factors.[10]

Indeed, exploring the apparent aberration between America's growth of national economic power in the immediate decades after the Civil War and the US late foreign expansionism at the end of the nineteenth century, he stressed that top policymakers in Washington "were well aware of its economic strength and proudly proclaimed it, [but] the country hewed to a relatively isolationist line, with few exceptions, until the 1890s."[11] The anomaly is attributed to the changing attributes of the American federal government, which transitioned from a weak, divided, and decentralized state in the 1870s and 1880s into a more unitary presidential-dominant government in the late 1890s. Zakaria posits:

> The American economy grew rapidly during the 1870s and 1880s, and by the early 1880s it had overtaken even Britain by most important measures. But, this national power was obscured by a state that was too weak to consistently extract resources to fulfill its objectives and that was too divided to act in a coherent fashion. Expansion was often proposed but rarely consummated. When state power was lowest, almost no expansion occurred. In the 1870s and 1880s, as industrialization proceeded and the need arose for an extensive regulatory state, the scope and strength of the central government increased. Power shifted from the states to the federal government and from the legislative branch to the executive branch. By the 1890s, the expansionist pipe dreams of the 1860s and 1870s could become reality.[12]

Hereafter, the USA grew so strong and had so many resources at its disposal that its behavior came to resemble that of other great power states.

---

[10] Fareed Zakaria, *From Wealth to Power*, pp. 16–17.
[11] Ibid., p. 5.
[12] Ibid., p. 184.

This included the enlargement of its national-security apparatus, annexation of overseas territories and basing rights, winning the World Wars, fighting the Cold War, leading multilateral conferences, and projecting hegemonic influence beyond even limited security objectives.[13]

In another study on America's foreign interventionist policy, Colin Dueck observes,

> Insofar as domestic conditions are restrictive and constraining, [central decision-makers] face a difficult choice. They can give up pursuing what they believe to be a necessary policy course, or they can redouble their efforts to mobilize and build support for intervention. In the latter case, this may involve pursuing or packaging the decision in such a way as to create new sources of domestic support. Yet, these very efforts to increase support at home may cause a particular military intervention to be implemented in a manner that is puzzling from a neorealist perspective.[14]

For instance, though the Truman administration's military response toward North Korea's aggression in June 1950 was primarily based on a realist national interest consideration, the president's subsequent deployment of the Seventh Fleet to the Taiwan Strait was motivated partly by domestic McCarthyism. "The issue of supporting the Chinese Nationalists [KMT] was a longtime favorite of conservative Republicans," observes Dueck. "[T]he administration had just been subjected to months of withering criticism on this very matter. The prospect of silencing or at least appeasing his critics on the issue of Taiwan must have been attractive to Truman, under the circumstances."[15]

Neoclassical Realism from the Works of Christensen, Dueck, and Layne

In addition, three other seminal studies which rely on the neoclassical realism model will be briefly examined here in order to further illustrate the theory's causal logics: (1) Thomas Christensen's *Useful Adversaries*; (2) Colin Dueck's *Reluctant Crusaders*; and (3) Christopher Layne's

---

[13] Ibid., p. 182.
[14] Colin Dueck, "Neoclassical Realism and the National Interest: Presidents, Domestic Politics, and Major Military Interventions," in Steven Lobell et al, eds., *Neoclassical Realism, the State, and Foreign Policy*, p. 146.
[15] Ibid., p. 155.

The Peace of Illusions. Christensen posits that a major shortcoming of the realist analysis is that it assumes that the state, defined as a black box or rational unitary actor, can simply mobilize their material and human resources in responding to international challenges and opportunities. Public willingness to sacrifice lives and wealth for national security is taken for granted. His "domestic mobilization model," however, places the "state's ability to mobilize the public as a key intervening variable between the international challenges facing the nation and the strategies eventually adopted by the state to meet those challenges."[16] If the domestic political hurdles to mobilize are relatively low, one should expect policies that are consistent with the expectations of black box realists. Nonetheless, if the hurdles are high, as in the USA, then policies could be either "over-reaction" or "under-reaction" to international environment facing the nation. Policymakers often tailor their policies to mobilize the support of the public by resorting to crusading rhetoric, ideologies, or initiating reckless foreign crises. Christensen examines two cases: US China policy, 1947–50, and Mao's Great Leap Forward policy and the 1958 Taiwan Strait Crisis.

On the other hand, Dueck argues that at moments of international flux and crisis, a window of opportunity is opened for new grand strategy options. Here, America's strategic cultures, predicated upon the notions of liberalism and limited liability, play an important role through two domestic political mechanisms: agenda setting and coalition building. He notes that "Americans have been 'crusaders'—crusaders in the promotion of a more liberal international order. But, Americans have also frequently been 'reluctant'—reluctant to admit the full costs of promoting this liberal international vision. These two strains within the American foreign policy tradition have not only operated cyclically; they have operated simultaneously. In this sense, the history of American grand strategy is a history of 'reluctant crusaders.'"[17] So, any strategies that seem to be contradicting the nation's dominant culture are unlikely to be considered in the first place. He looks at American grand strategic adjustment in four historical periods: 1918–21, the defeat of the League Nation; 1945–51, the origins and consolidation of containment; 1992–2000, the immediate post-Cold War era; and 2001–06, the George W. Bush administration. The author argues that, for instance, the "crucial point about containment is that it

[16] Christensen, *Useful Adversaries*, p. 13.
[17] Colin Dueck, *Reluctant Crusaders*, p. 4.

was not the only internationally viable grand strategy open to U.S. foreign policymakers in 1945–46; rather it was the only internationally viable grand strategy that also resonated with American [domestic strategic] cultural—which is to say, liberal assumptions."[18]

Finally, examining US grand strategy since the 1940s, Christopher Layne asserts that America has consistently pursued "extra-regional hegemony," which aims to establish preponderance outside of the Western Hemisphere and into three other regions: Western Europe, East Asia, and the Middle East. "Structural factors in 1945 and 1989," writes Layne, "gave the United States both the opportunity and the means to expand beyond the Western Hemisphere; however, structural factors do not tell us *why* the United States *chose* to do so, [and] to find the motive for America's hegemonic expansion we must look at domestic factors."[19] Essentially, structural realism cannot explain adequately why an "offshore great power" that is already "extraordinarily secure" would follow an expansionist grand strategy that would eventually result in counterbalancing and overstretch.[20] Layne therefore attributes the choice of hegemonic strategy to the domestic "Open Door tradition," underpinned by Wilsonian liberal internationalism. The Open Door principle envisions "an international system or world order made up of states that are open and subscribe to the United States' liberal values and democratic institutions and are open to America's economic penetration."[21]

An Open Door world rests on two pillars: the economic Open Door (maintaining an open international economic system) and the political Open Door (spreading liberalism and democracy abroad). These are vital to US national security because "closure" abroad threatens the survival of American core values at home. The assumption is that political and economic liberalism cannot flourish in the American homeland unless they are also implemented abroad. "U.S. policymakers," argues Layne, "fear that important regions of the world—especially in Europe and Asia—will be closed to the United States economically and ideologically, cutting off the oxygen without which American society, and liberal institutions generally, would asphyxiate."[22] Hence, notwithstanding structural conditions,

---

[18] Ibid., p. 99.
[19] Christopher Layne, *The Peace of Illusions*, p. 8.
[20] Ibid., p. 22.
[21] Ibid., p. 30.
[22] Ibid.. p. 32.

America has chosen extra-regional hegemony over offshore balancing as its grand strategy in the postwar era, which in Layne's opinion would actually engender greater insecurity for the USA.

While the foregoing neoclassical realist works examined mainly the transformations of American grand strategies, their theoretical framework and empirical findings clearly attested to the importance of bringing domestic politics into a realist analysis of international affairs.

Neoclassical Realism and Taiwan–China Relations

In recent years, a plethora of studies have focused on the coexistence of deepening economic ties and hostile political relations between Taiwan and China. This "perplexing duality"[23] is revealed by the fact that despite persistent and severe bilateral political confrontations, especially during the Lee Teng-hui and Chen Shui-bian administrations, cross-strait economic interdependence has "grown rapidly, and mainland China [even] displaced the United States as Taiwan's primary trading partner; mainland China is also the primary destination for Taiwan's outward foreign direct investment by a large margin."[24] For instance, notwithstanding Taiwan's restrictive laws and controls on cross-strait commerce, bilateral trade between China and Taiwan increased from $3.8 billion in 1987, to $14.5 billion in 1992, to $30 billion in 2000, to $90 billion in 2006, and to $105 billion in 2008. In the decade of 2000 alone, the growth of two-way trade averaged 16 percent annually.[25] As China accelerated its market reforms after 1992, it also became a global manufacturing final assembler.

---

[23] Chu Yun-han, "The Political Economy of Taiwan's Mainland Policy," in Suisheng Zhao, ed., *Across the Taiwan Strait* (New York: Routledge, 1999), p. 164.

[24] Scott Kastner, *Political Conflict and Economic Interdependence Across the Taiwan Strait*, p. 30. See also Suisheng Zhao, "Economic Interdependence and Political Divergence," in Suisheng Zhao ed., *Across the Taiwan Strait*, pp. 21–40; Paul Bolt, "Economic Ties Across the Taiwan Strait: Buying Time for Compromise," *Issues & Studies* 37, no. 2 (2001), pp. 80–105; Karen Sutter, "Business Dynamism across the Taiwan Strait: The Implications for Cross-Strait Relations," *Asian Survey* 42, no. 3 (2002), pp. 522–540; Chao Chien-min, "Will Economic Integration Between Mainland China and Taiwan Lead to a Congenial Political Culture?" *Asian Survey* 43, no. 2 (2003), pp. 280–304; Cal Clark, "The China-Taiwan Relationship: Crowing Cross-Strait Economic Integration," *Orbis* 46, no. 4 (2002), pp. 753–766; and Daniel Rosen and Zhi Wang, *The Implications of China-Taiwan Economic Liberalization* (Washington, DC: Peterson Institute, 2011).

[25] Scott Kastner, *Political Conflict and Economic Interdependence Across the Taiwan Strait and Beyond*, p. 48; Daniel Rosen and Zhi Wang, *The Implications of China-Taiwan Economic Liberalization* (Washington, DC: Peterson Institute, 2011), p. 10.

Taiwan's businesses saw the profitability of exporting high-value intermediate goods (e.g., electrical machinery and optical equipment) to factories in China, where the final production and assembly would take place, and then re-exporting to markets around the world.[26] Between 1995 and 2008, approximately 70 percent of Taiwan's exports to China belonged to those intermediate "processing trades."[27] By the time Chen Shui-bian left office in 2008, more than 30 percent of Taiwan's total world export went to China.[28] On the other hand, Taiwan's outward investments to China also rose from $4.3 billion in 1997 to more than $10.7 billion in 2008. Most of these investments traveled to China either by exploiting loopholes in Taiwan's regulations or indirectly through other countries. Since 2002, a great majority of Taiwan's total foreign investments went to mainland China.[29] As will be elaborated in Chap. 4, cross-strait socioeconomic exchanges continued to grow after Ma Ying-jeou became the ROC's president in May 2008.

Much of the international relations literature has focused on the causal connections between economic trade and security conflicts, that is, whether growing commercial interdependence would reduce military disputes.[30] Nevertheless, these dichotomous tendencies of economic liberalization and political feuds have raised an important question: How is it possible for states that are engaged in an active security contention to continue trading with each other? Using neoclassical realism, Scott Kastner and Jennifer Sterling-Folker sought to untangle the specific domestic conditions under which states with long-standing political

---

[26] Ibid., p. 12.

[27] Ibid., p. 13.

[28] Ibid., p. 72.

[29] Ibid., pp. 30–33. Shirley Lin, *Taiwan's China Dilemma*, p. 5. In 2008, the cumulative Taiwan's investments to China stood at about $76 billion. Given many indirect investments through other locations, however, the actual total investments from Taiwan to China could be larger than these official figures. According to the US Department of State, many unofficial estimates put the actual value of Taiwan's investments in China at over $300 billion by 2008. Robert Sutter, *U.S.-Chinese Relations,* p. 232 (the 2010 edition).

[30] See Edward Mansfield and Brian Pollins, "Interdependence and Conflict: An Introduction," in Edward Mansfield and Brian Pollins eds., *Economic Interdependence and International Conflict* (Ann Arbor: University of Michigan Press, 2005), pp. 1–28; Gerald Schneider, Katherine Barbieri, and Nils Petter Gleditsch, "Does Globalization Contribute to Peace? A Critical Survey of the Literature," in Gerald Schneider, Katherine Barbieri, and Nils Petter Gleditsch eds., *Globalization and Armed Conflict* (New York: Rowman & Littlefield, 2003), pp. 3–29; and Katherine Barbieri, *The Liberal Illusion: Does Trade Promote Peace?*(Ann Arbor: University of Michigan Press, 2006), especially Chapter 2.

antagonism (an international structural constraint) can still maintain close economic relations with one another.[31] Kastner posited that the negative impacts of international political conflict on trade tend to be less severe when "internationalist economic interest coalitions" hold strong political clout in the states involved. Leaders, whose domestic support depends on those internationalist interests, would pay higher political costs (i.e., penalized electorally if in a democracy) for taking actions detrimental to commerce.[32] Taiwan's major business associations and high-profile tycoons have tended to be very outspoken in their support for open foreign economic policies, especially vis-à-vis mainland China. The DPP president Chen Shui-bian, at least in the early years of his presidency, wanted to cultivate better relations with the entrepreneurial sectors in order to enlarge the DPP's constituent base and to mitigate Taiwan's declining economic conditions. Hence, Chen was pressured by the business elites to liberalize trade and investment policies toward the PRC.[33] But, when running for and after winning his second term in 2004, the president opted for a more provocative approach toward China as he "was able to craft a winning coalition that included both those seeking to build a stronger Taiwanese identity and those who are threatened, economically, by growing commercial links with mainland China."[34]

Capitalist interests, nonetheless, are not the only pressure groups that influence cross-strait policymaking. Chapter 1 has noted that, as a result of democratization in the late 1980s and early 1990s, Taiwan's identity politics—the "lingering sub-ethnic tensions between the native Taiwanese and the mainlanders"—has also constituted a well-entrenched domestic fault line that "provides the institutional space for airing nativist messages and agitating for separatist goals."[35] According to Sterling-Folker, between 1947 and 1987, the KMT's mainlander rule and its martial law

---

[31] Scott Kastner, "When Do Conflicting Political Relations Affect International Trade?" *Journal of Conflict Resolution* 51, no. 4 (2007), pp. 664–688. See also J. Sterling-Folker, "Neoclassical Realism and Identity," in Steven Lobell et al, eds., *Neoclassical Realism, the State, and Foreign Policy*, pp. 99–138.

[32] Kastner, "When Do Conflicting Political Relations Affect International Trade?" p. 671.

[33] Ibid., pp. 679–680.

[34] Scott Kastner, "Does Economic Integration across the Taiwan Strait Make Military Conflict Less Likely?" *Journal of East Asian Studies* 6 (2006), p. 332.

[35] Wu Yu-shan, "Taiwan's Domestic Politics and Cross-Strait Relations," *The China Journal* 53 (Jan 2005), p. 36.

on Taiwan alienated the native Taiwanese population.[36] Though transforming Taiwan into an advanced industrial economy, the KMT authority, in order to perpetuate its sole Chinese ruling legitimacy, sought to socialize the Taiwanese people to maintaining a collective Chinese identity.[37] The KMT's policies therefore included "insisting that Mandarin be the ROC's official language while other local languages were banned, the adoption of Chinese-related textbooks and curriculums in schools, and restrictions on ethnic programming in TV and radio broadcasts."[38] Since any hint of Taiwanese identity was discouraged, the concept of "Taiwan" was naturally subordinated to "China" or the "Republic of China." The people of Taiwan naturally felt "socio-culturally disadvantaged."[39] In the words of Cal Clark and Alex Tan, "the authoritarian era bequeathed a legacy of strong ethnic resentments that created a potential for cultural conflict but did not develop a tradition of democratic compromise and policymaking, which inhibited resolving this conflict by creating an institutional imbroglio."[40]

The push for political liberalization as well as the abrogation of martial law by President Chiang Ching-kuo, in part pressured by the USA following its normalization of ties with Beijing, in the late 1970s and throughout the 1980s, unleashed Taiwan's democratization movement, opening the Pandora's Box that gave rise to the DPP and its pro-independence-Taiwanization advocacy.[41] As will be discussed in Chap. 4, Taiwan's national consciousness and identity have risen considerably since then: the native Taiwanese populations are seeing themselves as more and more distinct from the mainland Chinese. Both the Lee Teng-hui and Chen Shui-bian administrations fervently fostered the "de-Sinification" campaign, including revamping school textbooks and encouraging native literature, history, music, and performing arts to "promote the burgeoning Taiwanese consciousness while deemphasizing Chinese culture and history."[42]

---

[36] J. Sterling-Folker, "Neoclassical Realism and Identity," p. 128.
[37] Wu Yu-shan, "Taiwan's Domestic Politics and Cross-Strait Relations," pp. 35–36.
[38] J. Sterling-Folker, "Neoclassical Realism and Identity," p. 128.
[39] Hui-Ching Chang and Rich Holt, "Taiwan and ROC: A Critical Analysis of President Chen Shui-bian's Construction of Taiwan Identities in National Speeches," *National Identities* 11, no. 3 (September 2009), p. 302.
[40] Clark and Tan, *Taiwan's Political Economy*, p. 140.
[41] Wu Yu-shan, "Taiwan's Domestic Politics and Cross-Strait Relations," pp. 42–44.
[42] J Sterling-Folker, "Neoclassical Realism and Identity," p. 132.

Externally, Lee and Chen emphasized that Taiwan and mainland China are essentially two different independent countries, as demonstrated by the former's "special state-to-state relations" theory (also known as the two-states theory) in July 1999 and the latter's "one country on each side of the Taiwan Strait" statement in August 2002.[43] Starting in late 2003 and well beyond into his second term after 2004, President Chen also actively pushed for referenda that called for drafting a new Taiwanese Constitution to replace the ROC and for Taiwan's entry into the United Nations. He further sought "name rectifications" to rename Taiwan's state enterprises, government institutions, and foreign offices that bear the name "China," "Chinese," or the "ROC" in order to purge "Chinese content as much as possible."[44] Because these policy initiatives were perceived by Beijing and Washington as major strides toward establishing de jure independence, USA–China–Taiwan relations experienced an extremely tumultuous period.[45] In her analysis, Sterling-Folker juxtaposed identity and capitalist interests and posited that Taiwanese politicians, in order to win office, must court the business community as well as stress their Taiwanese roots and identity.[46] However, it may be fair to emphasize that as the Taiwanese

[43] Su Chi, *Taiwan's Relations with Mainland China*, Ch. 3–4.

[44] S. Philip Hsu, "Between Identity Quest and Risk Aversion: Lessons from the Chen Shui-bian Presidency for Maintaining Cross-Strait Stability," *Journal of Contemporary China* 19, no. 66 (2010), pp. 695–696. Many excellent works have examined and analyzed Chen Shui-bian's mainland policy. See also Nancy Tucker, *Strait Talk* (Cambridge, MA: Harvard University Press, 2009); Alan Romberg, *Rein In at the Brink of the Precipice* (Washington, DC: The Henry L. Stimson Center, 2003); Shelley Rigger, *Why Taiwan Matters*, T.Y. Wang, "'One China, One Taiwan': An Analysis of the Democratic Progressive Party's China Policy," *Journal of Asian and African Studies* 35, no. 1 (2000), pp. 159–182; Chao Chien-min, "One Step Forward, One Step Backward: Chen Shui-bian's Mainland Policy," *Journal of Contemporary China* 12, no. 34 (2003), pp. 125–143; Chao Chien-min, "National Security vs. Economic Interests," *Journal of Contemporary China* 13, no. 41 (2004), pp. 687–704; Jonathan Sullivan and Will Lowe, "Chen Shui-bian: On Independence," *The China Quarterly* 203 (2010), pp. 619–638; and Robert Ross, "Explaining Taiwan's Revisionist Diplomacy," *Journal of Contemporary China* 15, no. 48 (2006), pp. 443–458.

[45] Dennis Hickey, *Foreign Policy Making in Taiwan* (New York: Routledge, 2007), p. 100.

[46] J. Sterling-Folker, "Neoclassical Realism and Identity," pp. 132–133. In fact, when running against Chen in the 2004 presidential election, Lien Chan and James Soong, the presidential and vice-presidential candidates, respectively, of the Pan-Blue coalition (the KMT and the People's First Party, PFP), embraced some of Chen Shui-bian's positions. For instance, in December 2003, Lien declared that both the ROC and PRC are two sovereign countries and that independence is also one of the options. See Wu Yu-shan, "Taiwan's Domestic Politics and Cross-Strait Relations," pp. 51–52. Lien also frequently spoke Minanese to emphasize his ethnic Taiwanese background. Lastly, during their final massive campaign ral-

national identity continues to rise and dominate political debates, identity politics has, to a great extent, superseded the importance of economic interests.[47] Sterling-Folker writes, "The pursuit of profits via economic exchange—whether for the benefit of society or particular constituents—is secondary to the goal of maintaining political separation from China."[48]

The work by Shirley Lin entitled *Taiwan's China Dilemma*[49] was built upon the similar neoclassical realist frameworks established by Kastner and Sterling-Folker. Examining Taiwan's economic approaches toward mainland China over the past 20 years since 1996, Lin assessed the impact of changing Taiwanese identity on cross-strait economic policies of the Lee, Chen, and Ma administrations, noting that, by 2006, contestation over Taiwan's national identity had largely been resolved. "The identity that has emerged is no longer defined on the basis of ethnicity, but rather on common residence on Taiwan and a strong commitment to Taiwanese civic values and institutions, which are very different from China's. Therefore, few Taiwanese regard themselves as even partially Chinese, especially among new generations. This has important implications for their preferred relationship with China."[50] Due to this more condensed or consolidated identity, Taiwan's public has moved away from the more extremist dichotomous economic preferences of the Lee Teng-hui and Chen Shui-bian eras, which favored either strong restriction or total integration. Instead, the mainstream position today is oscillating between moderate protectionism and moderate liberalization.

> Most occupy a new center characterized by willingness to liberalize trade with China, but also insistence on government action to ameliorate the negative consequences of liberalization for Taiwanese society. Within that new center, Moderate Restrictionists believe that the government should play a role in actively promoting Taiwanese interests through strategic economic policy that selectively opens or restricts sectors to Chinese trade and investment, while Moderate Liberalizers see the market as a dominant force

---

lies in 2004, Lien and Soong kissed the ground in Taipei and Taichung, respectively, to further demonstrate their devotion and loyalty to Taiwan. See Clark and Tan, p. 146.

[47] Malte Kaeding, "Taiwanized "New Taiwanese": The Effect of Taiwanization on the 2008 Presidential Election Campaign of Ma Ying-jeou," *Asia Pacific Social Science Review* 9, no. 2 (2009), pp. 19–34.

[48] J. Sterling-Folker, "Neoclassical Realism and Identity," p. 136.

[49] Shirley Lin, *Taiwan's China Dilemma* (Stanford, CA: Stanford University Press, 2016).

[50] Ibid., p. 209.

that the government should regulate only to the extent necessary to provide social stability and security.[51]

Despite China's ascending global influence and leverage over Taiwan, the latter continues to resist commercial policies that would undermine the island's identity, competitiveness, democracy, stability, and autonomy. "Neither China's growing power nor the supposed logic of interdependence has disposed the public opinion more favorably toward unconditional liberalization or across-the-board restriction. Although they live in a small territory with a small population, the Taiwanese do not accept that they lack options in their national economic policy."[52] In other words, the ROC's cross-strait commercial policies, while constrained by external economic structure, result primarily from "domestic factors." Thus, both Chen Shui-bian and Ma Ying-jeou were punished electorally when they overreached with their cross-strait economic policies that threatened to destabilize this new Taiwanese inclusive civic identity.

Though Kastner, Sterling-Folker, and Lin successfully demonstrated how a neoclassical realist model could be used to explicate cross-strait economic ties, they did not pay much attention to the increasingly heightened Sino-American competitions and how Ma's China-leaning policy not only under-reacted to the PRC but went against the USA's national security interests.

2   Proposing a Neoclassical Realist Explanation of Ma Ying-jeou's China Policy

Consequently, prevailing literatures on cross-strait relations have mostly concentrated on the uneasy coexistence of political conflicts and economic interdependence, as well as the rise of Taiwanese identity and consciousness which pulls the Taiwanese people further away from reuniting with China. To be sure, there have been important scholarships which analyze the implications of President Ma's engagement policy after 2008.[53]

---

[51] Ibid., p. 214.
[52] Ibid., p. 224.
[53] See, for instance, Dennis Hickey, "Rapprochement between Taiwan and the Chinese Mainland: Implications for American Foreign Policy," *Journal of Contemporary China* 20, no. 69 (2011), pp. 231–247. See also Jean-Pierre Cabestan and Jacques deLisle eds., *Political Changes in Taiwan under Ma Ying-jeou* (New York: Routledge, 2014).

However, an important question is missing from their discussions, especially given Beijing's power ascendancy and America's rebalancing to the Asian Pacific: Why did the Ma administration remain persistent in pursuing a China-leaning policy when both Taiwan's domestic political predispositions and changes in USA–China relations should cause Taipei to react more circumspectly toward the PRC? During his tenure as Taiwan's president, from 2008 to 2016, Ma Ying-jeou championed a détente policy toward the PRC, predicated on the "1992 consensus" or "one China, respective interpretations" formulation. Ma's KMT government explicitly defined "one China" as the Republic of China, which was established on the Chinese mainland in 1912 and, according to its Constitution effective in 1947, has legal sovereignty over both Taiwan and mainland China regions (also known as "one ROC, two areas") even though the ROC currently only has effective control over Taiwan, Penghu, Jinmen, and Mazu.

However, sandwiched between the People's Republic of China—Taiwan's primary security threat but also its chief commercial partner—and the USA—the island's long-standing and major security guarantor—the ROC has been vividly described by Dennis Hickey as a "shrimp between whales" whose fate has been shaped largely by the dynamics of these two great power states.[54] Based on its national interest imperative, Taiwan should pursue a prudent and strategically rational course of policy to avoid either a purely confrontational or concessionist strategy toward mainland China.[55] The logic is simple: hard balancing or provocations (i.e., a declaration of de jure independence and forging strong military alliance with Washington and Tokyo) would definitely arouse enmity from Beijing, thereby exacerbating Taiwan's security and economic interests while instigating tensions across the strait. On the other hand, by overly accommodating to or appeasing the PRC, Taiwan risks losing its political autonomy and inviting Beijing's dominance and even forceful unification. Having an

---

[54] Dennis Hickey, *Foreign Policy Making in Taiwan*, p. 26.

[55] According to the realist theory of international relations, a pure balancing strategy consists of both internal balancing (bolstering one's military capabilities and mobilizing domestic resources for national security enhancement) and external balancing (forging formal or informal security alliances). See Kenneth Waltz, *Theory of International Politics* (New York: McGraw-Hill, 1979), p. 168. See also Stephen Walt, *The Origins of Alliances* (Ithaca: Cornell University Press, 1987); Randall Schweller, "Managing the Rise of Great Powers: History and Theory," in Alastair Johnston and Robert Ross, eds., *Engaging China* (New York: Routledge, 1999), pp. 9–10.

enduring interest in the peaceful resolution of the Taiwan Strait impasse, the USA supports neither scenario through its long-standing policy of strategic ambiguity.[56]

Although the Ma administration pledged to a status quo policy of "no unification, no independence, and no use of force"[57] and that no political agreements would be negotiated with Beijing without Taiwan's public consent, the president's policy approach illustrated an obvious China-leaning predisposition that went far beyond the strategic requirements to satisfy international pressures for a stable and peaceful cross-strait relationship. Indeed, his policy direction was, to some extent, incongruent with the interests of Taiwan's traditional allies and regional partners, the USA, Japan, and other Asian states, especially over the East and South China Seas' territorial and maritime contentions.[58] Meanwhile, the KMT's détente policy also galvanized a higher level of domestic opposition and discontent, which, to a great degree, contributed to the KMT's major electoral routs in Taiwan's 2014 and 2016 elections. In short, there had been an apparent inconsistency in President Ma Ying-jeou's China policy. Despite its call for peaceful relations, the strategy had enhanced Beijing's economic and political leverage over Taiwan, thus posing a strategic challenge for Washington, whose relations with Beijing have become more competitive since 2010.

A Neoclassical Realist Model of Under-balancing: Divided Polity and Fragmented Views on "One China"

Accordingly, building upon the theory of neoclassical realism, my argument makes three claims. First, Taipei's rapprochement toward the PRC began, initially in May 2008, as a rational national interest policy to stabilize Taiwan's precarious strategic and economic positions after years of cross-strait tensions under the former Chen Shui-bian administration

---

[56] Richard Bush and Alan Romberg, "Cross-Strait Moderation and the United States—A Response to Robert Sutter," *PACNET* no. 17A (March 12, 2009), p. 1.

[57] Baohui Zhang, "Taiwan's New Grand Strategy," *Journal of Contemporary China* 20, no. 69 (March 2011), pp. 269–285; and T.Y. Wang et al., "Taiwan's Expansion of International Space: Opportunities and Challenges," *Journal of Contemporary China* 20, no. 69 (March 2011), pp. 249–267.

[58] Christopher Hughes, "Revisiting Identity Politics under Ma Ying-jeou," in Jean-Pierre Cabestan and Jacques deLisle, eds., *Political Changes in Taiwan under Ma Ying-jeou* (New York: Routledge, 2014), p. 125.

that severely strained Taipei's ties with both Beijing and Washington. The USA, as will be noted in Chap. 5, welcomed President Ma's conciliatory initiatives to mend fences with Beijing and repair their relations by promoting deeper economic cooperation through the direct three-links agreement in November 2008 and the much broader Economic Cooperation Framework Agreement (ECFA) in June 2010.

Second, even though improving relations with Beijing could cultivate more benign socioeconomic interactions across the strait—an outcome lauded by the USA—Taipei's revitalization of a China-centric national identity and political conciliation on "one China," despite its different interpretations of the term, were also tantamount to under-reacting or under-balancing toward the PRC's coercive threat to reunify with Taiwan. In light of the increasingly tense relationship among China, the USA, Japan, and other Asian states, the Ma administration's mainland policy therefore generated an impression, if not a reality, that Taipei is tacitly siding with Beijing in establishing a "pan-Chinese" union at the expense of its traditional allies. In the words of Christopher Hughes,

> Ma's embrace of Chinese identity for Taiwan was not a necessary response to…the impact of broader international factors, including the views of the United States. The retreat from Chen Shui-bian's use of identity politics to mobilize voters and raise Taiwan's international status was welcomed in Washington. Yet, there has also been a degree of wariness in the U.S. over just how close the Ma administration may move towards a new alignment with the PRC.[59]

Nevertheless, to survive in an anarchic international system, states are not necessarily inclined to balance against an emerging or revisionist power. "Much of international life," according to Fareed Zakaria, "consists of grays: periods of ambiguous threats and opportunities." As a result of such uncertainty, states have a "greater range of choices than we might think, and they choose to highlight certain threats and downplay others based on their conception of their interests."[60] Yet, the structural conditions of Taiwan are less ambivalent. Even increasing cross-strait economic cooperation cannot be divorced from the PRC's inherent motive to create incentives for a future political union. "There can be little doubt,"

---

[59] Hughes, "Revisiting Identity Politics under Ma Ying-jeou," p. 127.
[60] Zakaria, *From Wealth to Power*, pp. 184–185.

Scott Kastner writes, "that China pushes for cross-strait economic integration in part because leaders in Beijing view this as conducive to China's political goals vis-à-vis Taiwan."[61] In short, a more assertive China which has never renounced the use of coercion to reunify with Taiwan and the deterioration of Sino-American strategic relationships in East Asia should have led the Ma administration to take up a more vigilant policy toward Beijing.

Third, a state's propensity to balance or not cannot be sufficiently deduced from the international security environment alone. Randall Schweller has testified that "states evaluate and adapt to changes in their external environment partly as a result of their peculiar domestic structures and political situations."[62] Domestic political institutions, interests, and norms act as "intervening variables" or "transmission belts" through which "systemic imperatives are translated into foreign policy responses."[63] Hence, while not being oblivious to the prevailing structural settings, central decision-makers must also carefully assess the domestic costs of balancing behavior against other viable strategic alternatives. States, especially in an era of democratic mass politics, "respond to threats and opportunities in ways determined by both internal and external considerations of policy elites, who must reach consensus within an often decentralized and competitive political process."[64]

More importantly, states suffering from deeply polarized domestic political climate, vulnerable regime institutions, and incoherent political visions are prone to under-balance as well. The viciously divisive politics in Taiwan has made "responding to China's threat to [its] sovereignty difficult because of the intense partisan dispute over what should be the policy toward the PRC."[65] As noted in Chap. 1, dangerous political divisions exist when political elites and their establishments within society do not confer loyalty to and legitimacy on the central political institutions and organizations. The situations are exacerbated when a significant proportion of these political forces wish to revolt against and topple the

---

[61] Kastner, *Political Conflict and Economic Interdependence across the Taiwan Strait and Beyond*, p. 95. See also Andrew Nathan and Andrew Scobell, *China's Search for Security* (New York: Columbia University Press, 2012), p. 219.

[62] Schweller, "Unanswered Threats," p. 164.

[63] Norrin Ripsman, "Neoclassical Realism and Domestic Interest Groups," in Steven Lobell et al. eds., *Neoclassical Realism, the State, and Foreign Policy*, p. 176.

[64] Schweller, "Unanswered Threats," p. 164.

[65] Clark and Tan, p. 133.

entire political order. Thus, for a highly fragmented polity with diverging political allegiances, the presence of an external threat may actually widen intra-groups' or intra-elites' contradictions, driving a wedge among these domestic actors and even prompting some members to collaborate with the foreign power. Internal cohesion is so low that "the group members have ceased to regard preservation of the [central government and institution] as worthwhile or actually see the outside threat to concern 'them' rather than 'us.'"[66] This is reinforced by the fact that political elites lack consensus on whether the foreign revisionist power constitutes a genuine national security threat. One major faction of the elites and/or societal forces may find it expedient to cooperate with the foreign power if the latter may help in justifying their domestic nation-state-building ideology and policies. In other words, under-balancing can result when some political leaders and societal actors perceive the revisionist power as a "useful ally" to jointly oppose the "enemies from within." Thus, Schweller writes, "The closer the policymaking process and actual state-society relations approximate a unitary actor, the more accurate realism's predictions. Conversely, when states are divided at the elite and societal levels, they are less likely to behave in accordance with balance of power predictions."[67]

In a similar vein, the impact of domestic-level elements in Taiwan—particularly partisan struggles and the elites' opposing nation-building initiatives—must be analyzed, in conjunction with international factors, to account for Taipei's China policy. This combination suggests that "external competitions with other states, internal competition for control of the state, and the process of national identity politics can be significantly entwined factors in foreign policy choices and the assessment of [foreign] threat."[68] Essentially, the Ma administration's commitment to the "1992 consensus" was not only a response toward the international pressures to create peace and stability across the strait, but also aimed at reconstituting Taiwan's national identity and re-integrating the island under the "one-China" framework of the ROC—which was deemphasized by the ruling Democratic Progressive Party between 2000 and 2008. The DPP's nation-building project under Chen Shui-bian was in itself a reaction to "China's economic and geopolitical accomplishments," as their architects

---

[66] Schweller, *Unanswered Threats*, p. 53.
[67] Randall Schweller, "Unanswered Threats," p. 161.
[68] Jennifer Sterling-Folker, "Neoclassical Realism and Identity," p. 103.

worried very much that "unless Taiwan can achieve formal independence soon, it will—peacefully or otherwise—be extinguished as an autonomous entity."[69]

In Taiwan, then, the deeply polarized domestic environment, underscored by the long-standing cleavages between the Chinese and Taiwanese-centered nationalisms, and between the KMT and DPP, constrains the behavior of top policymakers and prevents the enactment of a coherent and rational mainland strategy. President Ma strived to rehabilitate the ROC as the sole legal Chinese state which encompasses not only the mainland but also Taiwan, thereby supplanting the DPP's pro-independence proclivities and painting the latter's policy as "chauvinistic and divisive de-Sinicization."[70] Thus, while knowing that the PRC remains Taiwan's primary security threat, the KMT government relied on the "1992 consensus" and cross-strait economic interdependence to promote and deepen the island's Chinese identity. Figure 2.1 illustrates the causal linkages described thus far.

In a sense, as Dafydd Fell noted, Ma Ying-jeou was trying to bring Taiwan back to the "mythical golden era" of the pre-Lee Teng-hui period, when the old KMT government under Chiang Kai-shek and Chiang Ching-kuo used Chinese nationalism to justify the ROC's legitimacy over Taiwan.[71] Furthermore, Fig. 2.2 depicts how Taiwan's ruling elites (both the KMT and DPP) are more interested in promoting its nation-building visions irrespective of international structural constraints or the prevailing dynamics of Sino-American relationships. When the DPP was in charge, from 2000 to 2008, Taipei was eager to push for various anti-China initiatives and programs (represented by the upper arrow), with the ultimate aim of establishing an independent Taiwan without any linkages (political, historical, cultural, and economic) to mainland China. In contrast, the KMT's Ma Ying-jeou, from 2008 to 2016, was actively pursuing a China-centric political framework to strengthen the political, economic, cultural, and historical ties between Taiwan and the mainland (represented by the lower arrow). The upshots were that the DPP was over-balancing against China whereas the KMT was under-balancing. These policies, under the

---

[69] Daniel Lynch, "Taiwan's Self-Conscious Nation-Building Project," *Asian Survey* 44, no. 4 (2004), p. 513.
[70] Hughes, "Revisiting Identity Politics under Ma Ying-jeou," p. 123.
[71] Dafydd Fell, *Government and Politics in Taiwan* (New York: Routledge, 2012), p. 134, p. 167.

China's Rise + Increasing Sino-American rivalry since 2010 + Taiwan's longstanding internal divisions over the "one China" issue ⟶ Elite fragmentation (KMT vs. DPP) over the China threat and whether to balance against it ⟶ Elite and social fragmentation ⟶ Greater political and social instability and incoherence ⟶ Ruling elites' nation-building vision (KMT's "92 consensus") to supplant domestic oppositions (DPP and Taiwanese independence advocates) ⟶ Underbalancing in the form of accommodation, bandwagoning, appeasement, buck-passing, or other half-hearted measures toward Beijing

Fig. 2.1 Causal scheme of the KMT's pro-China policy, 2008–16 (Source: adopted and modified from Randall Schweller, *Unanswered Threats*, pp. 62–64)

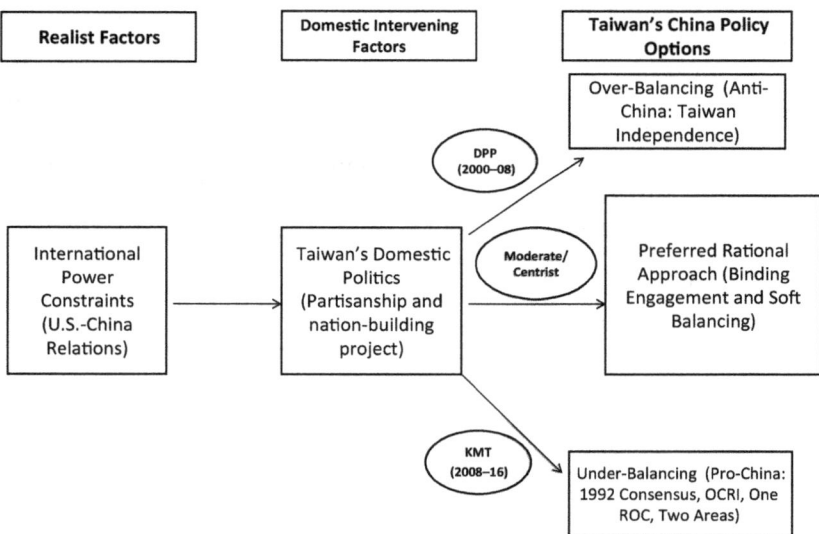

Fig. 2.2 A neoclassical realist model of Taiwan's mainland policy (2000–16)

respective parties, were launched in the midst of a highly polarized and contentious domestic environment and, ultimately, jeopardized Taiwan's national security and relations with the USA and China. A centrist and rational approach (represented by the middle arrow), however, has been missing from Taiwan's highly polarized domestic political climate. Chapter 6 will discuss about this centrist approach, based on soft balancing and binding engagement strategies.

3 Conclusion

Using a neoclassical realist analysis, this chapter argues that a national leader's foreign policymaking is affected not only by the prevailing global security considerations but also, more essentially, by the country's internal political situations and arrangements. In other words, while international power configurations certainly prescribe the perimeter of acceptable policy responses and behaviors, the specific contours of a decision and its final articulations are constituted by the domestic opportunities and constraints, including institutions, ideologies, and interests. The KMT government's "one-China" policymaking provides a pertinent case study, and there are three policy implications for the larger USA–PRC–Taiwan strategic relationships.

First, great powers always dictate the behaviors and policies of smaller and weaker states. This Thucydidean principle is certainly true for Taiwan, whose tenuous security-economic position requires the maintenance of a constructive as well as balanced relationship with both the USA and mainland China. Given the island's security dependency on Washington and its economic lifeline to Beijing, Taipei, be it under the DPP or KMT administration, cannot afford to alienate either power, for the repercussions of a "leaning to one-side" policy could be astronomically detrimental. Such is the reality of international politics. A neutral and non-aligned policy stance is probably the most rational approach, but it is also, at the same time, an exceedingly difficult one to undertake. Indeed, similar to Chen Shui-bian's "five no's" in 2000, Ma Ying-jeou, after being elected president in 2008, pledged to charter a moderate course of action, known as the "three no's" or "no unification, no independence, and no use of force." After years of crises across the Taiwan Strait, the KMT government's resumption of socioeconomic exchanges with the mainland, on the basis of the "1992 consensus," was welcomed by the USA, at least during the first term of Ma Ying-jeou's administration.

Second, as a result of Taiwan's democratization and rising national consciousness, the struggles between the KMT and DPP have focused less on socioeconomic issues than national state building. The two parties have vastly opposing views regarding whether Taiwan is an independent state or part of China, even though the KMT's interpretations of the "1992 consensus" have been predicated on the notion that "one China" is the Republic of China. As will be elaborated in Chap. 4, however, the DPP has treated the ROC as merely an instrumental cover-up for Taiwan, which is a genuinely independent sovereign state that has no connections with mainland China. Notwithstanding Tsai Ing-wen's moderation after being inaugurated as the ROC's new president in May 2016, the meaning of the "ROC" has been muddled by the DPP administration, which refrains from defining the term in the same manner as Ma Ying-jeou. The contradictions among political elites over their nationalist visions inevitably deny any chances of bipartisan cooperation because party leaders perceive each other not as loyal oppositions or competitors within the same nation but as "enemies," "foreigners," or "national traitors." Electoral politics thus becomes a ruthless zero-sum game in which one party's victory means the defeat of the other's "national state."

Hence, Chen's administration from 2000 to 2008 saw the denigration of the ROC and dismissal of its constitutional arrangements, whereas the Ma government between 2008 and 2016 resurrected the ROC's "one-China" legitimacy. Consequently, the DPP's mainland policy is confrontational (or, over-balancing) while the KMT's is conciliatory (or, under-balancing). Neither party can stay on the course of moderation for long because each must eventually embrace their respective ideological fundamentalisms to defend or construct their own nation-states. Neither policy stance is conducive to Taiwan's national security interests. Furthermore, when either party gets to the extremist level, it is rejected by Taiwan's mainstream voters, as illustrated by the DPP's electoral losses in 2005, 2008, 2010, and 2012. The KMT experienced the identical quandary in its huge losses of 2014 and 2016.

Third, while Ma was actively pursuing rapprochement with Beijing, his administration encountered both internal and external pushbacks. Domestically, fervent oppositions increased over Ma's lackluster domestic policy performance (i.e., long-term wage stagnation; worsening socioeconomic inequality; soaring price of gas and electricity; corruption scandals; cutbacks on retiree benefits of military personnel, government employees, and school teachers;, and the food safety debacles, to name just a few) and Taiwan's greater economic and political tilt toward mainland China.[72] The president's policies of national identification with China, though helping

---

[72] Min-Hua Huang, "Taiwan's Changing Political landscape: The KMT's Landslide Defeat in the Nine-in-One Elections," The Brookings East Asia Commentary (December 2014), accessible at: http://www.brookings.edu/research/opinions/2014/12/08-taiwan-political-landscape-elections-huang. See also Wu, "Heading towards Troubled Waters"? pp. 70–71.

to stabilize cross-strait relations and correcting some of Chen Shui-bian's excesses, went beyond what was needed to appeal to Taiwan's median voters.[73] While economically engaging China served Taiwan's interests, the "1992 consensus" should also be utilized to boost Taiwan's international profile and soft power. The island's democratic institutions and norms, according to some of President Ma's critics, should be further underscored in order to distinguish the ROC from the PRC.[74]

Internationally, as will be analyzed in Chap. 5, when Sino-American relations have grown more complex in light of Washington's rebalancing to Asia and China's growing assertiveness, the KMT's close political ties with Beijing have become a strategic liability for the party. Despite reaching some major agreements with President Xi Jinping in November 2014 and during the latter's state visit to Washington, DC, in September 2015, the Obama administration continues to view the PRC's "muscular foreign policy" with wariness.[75] A well-balanced position, consequently, is in the interests of Taiwan to survive in between these great power states.[76] Nonetheless, as long as Taiwan remains irreconcilable internally over the national identity issue, central leaders in Taipei, irrespective of which ruling party, will be unable to implement a rational strategic approach to the satisfaction of Taiwan's domestic and international audiences. The DPP's "one China, one Taiwan" and the KMT's "one China, respective interpretations" have no overlapping point and such cleavage is likely to persist. Each party's obsession with nation building inevitably leads to irrational national security policy and, when taken to the extreme, is also likely to be penalized by Taiwan's electorates.

[73] Hughes, "Revisiting Identity Politics under Ma Ying-jeou," pp. 120–136.

[74] "Editorial: Shredding the '1992 Consensus,'" *Taipei Times* (June 28, 2016), accessible at: http://www.taipeitimes.com/News/editorials/archives/2016/06/28/2003649621.

[75] Chris Buckley, "Xi Jinping's Rapid Rise in China Presents Challenges to the U.S.," *The New York Times* (November 11, 2014), accessible at: http://www.nytimes.com/2014/11/12/world/asia/president-xi-jinping-makes-it-his-mission-to-empower-china.html. See also Elizabeth Economy, "China's Imperial President," *Foreign Affairs* (November–December 2014), pp. 80–91; and David Nakamura, "China's Xi to Get a Pomp Heavy U.S. Welcome Friday, But Maybe Not a Warm One," *The Washington Post* (September 24, 2015), accessible at: http://www.washingtonpost.com/politics/chinas-xi-to-get-a-pomp-heavy-us-welcome-friday-but-maybe-not-a-warm-one/2015/09/24/a18e88ba-62ca-11e5-8e9e-dce8a2a2a679_story.html. See also Robert Blackwill and Kurt Campbell, *Xi Jinping on the Global Stage* (New York: Council on Foreign Relations, Special Report No. 74, February 2016).

[76] Tuan Cheng, "Taiwan-U.S. Relations," p. 382.

References

Barbieri, Katherine. 2006. *The Liberal Illusion: Does Trade Promote Peace?* Ann Arbor: University of Michigan Press.
Blackwill, Robert, and Kurt Campbell. 2016. *Xi Jinping on the Global Stage*. New York: Council on Foreign Relations, Special Report No. 74.
Bush, Richard, and Alan Romberg. 2009. Cross-Strait Moderation and the United States—A Response to Robert Sutter. *PACNET* 17A: 1–2.
Cabestan, J-Pierre, and Jacques deLisle (eds.). 2014. *Political Changes in Taiwan under Ma Ying-jeou*. New York: Routledge.
Chang, Hui-Ching, and Rich Holt. 2009. Taiwan and ROC: A Critical Analysis of President Chen Shui-bian's Construction of Taiwan Identities in National Speeches. *National Identities* 11(3): 301–330.
Chao, Chien-min. 2003. One Step Forward, One Step Backward: Chen Shui-bian's Mainland Policy. *Journal of Contemporary China* 12(34): 125–143.
———. 2004. National Security vs. Economic Interests. *Journal of Contemporary China* 13(41): 687–704.
Cheng, Tuan. 2013. Taiwan-U.S. Relations. *China Report* 49(4): 371–384.
Christensen, Thomas. 1996. *Useful Adversaries*. Princeton: Princeton University Press.
Chu, Yun-han. 1999. The Political Economy of Taiwan's Mainland Policy. In *Across the Taiwan Strait*, ed. Suisheng Zhao, 163–196. New York: Routledge.
Clark, Cal, and Alexander Tan. 2012. *Taiwan Political Economy*. Boulder: Lynne Rienner Publishers.
Dueck, Colin. 2006. *Reluctant Crusaders*. Princeton: Princeton University Press.
———. 2009. Neoclassical Realism and the National Interest: Presidents, Domestic Politics, and Major Military Interventions. In *Neoclassical Realism, the State, and Foreign Policy*, ed. Steven Lobell, N. Ripsman, and J. Taliaferro, 139–169. New York: Cambridge University Press.
Economy, Elizabeth. 2014. China's Imperial President. *Foreign Affairs* 93(6): 80–91.
Fell, Dafydd. 2012. *Government and Politics in Taiwan*. New York: Routledge.
Gitter, David, and Robert Sutter. 2016. Taiwan's Strong but Stifled Foundations of National Power. *The NBR Special Report* 54: 1–24.
Hickey, Dennis. 2007. *Foreign Policy Making in Taiwan*. New York: Routledge.
———. 2011. Rapprochement between Taiwan and the Chinese Mainland: Implications for American Foreign Policy. *Journal of Contemporary China* 20(69): 231–247.
Hsu, Philip. 2010. Between Identity Quest and Risk Aversion: Lessons from the Chen Shui-bian Presidency for Maintaining Cross-Strait Stability. *Journal of Contemporary China* 19(66): 693–717.

Hughes, Christopher. 2014. Revisiting Identity Politics under Ma Ying-jeou. In *Political Changes in Taiwan under Ma Ying-jeou*, ed. Jean-Pierre Cabestan and Jacques deLisle, 120–136. New York: Routledge.

Kaeding, Malte. 2009. Taiwanized "New Taiwanese": The Effect of Taiwanization on the 2008 Presidential Election Campaign of Ma Ying-jeou. *Asia Pacific Social Science Review* 9(2): 19–34.

Kastner, Scott. 2006. Does Economic Integration across the Taiwan Strait Make Military Conflict Less Likely? *Journal of East Asian Studies* 3(6): 319–346.

———. 2007. When Do Conflicting Political Relations Affect International Trade? *Journal of Conflict Resolution* 51(4): 664–688.

———. 2009. *Political Conflict and Economic Interdependence across the Taiwan Strait and Beyond*. Stanford: Stanford University Press.

Layne, Christopher. 2006. *The Peace of Illusions*. Ithaca: Cornell University Press.

Lin, Shirley. 2016. *Taiwan's China Dilemma*. Stanford: Stanford University Press.

Lynch, Daniel. 2004. Taiwan's Self-Conscious Nation Building Project. *Asian Survey* 44(4): 513–533.

Mansfield, Edward, and Brian Pollins. 2005. Interdependence and Conflict: An Introduction. In *Economic Interdependence and International Conflict*, ed. Edward Mansfield and Brian Pollins, 1–28. Ann Arbor: University of Michigan Press.

Rigger, Shelley. 2011. *Why Taiwan Matters*. Lanham: Rowman & Littlefield.

Romberg, Alan. 2003. *Rein In at the Brink of the Precipice*. Washington: The Henry L. Stimson Center.

Rose, Gideon. 1998. Neoclassical Realism and Theories of Foreign Policy. *World Politics* 51(1): 144–172.

Rosen, Daniel, and Zhi Wang. 2011. *The Implications of China-Taiwan Economic Liberalization*. Washington, DC: Peterson Institute.

Ross, Robert. 2006. Explaining Taiwan's Revisionist Diplomacy. *Journal of Contemporary China* 15(48): 443–458.

Schneider, Gerald, Katherine Barbieri, and Nils Petter Gleditsch. 2003. Does Globalization Contribute to Peace? A Critical Survey of the Literature. In *Globalization and Armed Conflict*, ed. Gerald Schneider, Katherine Barbieri, and Nils Petter Gleditsch, 3–29. New York: Rowman & Littlefield.

Schweller, Randall. 1999. Managing the Rise of Great Powers: History and Theory. In *Engaging China*, ed. Alastair Iain Johnston and Robert Ross, 1–31. New York: Routledge.

———. 2004. Unanswered Threats: A Neoclassical Realist Theory of Underbalancing. *International Security* 29(2): 159–201.

———. 2006. *Unanswered Threats*. Princeton: Princeton University Press.

Sterling-Folker, J. 2009. Neoclassical Realism and Identity. In *Neoclassical Realism, the State, and Foreign Policy*, ed. Steven Lobell, N. Ripsman, and J. Taliaferro, 99–138. New York: Cambridge University Press.

Su, Chi. 2009. *Taiwan's Relations with Mainland China*. New York: Routledge.
Sullivan, Jonathan, and Will Lowe. 2010. Chen Shui-bian: On Independence. *The China Quarterly* 203: 619–638.
Tucker, Nancy. 2009. *Strait Talk*. Cambridge, MA: Harvard University Press.
Walt, Stephen. 1987. *The Origins of Alliances*. Ithaca: Cornell University Press.
Waltz, Kenneth. 1979. *Theory of International Politics*. New York: McGraw Hill.
Wang, T.Y. 2000. 'One China, One Taiwan': An Analysis of the Democratic Progressive Party's China Policy. *Journal of Asian and African Studies* 35(1): 159–182.
Wang, T.Y., et al. 2011. Taiwan's Expansion of International Space: Opportunities and Challenges. *Journal of Contemporary China* 20(69): 249–267.
Wohlforth, William. 1993. *The Elusive Balance*. Ithaca: Cornell University Press.
Wu, Yu-shan. 2005. Taiwan's Domestic Politics and Cross-Strait Relations. *The China Journal* 53: 35–60.
———. 2016. Heading towards Troubled Waters? The Impact of Taiwan's 2016 Elections on Cross-Strait Relations. *American Journal of Chinese Studies* 23(1): 59–76.
Zakaria, Fareed. 1998. *From Wealth to Power*. Princeton: Princeton University Press.
Zhang, Baohui. 2011. Taiwan's New Grand Strategy. *Journal of Contemporary China* 20(69): 269–285.
Zhao, Suisheng. 1999. Economic Interdependence and Political Divergence. In *Across the Taiwan Strait*, ed. Suisheng Zhao, 21–40. New York: Routledge.

Author's Interviews

Interview with Robert Sutter, Professor of Practice of International Affairs at the Elliot School of International Affairs, George Washington University, February 24, 2016, Washington, DC, USA.

CHAPTER 3

Defining "One China"

There are legitimate concerns from skeptics of the "1992 consensus," asserting that the Ma Ying-jeou administration was merely engaging in self-deception because Beijing has never agreed to the KMT's "one China, respective interpretations" formulation. The PRC has not given any concessions to the continued existence of the ROC. The mainland, indeed, has frequently responded harshly to citizens or supporters of Taiwan waving the ROC national flag at international venues such as the Olympics or other sporting events. In major political and socioeconomic international and non-governmental organizational (NGO) gatherings, Taiwan is either barred from joining or, if participation is permitted, must use the designation of "Chinese Taipei" in order to specify its non-state status. The most recent incident was Chou Tzu-yu, the Taiwanese member of a South Korean K-pop girl group, who waved an ROC national flag during an appearance on a South Korean TV show in late 2015. Accused of being an advocate of Taiwanese independence, Chou was "sanctioned" and her commercial activities in China and South Korea were immediately curtailed. On the eve of Taiwan's elections on January 16, 2016, Chou was asked by her management company to issue a formal "apology" through a video-recording and to affirm that she has "always felt proud of being Chinese." While it was unclear how much impact Chou's video had on the election results, it surely sparked public indignation across Taiwan and led many to wonder whether the ROC could really be accepted by Beijing in line with the KMT's OCRI narratives.[1]

This chapter,[2] however, suggests that although Beijing is certainly not publicly recognizing the ROC (and, at times, even seeking to suppress it), one cannot dismiss the CCP authority's changing, and increasingly more flexible, conception of the "one-China" principle since 1992 and more receptive attitude toward Taiwan's ROC after 2008. As discussed in Chap. 1, the historic Xi–Ma meeting shows that the PRC is no longer taking a zero-sum position toward the ROC. Some observers even stressed that the summit represented an "important turning point" implying an "openness [on the part of Beijing leadership] to recognize two separate governments as legitimate entities [under one China]."[3] Even after Tsai Ing-wen and the DPP's resounding electoral victory in January 2016, the Xi Jinping administration, despite its stern and uncompromising insistence on the "1992 consensus" and warning against Taiwanese independence, has not entirely backtracked from its tacit acceptance of the ROC. The ROC's "one-China" route is clearly the more appealing choice for Beijing than the prospect of coping with a Republic of Taiwan.

Despite being the more powerful actor in cross-strait relations today, mainland China is becoming less compelling in its once-rigid stance of "one China." While setting the perimeter of acceptable discourse, Beijing has actually been "persuaded" by its former and defeated rival—the KMT—that the "1992 consensus" or OCRI proves to be the better argument than the pro-independence narratives propounded by the administrations of Lee Teng-hui and Chen Shui-bian. Indeed, as we shall see in the following subsections, starting in the early 1990s, Beijing's changing conception of "one China," as a result of cross-strait social and discursive interactions, has produced a new set of identities and interests for the

---

[1] "Editorial: Flush Away the 1992 Consensus," *Taipei Times* (January 19, 2016), accessible at: http://www.taipeitimes.com/News/editorials/archives/2016/01/19/2003637518. See also Wu Chung-li, "Games without Frontiers, War without Tears? The Process of Campaigning in the 2016 Taiwanese General Elections," *American Journal of Chinese Studies* 23, no. 1 (2016), pp. 35–36.

[2] This chapter is derived, in part, from an article written by this author. See Dean P. Chen, "Constructing Peaceful Development: The Changing Interpretations of 'One China' and Beijing's Taiwan Strait Policy," *Asian Security* 10, no. 1 (2014), pp. 22–46, DOI: 10.1080/14799855.2013.874337.

[3] Winberg Chai, "Xi Jinping and Ma Ying-jeou's Historic 2015 Meeting in Singapore," *Asian Affairs: An American Review* 42, no. 4 (2015), p. 201.

PRC with respect to Taiwan. On identity, Chinese leaders have eschewed the notion that "one China" means unequivocally the PRC. Instead of squarely identifying Beijing as the central government and Taiwan its subject, the CCP has opted for greater equality—that is, both mainland and Taiwan belong to "one China." Although national unification remains the top priority for China's leaders, they are assuming a more gradualist attitude. Since 2008, Beijing has focused on exploring mutually acceptable and reasonable political arrangements that would pragmatically reflect the present cross-strait realities. These suggest Beijing's implicit acknowledgment of the ROC's existence in cross-strait interactions even though the former continues to dismiss the ROC at the international/global level.

Although this chapter shifts its focus toward examining Beijing's "one-China" perspective, its objective is to lay out the origins or backgrounds on how the "1992 consensus" and subsequently more relaxed construction of the "one-China" principle have facilitated the KMT and CCP to find common ground to foster a new united front to jointly combat the DPP and Taiwanese independence forces. In short, without the PRC's acquiescence to the KMT's OCRI and ROC-centric position, one cannot fully understand the permissive cross-strait context under which President Ma Ying-jeou launched his nation-building projects in Taiwan.

1   Background

In the wake of Deng Xiaoping's economic opening and the establishment of Sino–US diplomatic relations in the late 1970s, the PRC has shifted its Taiwan policy from forceful liberation to a more peaceful and patient approach predicated on economic and cultural exchanges and political negotiations leading eventually to peaceful unification under the "one country, two systems" formula.[4] Certainly, while emphasizing more on "carrots" and pushing for closer cross-strait economic interdependence, Beijing has never given up on the use of "sticks" or military coercion should

---

[4] "NPC Standing Committee's Message to Compatriots in Taiwan," (Jan 1, 1979), accessible at: http://www.gwytb.gov.cn/en/Special/OneChinaPrinciple/201103/t20110317_1790061.htm; "Ye Jianying on Taiwan's Return to Motherland and Peaceful Reunification," (Sep 30, 1981), accessible at: http://www.gwytb.gov.cn/en/Special/OneChinaPrinciple/201103/t20110317_1790062.htm; "Deng Xiaoping on 'one country, two systems'" (June 22–23, 1984), accessible: http://www.gwytb.gov.cn/en/Special/OneCountryTwoSystem/201103/t20110316_1789244.htm. See also Shelley Rigger, "Taiwan in U.S.-China Relations," in David Shambaugh, ed., *Tangled Titans*, p. 294.

Taipei indefinitely procrastinate on unification or venture toward formal independence. The PRC's peaceful initiatives toward Taiwan have already been well explicated and analyzed in many seminal works.[5] In essence, three plausible determinants have been raised.[6] First, as a result of international pressure and, specifically, American hegemonic influence, central leaders in Beijing have come to terms with the fact that, in order to cultivate beneficial ties with foreign powers and improve US–China relations, it is rational to embrace a softer attitude on the Taiwan Strait impasse to assure the international community that its rise is not threatening and revisionist.[7] Second, because China today continues to face a myriad of socioeconomic challenges at home,[8] the CCP elites have greater interest in maintaining internal political stability and sustaining economic growth and modernization through its "peaceful development" grand strategy.[9] Consequently, Beijing has less incentive to stimulate troubles across the strait and to jeopardize its economic well-being. Finally, China's perception of Taiwan's

---

[5] See, for instance, Michael Swaine, "Decision-Making Regarding Taiwan, 1979–2000," in David Lampton, ed., *The Making of Chinese Foreign and Security Policy in the Era of Reform* (Stanford, CA: Stanford University Press, 2001), pp. 289–336.

[6] Suisheng Zhao, "Military Coercion and Peaceful Offense: Beijing's Strategy of National Unification with Taiwan," *Pacific Affairs* 72, no. 4 (Winter 1999–2000), pp. 495–512; and Chien-Kai Chen, "Comparing Jiang Zemin's Impatience with Hu Jintao's Patience Regarding the Taiwan Issue, 1989–2012, *Journal of Contemporary China* 21, no. 78 (November 2012), pp. 1–18.

[7] On Beijing's foreign policy and relations with Taiwan and other major powers, see Michael Swaine and Ashley Tellis, *Interpreting China's Grand Strategy* (Santa Monica, CA: RAND, 2000), pp. 112–150; Avery Goldstein, *Rising to the Challenge* (Stanford, CA: Stanford University Press, 2005), p. 39. See also Rosemary Foot, "Chinese Strategies in a U.S. Hegemonic Global Order," *International Affairs* 82, no. 1 (2006), pp. 77–94; Bates Gill, *Rising Star* (Washington DC: Brookings Institution Press, 2010); David Kang, *China Rising* (New York: Columbia University Press, 2010), Ch. 3; Evan Medeiros, *China's International Behavior* (Santa Monica, CA: RAND, 2009); Robert Sutter, *Chinese Foreign Relations* (Lanham, MD: Rowman & Littlefield, 2016).

[8] Susan Shirk, *China: Fragile Superpower*. See also David Lampton, *Following the Leader: Ruling China, from Deng Xiaoping to Xi Jinping* (Berkeley, CA: University of California Press, 2014).

[9] Initially, the term "peaceful rise" was used. However, critics cautioned the Hu Jintao administration that the very use of the word "rise" could create suspicion and wariness among other countries. Hence, the term was changed to "peaceful development" in April 2004. See Zheng Bijian, "China's 'Peaceful Rise' to Great Power Status," *Foreign Affairs* 84, no. 5 (September/October 2005), pp. 18–24. See also Goldstein, *Rising to the Challenge*, p. 192; Friedberg, *A Contest for Supremacy*, p. 148; and G. John Ikenberry, "The Rise of China, the United States, and the Future of the Liberal International Order," in David Shambaugh, ed., *Tangled Titans*, pp. 53–73.

political change and behavior also affects Beijing's decision-making. As Taiwan democratizes in the post-Cold War era, the political ascendancy of the pro-independence forces, such as the DPP, growing Taiwanese identity and sentiments, and diminishing popular support for unification have convinced Beijing that conciliatory economic policies should be implemented to win the hearts and minds of the Taiwanese people.

While the foregoing arguments have made valid assessments, their focus is mainly on Beijing's peaceful economic offense toward Taiwan and ignores the former's increasingly flexible interpretation of the "one-China" principle. Between 1949 and 1992, the Chinese official position on "one China" was firmly predicated on the so-called old "one-China" syllogism (*jiu yizhong sanduanlun*) that "there is only one China in the world; Taiwan is an inalienable part of China; and the seat of China's central government is in Beijing."[10] In other words, although Taiwan, like Hong Kong and Macau, would be given substantial autonomy in deciding and managing its own political and socioeconomic affairs after reunification with the mainland under the "one country, two systems" arrangement, it is, without any doubt, a local government subordinating to the PRC central state. However, starting in the early 1990s, Beijing's rigid stance on "one China" began to loosen. In November 1992, the Jiang Zemin administration did not refute the then KMT government's assertion of "one China, respective interpretations," in which both Taiwan and the mainland could verbally disagree over what "one China" means. Such implicit understanding was later coined by the then minister of the MAC, Su Chi, in April 2000, as the "1992 consensus" (more on Su's rationales behind the creation of the term "1992 consensus" in Chap. 4). Then, by the end of the decade, top CCP leaders, such as Qian Qichen and Wang Daohan, further suggested, through the "new one-China syllogism" (*xin yizhong sanduanlun*), that "there is only one China in the world; both mainland and Taiwan belong to one China; and China's sovereignty and territorial integrity cannot be divided." In a sense, Beijing no longer insists that "China" must be the PRC, implying that the relations between Beijing and Taipei are not "principal" and "subordinate," but "equal political entities."[11] Since 2008, the Hu Jintao and, subsequently, the Xi Jinping administrations even tacitly allowed the ROC—long taboo in the PRC's

---

[10] "The Taiwan Question and Reunification of China," *Taiwan Affairs Office of the State Council PRC* (August 1993), accessible at: http://www.gwytb.gov.cn/en/Special/WhitePapers/201103/t20110316_1789216.htm.

[11] Wu, "Heading towards Troubled Waters"? p. 66.

political lexicon—to resurface in the cross-strait discourse and dialogue. When President Ma Ying-jeou, in making his second inaugural address on May 20, 2012, openly stressed that "one China" is the ROC, which claims sovereignty over both the Taiwan and mainland regions, Beijing, to the surprise of many observers, was not particularly perturbed and did not directly challenge Taipei's contention.

Hence, three important points should be kept in mind when considering Beijing's changing postulations of its "one-China" principle. First, the Taiwan issue has long been identified as China's "internal affair" or "core interest," that the island's eventual integration is pivotal to China's national unity and territorial integrity. Hence, although China is concerned about developing salutary security and economic ties with the United States and other international powers, it has never concealed its intent to unify with Taiwan and to use military force when necessary.[12] For instance, the 1995–96 Taiwan Strait confrontation clearly shows China's intransigence on the sovereignty issue when Beijing launched a series of military exercise and live-fire missile tests to warn against Taipei's seemingly greater propensity toward independence.[13] Though America's superior deterrence power prevented the tension from escalating into militarized conflict, Beijing became deeply suspicious of Washington in covertly abetting Taiwanese independence to keep China permanently divided and weak.[14] To amend the rupture, President Bill Clinton, during his state visit to China in June 1998, stated, "We [the United States] don't support independence for Taiwan, or two Chinas, or one-China-one Taiwan. And, we don't believe that Taiwan should be a member in any organization for which statehood is a requirement."[15] The Clinton administration sought to reassure Beijing that it was not deviating from America's long-term commitment to the "one-China" policy. In the mid-2000s, despite Hu Jintao's commitment to a peaceful development grand strategy, the National People's Congress (NPC) passed the Anti-Secession Law, in March 2005, to legalize the use of "non-peaceful means" to deter Taiwanese independence.

Second, whereas Beijing, in light of its domestic problems, has a clear incentive to fashion a more moderate Taiwan policy by strengthening

[12] Thomas Christensen, "Posing Problems without Catching Up," *International Security* 25, no. 4 (Spring 2001), p. 36.
[13] Robert Ross, "The 1995–96 Taiwan Strait Confrontation."
[14] Nancy Tucker, *Strait Talk*, pp. 273–274.
[15] Romberg, *Rein In at the Brink of the Precipice*, pp. 183–184; Robert Sutter, *U.S.-Chinese Relations*, pp. 119–122.

cross-strait economic cooperation, fervent Chinese nationalism is also burgeoning and has become a critical source of the CCP's ruling legitimacy. "Nationalism," according to Robert Sutter, "supports the CCP administration's high priority to prevent Taiwan independence and restore this and other territory taken from China by foreign powers when China was weak and vulnerable during the nineteenth and twentieth centuries."[16] In fact, in the aftermath of the 2008 global financial crisis, Beijing has behaved more assertively toward the United States and the West, and, especially, its Asian neighbors over maritime and territorial disputes in the East and South China Seas.[17] Since coming to power in 2012–13, Xi Jinping has also repeatedly called for the "rejuvenation of the Chinese nation and Chinese dream."[18] President Xi's more confident foreign policy stance also propelled Beijing to coin the notion of establishing a "new type of major power relationship" between the PRC and United States, with the direct implication that mainland China should be treated as equal to America in global and regional affairs.[19] As a result, it is unclear why Beijing would relax and re-conceptualize its cardinal "one-China" stance at a time of rising power ascendancy and nationalism.

Finally, the PRC is, needless to say, utilizing economic instruments and benefits to win Taiwan's goodwill, to foster the island's greater dependency on the Chinese market, and promote unification in the long run. However, for a regime that has, since 1949, unequivocally based its ruling legitimacy on overthrowing the ROC and representing China's solely legitimate government, its modification in political discourse—the "one China"—cannot be easily accounted. More importantly, Taiwan's general public attitude toward the ROC is also much divided since the government is often associated with the KMT's past authoritarianism and martial law imposed by Presidents Chiang Kai-shek and Chiang Ching-kuo on the island between 1947 and 1987. As will be addressed in Chaps. 4 and 6,

---

[16] Sutter, *U.S.-Chinese Relations*, p. 140.

[17] Suisheng Zhao, "Foreign Policy Implications of Chinese Nationalism Revisited: The Strident Turn," *Journal of Contemporary China* 22, no. 82 (March 2013), pp. 543–545.

[18] "Xi Vows Peaceful Development while Not Waiving Legitimate Rights," *The Xinhua News Agency* (January 29, 2013), accessible at: http://news.xinhuanet.com/english/bilingual/2013-01/29/c_132136438.htm. See also Willy Lam, *Chinese Politics in the Era of Xi Jinping* (New York: Routledge, 2015); Blackwill and Campbell, *Xi Jinping on the Global Stage*, pp. 14–15.

[19] David Lampton, "A New Type of Major-Power Relationship: Seeking a Durable Foundation for U.S.-China Ties," *Asia Policy* no. 16 (July 2013), pp. 51–68.

the DPP and a substantial percentage of the Taiwanese people continue to reject the "1992 consensus," or "one China, respective interpretations," whether that China stands for the ROC or PRC. The people's eagerness to cultivate a self-consciously Taiwanese national identity has made the KMT's ROC legitimacy much less appealing. Consequently, Beijing's greater latitude on "one China" does not appear to offer clear payoffs and benefits, let alone winning the hearts and minds of the Taiwanese people. Indeed, the KMT's landslide electoral defeats in 2014 and 2016 are both cases in point for Beijing. Nevertheless, the greater tolerance of the ROC at least puts Beijing in a relatively less intransigent position and facilitates sturdier partisan cooperation between the CCP and KMT.

2 Neoclassical Realism and Social Constructivism

To be sure, Beijing's reconstruction or reconstitution of the "one-China" principle does not imply it is surrendering its objective in national reunification. Rather, it is propounding an argument that both the mainland and Taiwan should explore and make reasonable political arrangements under the special condition that China is yet to be reunified. Therefore, a future unified "one China" remains the bottom line, but, meanwhile, Beijing and Taipei cannot deny their "splitting status" and that each is governed by its own functioning and legal governing institutions. Thus, this chapter contends that the "one-China" principle is a socially constructed discourse subject to competing deliberations and persuasions from both China and Taiwan. In line with neoclassical realism noted in Chap. 2, it's important to recall that foreign policy limited to international systemic or structural factors alone is bound to be inaccurate much of the time. The central decision-makers' perception, identity, normative commitment, and policy discourse are also indispensable for our understanding as these factors bridge between systemic pressures or constraints and foreign policy outcomes. Thus, neoclassical realism and ideational theories are, in fact, complementary.[20] Gideon Rose maintained that "neoclassical realists occupy a middle ground between pure structural theorists and

---

[20] See Alexander Wendt, "Anarchy Is What States Make of It," *International Organization* 46, no. 2 (Spring 1992), pp. 391–425. See also Jutta Weldes, *Constructing National Interests* (Minneapolis: University of Minnesota Press, 1999) and Peter Katzenstein, ed., *The Culture of National Security* (New York: Columbia University Press, 1996).

constructivists.... Neoclassical realists assume that there is indeed something like an objective reality of relative power which will have dramatic effects on the outcomes of state interactions. They do not assume, however, that states necessarily apprehend that reality accurately on a day-to-day basis.... The world states end up inhabiting, therefore, is indeed partly of their own making."[21]

Hence, the end of the Cold War and Taiwan's democratization have gradually opened up a "communicative space" across the strait for competing views and propositions on what "one China" is and how cross-strait relations should unfold. In 1992, the then KMT government put forward "one China, respective interpretations" or OCRI. Though Beijing did not repudiate such postulation, it continued to insist that the PRC is the "one China" and Taiwan its local subject. Nevertheless, between 1995 and 2008, the emergence of the pro-independence Lee Teng-hui and Chen Shui-bian administrations promoted, respectively, the "special state-to-state relations," also known as the "two-states theory," in July 1999 and the "one country on each side of the strait" statement in August 2002. As the DPP won consecutive presidential elections in 2000 and 2004, Beijing realized that there is a rising "Taiwanese self-consciousness" among the Taiwan citizens who increasingly view themselves as not Chinese and strongly oppose "any form of reunification under which the mainland authorities would exercise real power over them."[22]

Cross-strait communicative action or the "logic of arguing"[23] has modified the Beijing leadership's perception of Taiwan's changing political situations. Although the PRC remains steadfast in upholding the "one-China" principle and firmly opposes the Taiwanese pro-independence policy narratives, it begins to re-conceive its identity and interest under the "one-China" rubric to search for a mutually acceptable consensus. First, Beijing had, by the late 1990s, defined that the mainland and Taiwan are equal political entities and mutually belong to the same "one China."

---

[21] Rose, "Neoclassical Realism and Theories of Foreign Policy," pp. 152–153. See also Norrin Ripsman et al., *Neoclassical Realist Theory of International Politics*, pp. 157–159.

[22] Andrew Nathan & Andrew Scobell, *China's Search for Security*, p. 216.

[23] On the theory of argumentative persuasion, see Thomas Risse, "'Let's Argue!' Communicative Action in World Politics," *International Organization* 54, no. 1 (Winter 2000), pp. 1–39. See also Marc Lynch, "Why Engage? China and the Logic of Communicative Engagement," *European Journal of International Relations* 8, no. 2 (2002), pp. 187–230; and Ronald Krebs & Patrick Jackson, "Twisting Tongues and Twisting Arms," *European Journal of International Relations* 13, no. 1 (2007), pp. 35–66.

Second, refraining from identifying which China, the CCP leaders are problematizing the identity of the Chinese state and creating an ambiguity conducive to ameliorating cross-strait tensions. Third, as shown in the policy rhetoric made by the Hu Jintao and Xi Jinping administrations, Beijing is urging both parties to search and to construct reasonable arrangements that will accommodate the present political reality across the strait, that is, reunification has yet to be accomplished. These remarks suggest that Beijing is altering its interest by tacitly accepting the KMT's "one China, respective interpretations" and, by extension, the coexistence of the PRC and ROC under a greater "one-China" framework. The ROC provides a linkage between the CCP and KMT, which have shared common Chinese heritage, history, and memories during the ROC era on the mainland. Moreover, from the perspectives of Beijing and most Taiwanese, the ROC also appears to be the "lesser of two evils" compared, respectively, to an independent Taiwan and unification with the PRC.

Beijing's flexibility does not mean that it has recognized the ROC to reemerge in the international arena. On the contrary, while Beijing has, since 2008, allowed Taiwan to participate in more NGOs and international forums where statehood is not required, the former has persisted in restricting the latter's international space. Taipei is not permitted to use the ROC openly in any context. Sovereignty, according to Stephen Krasner, has three elements: (1) Westphalian, (2) domestic, and (3) international legal sovereignty.[24] Beijing has not loosened up the PRC's international legal sovereignty, though it does not refute the fact that the ROC has effective Westphalian and domestic sovereign controls over Taiwan.

3 The Evolution of "One China" in Cross-Strait Interactions

The Era of Rigidity, 1949–92

As discussed in Chap. 1, since coming to Taiwan after losing the Chinese Civil War in 1949, the KMT government, under Chiang Kai-shek and Chiang Ching-kuo, had continued to regard Mao Zedong's PRC regime as merely a "rebellious bandit group" whereas Taipei is China's authentic and legal government. Until the 1970s, the ROC held on to interna-

---

[24] Stephen Krasner, "Sharing Sovereignty: New Institutions for Collapsed or Failing States," *International Security* 29, no. 2 (Fall 2004), pp. 88–89.

tional recognition and support from most countries, including the United States, and represented mainland China in the United Nations' Security Council. On the other hand, Beijing also perceived Chiang's KMT forces as lackeys of American imperialism and that the CCP must eliminate and "wash out" the Nationalist remnants to "liberate" Taiwan. Nonetheless, after Beijing replaced Taipei in the UN in 1971 and normalized relations with Washington in 1979, the CCP leaders began to extend more conciliatory gestures toward its Taiwanese counterpart. Instead of calling the island "Chiang's clique" and stating that the CCP would "liberate Taiwan," Beijing has begun to address the ROC as "Taiwan authorities" and stress on "peaceful reunification."[25]

In the "New Year Day's Message to Taiwan Compatriots," issued on January 1, 1979, the NPC's Standing Committee pledged to "take present realities into account in accomplishing the great cause of reunifying the motherland and respect the status quo on Taiwan and the opinions of people in all walks of life there and adopt reasonable policies and measures in settling the question of reunification so as not to cause the people of Taiwan any losses."[26] Then, on September 30, 1981, Ye Jianying, the chairman of the NPC's Standing Committee, elaborated on peaceful reunification under his "Nine Points Proposal," in which Taiwan is promised a "high degree of autonomy" after reunification. This statement also brought up the notion of "three links" across the Taiwan Strait in trade, transportation, and postal exchanges, as well as "four exchanges" in culture, academics, economics, and sports.[27] Ye essentially underscored Deng Xiaoping's "one country, two systems" principle.[28] Notwithstanding the more amicable attitudes in these statements, the "one China" is always defined as the PRC and Taiwan its local administrative unit. Deng said, "We are pursuing a policy of 'one country, two systems.' More specifically, this means that within the People's Republic of China, the mainland…will

---

[25] Zhao, "Chinese Nationalism and Beijing's Taiwan Policy," p. 94.

[26] "NPC Standing Committee's Message to Compatriots in Taiwan," (Jan 1, 1979), accessible at: http://www.gwytb.gov.cn/en/Special/OneChinaPrinciple/201103/t20110317_1790061.htm.

[27] "Ye Jianying on Taiwan's Return to Motherland and Peaceful Reunification," (Sep 30, 1981), accessible at: http://www.gwytb.gov.cn/en/Special/OneChinaPrinciple/201103/t20110317_1790062.htm.

[28] "Deng Xiaoping on 'One Country, Two Systems'" (June 22–23, 1984), accessible: http://www.gwytb.gov.cn/en/Special/OneCountryTwoSystem/201103/t20110316_1789244.htm.

maintain the socialist system while Hong Kong and Taiwan continue under the capitalist system."[29] Reunification, according to the CCP leader, is the "aspiration of the whole nation."

The Hong Kong Meeting in 1992

In 1987, responding to increasing demand for liberalization and democratization, President Chiang Ching-kuo, whose health was deteriorating, decided to lift Taiwan's martial law and permitted political parties to freely assemble and contest in elections. He also opened up cross-strait economic and cultural contacts, marking the "beginning of the current cross strait relations."[30] Between the end of 1987 and June 1995, Taipei and Beijing worked incessantly to dispatch secret envoys and construct formal and informal institutions and agencies, including Taiwan's MAC and Strait Exchange Foundation (SEF) and the PRC's Taiwan Affairs Office and Association for Relations Across the Strait (ARATS), to promote trust and constructive dialogues.[31]

In spite of their differences, the KMT and CCP concurred on China's territorial integrity and national unification with Taiwan. The only question is whose China. On August 1, 1992, Taipei provided an answer as the ROC's National Unification Council (NUC) passed the "Definition of One China Resolution," which stipulates:

> The two sides of the Taiwan Strait uphold the one China principle, but the interpretations of the two sides are different.... Our side believes that one China should mean the Republic of China, established in 1912 and existing today, and its sovereignty extends throughout China, but its current governing authority is only over Taiwan, Penghu, Kinmen, and Matzu. Admittedly, Taiwan is a part of China, but the mainland is also a part of China.[32]

---

[29] "Deng Xiaoping on 'One Country, Two Systems.'"
[30] Su Chi, *Taiwan's Relations with Mainland China*, p. 1.
[31] SEF and ARATS are semi-government organizations (also known colloquially as the "white gloves") representing Taipei and Beijing, respectively, to negotiate socioeconomic, technical, and functional issues between the two sides. The official government organizations—ROC's MAC and the PRC's Taiwan Affairs Office of the State Council (TAO)—are responsible for managing cross-strait relations but did not meet directly. It was not until 2014 that heads from both the MAC and TAO meet in person and address each other in their official capacities.
[32] Ibid., p. 13.

The NUC resolution furnished the basis for the quasi-governmental SEF-ARATS negotiations in October–November 1992. SEF stated, in a press release on November 3, that "each side expresses its own interpretation *verbally* in order to solve this sticky problem of [one China] and thereby reaffirmed the August 1st NUC resolution as SEF's interpretation of one China."[33] In response, ARATS, on the same day, telephoned SEF, informing that the former "fully respected and accepted" Taipei's proposal to use a verbal declaration of each side's position on the matter. On November 16, ARATS sent a formal letter to SEF, stating that ARATS "fully respect and accept your Foundation's suggestion" and, simultaneously, affirming the content of its own interpretation, which was that "both sides of the strait uphold the principle of one China, and actively seek national unification, but the political interpretation of the one China will not be referred to in the cross-strait negotiations on functional issues."[34] This, in the KMT's view, is "one China, respective interpretations."

By late November 1992, both SEF and ARATS moved on to focus on the preparation works for the upcoming meeting between Koo Chen-fu, chairman of SEF, and Wang Daohan, head of ARATS, which took place in April 1993 in Singapore. The Koo-Wang talks launched subsequent rounds of negotiations and sub-meetings, centering on technical issues including fishing disputes, hijacking, cross-strait document notarization, express mailings, and other civil matters. In the words of Su Chi, OCRI was not "coined by either government but by the Taipei media in nearly unanimous fashion, which the Taipei government later adopted. [Thus], the mainland had never fully accepted this characterization since 1992, but it never completely rejected it either."[35] While Beijing emphasized that "both sides of the strait uphold the principle of one China," and that Taiwan is part of China, Taipei construed that both Taiwan and the mainland belong to China, which, based on the ROC Constitution and the NUC resolution, is the ROC. The ambiguity inherent in such a formulation allowed cross-strait relations to progress and consolidate in the early 1990s.

However, as President Lee Teng-hui opted for a more independence-oriented policy from the mid-1990s onward, Beijing began to criticize

---

[33] Ibid.
[34] Su, *Taiwan's Relations with Mainland China*, p. 14. See also ARATS eds., *Jiuer Gongshi Lishi Cunzheng [The Historical Documents of the 1992 Consensus]* (Beijing: Jiuzhou Press, 2005), p. 11.
[35] ARATS, eds., *Jiuer Gongshi Lishi Cunzheng*, p. 14.

OCRI as "deliberate distortion," a mere disguise utilized by independence advocates to promote either "two Chinas" or Taiwan's formal separation.[36] Indeed, in July 1999, in an interview with Germany's *Radio Deutsche Welle* at Taipei, Lee declared that cross-strait relations were in fact "special state-to-state relations." The "two-states theory" invoked consternation in both Washington and Beijing just three years after the 1995–96 Taiwan Strait crisis. The PRC not only launched incessant recriminations and polemical attacks against the Taiwan leader but also canceled ARATS chairman Wang Dao-han's scheduled visit to Taiwan in the fall of 1999. After this, SEF-ARATS talks ran into the doldrums, even though limited pacts were negotiated between Beijing and Taipei to facilitate economic and culture exchanges. When Chen Shui-bian came to office in May 2000, he initially embraced a more moderate approach toward the PRC, even at one point suggesting his willingness to accept the OCRI or "1992 consensus" formulation. Yet, Chen's position was immediately denied by Tsai Ing-wen, who was then minister of the MAC. As former president Lee Teng-hui's protégé, Tsai asserted that no consensus was attained in the Hong Kong meeting of 1992. Instead of going along with the KMT's OCRI position, Lee and Tsai stressed on the independent sovereignty of the ROC on Taiwan, which was not related to the Chinese mainland.[37] In August 2002, President Chen also became more vocal on the independence issue when proclaiming that "Taiwan and China are each one country on each side of the strait." Between then and May 2008, cross-strait relations severely worsened and all SEF-ARATS talks were effectively suspended. Chen and the DPP further denounced the existence of the "1992 consensus" and OCRI altogether as they sought to move Taiwan further away from China.[38]

Equality: "Both Mainland and Taiwan Belong to One China"

By the mid- and late 1990s, China's Jiang Zemin administration, responding to Taiwan's greater tilt toward independence, took a more flexible

---

[36] Ibid., pp. 12–15; Chen Qimao, "The Taiwan Straits Situation since Ma Came to Office and Conditions for Cross-Straits Political Negotiations," *Journal of Contemporary China* 20, no. 68 (January 2011), pp. 157–58.

[37] Wu, "Heading towards Troubled Waters"? pp. 66–68.

[38] Dennis V. Hickey, *Foreign Policy Making in Taiwan* (New York: Routledge, 2007), Su, *Taiwan's Relations with Mainland China*, and Shelley Rigger, *Why Taiwan Matters* (Lanham, MD: Rowman & Littlefield, 2011), especially Ch. 4.

approach on the "one-China" issue. In essence, Jiang's so-called Eight-Point Proposal, announced in January 1995, suggested a gradualist and "phased" process of rapprochement and negotiations leading eventually to reunification.[39] While building his pronouncement on the "one country, two systems" formula, Jiang put more emphasis on maintaining the status quo, facilitating cross-strait economic exchanges and the "three links," and deterring Taiwan's attempt to separate from the mainland. More importantly, as long as the island accepts the "one-China" principle, Beijing would consider and address all of Taiwan's concerns, including renouncing the use of force, treating Taipei as an equal political entity, and allowing Taiwan greater international space.[40]

On the other hand, Jiang's initiative also encompasses a clear hardline dimension in order to prevent Taiwanese independence.[41] As a result of the Taiwan Strait crisis of 1995–96 and the growing influence of the pro-independence political forces in Taiwan, Beijing's focus on a more coercive measure intensified in the latter half of the 1990s. Chinese military modernization has increased rapidly to prepare for a possible Taiwan Strait contingency and to prevent, delay, and deter America's timely involvement in the region. Moreover, the policies of Lee and Chen further reinforced Chinese pessimism regarding Taiwan's future. In fact, Beijing issued *The One-China Principle and Taiwan Issue White Paper* in February 2000 to sternly warn against Taiwan separatism and to state explicitly that the PRC would consider the use of force if Taipei continued to avoid meaningful talks with China indefinitely.[42]

Nonetheless, an even more notable change in Beijing's Taiwan policy had emerged by the end of Jiang's tenure, that is, top CCP elites have begun to identify both sides as "equal political entities." This important shift, from the previous principal-subordinate relationship, has had a lasting impact on the cross-strait policy discourse and re-conceptualized Beijing's identity and interests in "one China." In an effort to reconcile

---

[39] For a full transcript of Jiang's propositions, see "Jiang Zemin's Eight-Point Proposal," *Taiwan Affairs Office of the State Council PRC*, accessible at: http://www.gwytb.gov.cn/en/Special/Jiang/201103/t20110316_1789198.htm.

[40] Swaine, "Decision-Making Regarding Taiwan, 1979–2000," pp. 313–314.

[41] Chien-Kai Chen, "Comparing Jiang Zemin's Impatience with Hu Jintao's Patience Regarding the Taiwan Issue," pp. 16–17.

[42] "The One China Principle and the Taiwan Issue," *The Taiwan Affairs Office of the State Council of PRC* (February 2000), accessible at: http://www.gwytb.gov.cn/en/Special/WhitePapers/201103/t20110316_1789217.htm.

with Taipei after the 1995–96 strait crisis, Foreign Minister Qian Qichen, in September 1997, suggested resuming the stalled cross-strait negotiations under the condition of the "one-China" principle. But he did not make the usual reference to the PRC as the sole legitimate government of all of China. This explicit omission of any reference to the PRC in the standard definition of "one China" by a senior Chinese official was unprecedented.[43] Beijing also became increasingly explicit that it would treat Taipei as equal in cross-strait negotiations. The then Taiwan Affairs Office (TAO) director Chen Yunlin posited that "cross-strait negotiations are equal talks based on the principle of one China, not in the name of talks between the central government and a local government."[44]

In 1998, Wang Daohan said that "one China" does not refer to "either the ROC or the PRC. [It] indicates a unified China that will be created by the Chinese people of the two sides in the future."[45] On January 4, 2001, Qian, in an interview with the *Washington Post* at Zhongnnanhai, provided a more inclusive definition of the "one-China" policy. While reaffirming Beijing's goal in national unification, he stated that:

> In the past, Chinese officials said "one China" meant Communist China [and] that Taiwan was a breakaway province and the Beijing government was the only legal government. When Taiwan's leaders thought of one China, they were trapped. In order to ease their doubts, we said "one China" not only includes the mainland, but also Taiwan. We think of this China as an integral whole which can't be separated in sovereignty or territory. This is the true meaning of "one China." And, they had another doubt.... They think that Taiwan being part of Chinese territory means Taiwan and China are not equal.... To ease this doubt, we said the mainland and Taiwan belong to the same one China. At least, it shows some kind of equality. I think it can help ease their doubt."[46]

Another Chinese official was quoted in the same report, stressing: "Once we said we would liberate Taiwan, then we said Taiwan was just a province of China, now we are saying Taiwan can be our equal.... For the mainland to make these kinds of adjustments in policy is not an easy thing."[47]

---

[43] Swaine, "Decision Making Regarding Taiwan," p. 330.
[44] Zhao, "Chinese Nationalism and Beijing's Taiwan Policy," p. 96.
[45] Ibid.
[46] John Pomfret, "Beijing Signals New Flexibility on Taiwan: Comments Appear Aimed at Bush," *Washington Post* (January 5, 2001), p. A01.
[47] Ibid.

This broader understanding of "one China" has become more similar to the KMT's OCRI interpretation of the "1992 consensus." In a speech delivered on January 24, 2002, Qian noted that "both the mainland and Taiwan belong to one China. Despite the absence of reunification at present, the two sides should work hard to create conditions for it by reducing contentions, improving cross-straits relations and breaking the political deadlock.... The importance of the '1992 consensus' lies in the fact that, under the prerequisite of adhering to the 'one-China' principle, both sides seek common ground while reserving differences in a flexible way and take the interests of both sides into consideration with a view to building mutual trust, negotiating matters in a practical manner and always looking towards the future."[48]

Tacitly Accepting the ROC?

Indeed, as Hu Jintao came to power in 2002–03, he urged Taiwan's DPP administration to resume cross-strait dialogues on the basis of the "1992 consensus."[49] However, by the mid-2000s, Chen Shui-bian took a more radical turn, abolishing the NUC, calling to draft a new Taiwanese Constitution to replace the ROC, and pushing Taiwan to rejoin the UN. He aimed at severing any ties between the mainland and Taiwan. Had the Bush administration not intervened to restrain Taipei, a new round of the Taiwan Strait crisis would have erupted. Witnessing Taiwan's rising independence sentiments, Beijing seeks to promote greater peace-

---

[48] "Speech by Vice Premier Qian Qichen at the Forum to Commemorate the Seventh Anniversary of Jiang Zemin's Speech Entitled 'Continuing to Endeavor for the Accomplishment of the Grand Cause of Reunification of the Motherland,'" *Ministry of Foreign Affairs of the People's Republic of China* (January 24, 2002), accessible at: http://www.fmprc.gov.cn/eng//wjdt/zyjh/t25047.shtml.

[49] Su, *Taiwan's Relations with Mainland China*, p. 122. On April 29, 2005, in the first meeting since 1945 between the heads of the KMT and CCP, Lien Chan and Hu Jintao issued a joint statement on the "peaceful development" of a cross-strait relationship, outlining five major goals: (1) resume cross-strait negotiations on the basis of the "1992 consensus"; (2) cease hostilities, conclude a peace agreement, and launch confidence building measures (CBMs); (3) comprehensively expand economic engagements; (4) negotiate Taiwan's international participation; and (5) set up a party-to-party platform. See Shirley Kan, "China/Taiwan: Evolution of the 'one China' Policy—Key Statements from Washington, Beijing, and Taiwan," *Congressional Research Service Report for Congress* (June 24, 2011), p. 75. The full press communique on Lien-Hu's five major goals, see: http://www.cctv.com/english/20050430/100193.shtml. On Hu's patient policy, see Chen, "Comparing Jiang Zemin's Impatience with Hu Jintao's Patience Regarding the Taiwan Issue," p. 4. See also Susan Shirk, *China: Fragile Superpower*, pp. 203–209.

ful development across the strait. Thus, at the 17th CCP Party Congress in October 2007, Hu raised the idea of a "common destiny community," implying a reorientation of the political status across the Taiwan Strait, in which the "one China does not mean PRC's China, but [simply] a common homeland for both sides."[50]

After the KMT returned to power in May 2008, Beijing showed more tolerance on the Ma administration's OCRI position and more literal and explicit interpretation of China as the ROC.[51] Essentially, three sets of discourse from Hu Jintao suggested Beijing's greater receptivity of the ROC. First, shortly after Ma's electoral victory on March 22, 2008, Hu, in a telephone conversation with President George W. Bush, expressed that both China and Taiwan should "restore consultation and talks on the basis of the '1992 consensus,' which sees both sides recognize there is only one China, but agree to differ on its definition." Bush welcomed the Chinese leader's flexibility.[52] Second, on December 31, 2008, Hu formally described that "both the mainland and Taiwan belong to one China" and urged both sides to "make *pragmatic explorations* in their political relations under the *special circumstances* where the country has not yet been reunified."[53] Finally, in March 2012, when meeting with the KMT's honorary chairman Wu Poh-hsiung, the Chinese president remarked that the CCP should view cross-strait situations "objectively," that is, the "fact that [both] the mainland and Taiwan belong to one China [is] in line with the *current cross-strait rules and regulations* and should be observed by both sides."[54]

---

[50] Qiang Xin, "Beyond Power Politics," *Journal of Contemporary China* Vol. 19, No. 65 (April 2010), p. 529.

[51] Su, *Taiwan's Relations with Mainland China*, p. 14.

[52] See "Chinese, U.S. Presidents Hold Telephone Talks on Taiwan, Tibet," *The Xinhua News Agency* (March 27, 2008); accessible at: http://news.xinhuanet.com/english/2008-03/27/content_7865209.htm. See also David G. Brown, "Taiwan Voters Set a New Course," *Comparative Connections* 10, no. 1, (April 2008), p. 4.

[53] See the full text of Hu's speech at the "Forum Marking the 30th Anniversary of the Issuance of the Message to Compatriots in Taiwan," (December 31, 2008), accessible at: http://www.gwytb.gov.cn/en/Special/Hu/201103/t20110322_1794707.htm. *Emphasis added*.

[54] "Hu Reiterates Opposition to 'Taiwan Independence,'" *The Xinhua News Agency* (March 22, 2012), accessible at: http://news.xinhuanet.com/english/china/2012-03/22/c_131483663.htm. *Emphasis added*. In fact, Hu already raised the idea as early as March 2004. See "Hu's Four-Point Guidelines on Cross-Strait Relations," *Taiwan Affairs*

Even though national unification is non-negotiable, Hu is recognizing the fact that, as of now, both sides have not been unified. Consequently, to explore "pragmatic arrangements for the existing cross-strait political relations" is to find reasonable accommodation for current situations that the PRC and ROC have effective sovereign controls over their respective territories: the mainland and Taiwan. While both cannot formally recognize each other, neither can they deny their existence. This echoes Ma Ying-jeou's "mutual non-recognition and mutual non-denial" description of cross-strait relations. The remarks that "one China is in line with current cross-strait rules and regulations" implies that both the ROC and PRC Constitutions agree on "one China" though they differ on what that China is.[55]

Hence, in April 2012, while expressing the hope of eventually creating conditions conducive for a cross-strait political agreement, the TAO director Wang Yi acknowledged that more time is needed to overcome difficulties and differences between the two sides. The "1992 consensus" was referred to as the political foundation, in which both sides "adhered to the common ground of one China and setting aside political differences."[56] After 2008, President Ma has more frequently stipulated that "one China" refers to the ROC, which incorporates the mainland region and Taiwan.[57] During his second inaugural address on May 20, 2012, Ma maintained:

> When we speak of "one China," naturally it is the Republic of China. According to our Constitution, the sovereign territory of the Republic of China includes Taiwan and the mainland. At present, the ROC government has authority to govern only in Taiwan, Penghu, Kinmin, and Matsu. In other words, over the past two decades [since 1992], the two sides of the

Office of the State Council PRC (March 4, 2004), accessible at: http://www.gwytb.gov.cn/en/Special/OneChinaPrinciple/201103/t20110317_1790120.htm.

[55] Huang Nian, *Liangan Da Jiagou: Da Wuding Xia De Zhongguo [The Cross-Strait Framework: A One China Roof]* (Taipei, Tianxia Wenhua Publishers, 2013), pp. 17–18.

[56] Wang's position on cross-strait relations after Ma's reelection is clearly outlined in "Consolidating Cross-Strait Relations: Starting a New Era of Peaceful Development," (April 16, 2012), accessible at: http://www.qstheory.cn/zxdk/2012/201208/201204/t20120412_150797.htm.

[57] See Office of the President, Republic of China, "Zongtong Chuxi Zhonghua Minguo Shinxian 60 Nian Yantao Hui"[President Ma Attending the Conference on the 60th Anniversary of the ROC Constitution], *Office of the President of the Republic of China* (December 21, 2008); accessible at: http://www.president.gov.tw/Default.aspx?tabid=131&itemid=14549&rmid=514&sd=2008/12/21&ed=2008/12/25.

Taiwan Strait have been defined as "one Republic of China, two areas." This status has remained unchanged throughout the administrations of the [past] three presidents.... [One ROC, two areas] is an eminently rational and pragmatic definition, and constitutes the basis for assuring the ROC's long-term development and safeguarding Taiwan's security. Both sides of the Taiwan Strait ought to squarely face up to this reality, seek common ground while respecting differences, and establish a consensus regarding "mutual non-recognition of sovereignty and mutual non-denial of authority to govern." Only in this way can the two sides move forward with confidence.[58]

Beijing's reaction toward Ma's second inaugural address was poised. While many Chinese observers voiced their disappointment that Ma did not more forcefully uphold the "one-China" principle,[59] the TAO spokesman, Yang Yi, coolly asserted that the "mainland was not surprised to hear Ma's statement, as it was consistent with his previous policies." He also noted that "the fact that both sides of the Taiwan Strait are part of one China has never changed.... We consider any statements, ideas or policies that adhere to this fact to be positive and conducive to the peaceful development of cross-strait relations."[60]

Although cross-strait discourse on "one China" has reproduced a set of identities and interests for Beijing in dealing with Taiwan, it is important to note that the Taiwanese people are very much ambivalent in their views about the "one-China" issue and the ROC. These issues will be explored in subsequent chapters. While Beijing perceives the ROC as the relatively better alternative to an independent Taiwan, the Taiwanese people in general are not overwhelmingly supportive of that regime. A case in point was Taiwan's Sunflower movement in March 2014, in which young students and social activists stormed into and occupied the Legislative Yuan to oppose the KMT majority's allegedly autocratic push for a rapid ratification of the Cross-Strait Service Trade Agreement. The episode revealed an increasing wariness among young Taiwanese, who were concerned that the Ma administration had been negotiating with Beijing without

---

[58] "Full Text of President Ma Ying-jeou's Second Inaugural Address," *Office of the President of the Republic of China* (May 20, 2012); accessible at: http://english.president.gov.tw/Default.aspx?tabid=491&itemid=27199&rmid=2355.

[59] Alan Romberg, "Shaping the Future," *China Leadership Monitor* no. 38 (August 2012), pp. 6–7.

[60] "Mainland Hopes to Enhance Political Trust across Taiwan Strait," *CCTV News* (May 30, 2012), accessible at: http://english.cntv.cn/20120530/113651.shtml.

much transparency and that Taiwan's continued economic tilt toward the mainland might very well compromise the island's security and political autonomy in the long run.[61] Thus, the PRC's greater receptivity toward the ROC does not necessarily guarantee winning the hearts and minds of the Taiwanese people. But Beijing's greater concession toward the ROC is, at least, moving in a less stringent direction than the CCP's traditionally orthodox embrace of the PRC as China's only and legitimate central government.

Love and Hate Relationship: Beijing Persists to Isolate the ROC Internationally

To be sure, Beijing also has mixed feelings toward the ROC.[62] On the one hand, the CCP authority, since Mao, has never stopped commemorating Sun Yat-sen and the 1911 Revolution, which overthrew the decadent Qing Dynasty and gave rise to the ROC.[63] But, according to the Chinese Communists, Sun's "bourgeoisie democratic revolution" was incomplete and failed in its mission to promote democracy and equality to the Chinese people because the reactionary and counterrevolutionary forces (imperialists, feudal lords, and bureaucratic capitalists) eventually dominated the KMT's republican government. The CCP, therefore, has shouldered the responsibility to continue the revolutionary struggle and create the necessary changes for China's unity and well-being.[64]

The shared 1911 Revolutionary heritage and reverence toward Sun Yat-sen have forged a unique bond between the CCP and KMT, as both celebrated the revolution's centennial anniversary on October 10, 2011.[65] Indeed, Ma Ying-jeou emphasized that "the people of the two sides of the

---

[61] "Politics in Taiwan: Sunflower Sutra," *The Economist* (April 8, 2014), accessible at: http://www.economist.com/blogs/banyan/2014/04/politics-taiwan.

[62] Hickey, "Waking Up to Reality," pp. 10–11.

[63] Zhang Hai-peng, "Commemorations and Assessments of the 1911 Revolution in the Chinese Mainland over the Past 50 Years," *Contemporary China History Studies* 8, no. 6 (Nov 2001), pp. 6–12. See also Rana Mitter, "1911: The Unanchored Chinese Revolution," *The China Quarterly* 208 (Dec 2011), pp. 1009–1020.

[64] Mitter, "1911," p. 1018.

[65] "President Hu Speaks Highly of 1911 Revolution," *The Xinhua News Agency* (Oct 9, 2011), accessible at: http://news.xinhuanet.com/english2010/china/2011-10/09/c_131180598.htm. "President Ma Ying-jeou's National Day Address," *Office of the President of the Republic of China* (Oct 10, 2011), accessible at: http://english.president.gov.tw/Default.aspx?tabid=491&itemid=25514.

strait share a common Chinese ethnic heritage. We share common blood lines, history and culture. We both revere our nation's founding father, Dr. Sun Yat-sen."[66] In recent years, cross-strait scholars and historians have substantially increased their contacts and exchanges through research visits, academic conferences, and seminars. China's renewed research interest in the Republican period and Chiang Kai-shek's diaries has led to a more objective and positive depiction of the KMT leader than had been possible before the 1990s.[67] Moreover, PRC officials also applauded the KMT's contributions and sacrifices in resisting Japanese aggression during the Second World War, even though the CCP is still depicted as the primary force that waged the struggle and Chiang Kai-shek is portrayed as more interested in fighting the Chinese Communists.[68] Yet, it is no small breakthrough for the CCP to reconcile with its longtime rival whose destruction has always been a top priority for the PRC.

On the other hand, the republic was annihilated by the CCP in 1949 and, therefore, ceased to exist. Beijing's official position remains that (1) when the central government of the PRC was proclaimed on October 1, 1949, the ROC government was "replaced" as the government of all of China and its "historical status" was brought to an end; and (2) even though the "KMT ruling clique" continued to use the terms "Republic of China" and "government of the Republic of China," it had "long since forfeited its right to exercise state sovereignty on behalf of China and, in reality, has always remained only a local authority in Chinese territory."[69] As noted, the Chinese government has never renounced the use of force to resolve cross-strait impasse. Despite some concessions since 2009, China has also not given up on restricting Taiwan's international space. Accordingly, it is probably fair to say that Beijing is only more receptive

[66] See "Ma's Second Inaugural Address," *Office of the President of the Republic of China*, (May 20, 2012), accessible at: http://english.president.gov.tw/Default.aspx?tabid=491&itemid=27199&rmid=2355.

[67] Mitter, "1911," p. 1014. See also Jay Taylor, *The Generalissimo: Chiang Kai-shek and the Struggle for Modern China* (Cambridge: Harvard University Press, 2009).

[68] "Official Lauds KMT Role in Anti-Japanese War," *The China Daily* (August 31, 2005), accessible at: http://www.chinadaily.com.cn/english/doc/2005-08/31/content_473662.htm. See also "Achieving a Third Round of CCP-KMT Cooperation," *China Org* (October 12, 2011), accessible at: http://www.china.org.cn/opinion/2011-10/12/content_23603712.htm.

[69] "The One China Principle and the Taiwan Issue," *The Taiwan Affairs Office of the State Council of PRC* (February 2000), accessible at: http://www.gwytb.gov.cn/en/Special/WhitePapers/201103/t20110316_1789217.htm.

to the ROC at the "domestic" or "cross-strait" level instead of the "international level." Since the PRC leaders have recognized the current splitting status between both sides, Beijing lacks domestic and Westphalian sovereignty over Taiwan. Krasner wrote that "the fundamental rule of Westphalian sovereignty is to refrain from intervening in the internal affairs of other states," while domestic sovereignty envisions an authority structure that would "ensure a society that is peaceful, protects human rights, has a consultative mechanism, and honors rules of law based on shared understanding of justice."[70] In terms of international legal sovereignty, however, Beijing continues to insist that the PRC represents China externally. This author agrees that it is unlikely, in the foreseeable future, that Beijing would allow the ROC to be recognized internationally. However, if sovereignty is conceived in terms of these three dimensions, the PRC is, to a great degree, accepting the ROC's Westphalian and domestic sovereignty. In other words, Beijing may tacitly recognize dual central governments under a "one-China" framework.

4 Conclusion

In November 2012, on the eve of China's political transition, Hu Jintao restated the importance of following the "1992 consensus" and urged both sides to "jointly explore cross-strait political relations and make *reasonable arrangements* for them under the special condition that the country is yet to be reunified."[71] In turn, President Ma, in his New Year address on January 1, 2013, expressed his aspiration to cooperate with the incoming Xi Jinping administration in continuing to "promote peaceful development across the Taiwan Strait on the basis of the '1992 consensus,' whereby each side acknowledges the existence of 'one China' but maintains its own interpretation of what that means."[72]

On February 25, 2013, during his meeting with the KMT's honorary chairman Lien Chan, Xi Jinping posited, "Nothing can change the fact that both sides on the Taiwan Strait belong to one China." He also

---

[70] Krasner, "Sharing Sovereignty," p. 88.

[71] "Full Text of Hu Jintao's Report at the 18th Party Congress," *The Xinhua News Agency* (November 17, 2012), accessible at: http://news.xinhuanet.com/english/special/18cpcnc/2012-11/17/c_131981259_11.htm. Emphasis added.

[72] "Full Text of President Ma's New Year Day Address," *Focus Taiwan* (January 1, 2013), accessible at: http://focustaiwan.tw/ShowNews/WebNews_Detail.aspx?Type=aIPL&ID=201301010005.

pledged to carry forward the "peaceful development of cross-strait ties," suggesting that his administration will continue to "maintain consistencies in policies toward Taiwan, by unswervingly upholding the one-China principle and continuing to promote cross-strait exchanges and cooperation."[73] Like Hu, Xi agreed that "both Taipei and Beijing base their *legal and government systems* on the one-China principle, under which Taiwan is a part of China, as is the Chinese mainland."[74] The new leader stressed that: "Of course, we also are soberly aware that historical problems remain in cross-strait relations, and that there will be issues in the future that will require time, patience, and joint effort to resolve."[75] In his meeting with Xi on June 14, 2013, Wu Poh-hsiung was very explicit in summing up current cross-strait relations, stating that the two sides are not "state-to-state" but base their "respective laws and systems on the one-China framework." Taiwan's MAC later commented that Wu's "one China" is obviously the ROC.[76] Xi responded that "seeking common grounds and shelving differences requires both sides to rally political wisdom, pool, and expand consensus on promoting development of cross-strait ties and manage differences appropriately."[77] On February 11, 2014, the minister of the MAC, Wang Yu-chi, met, in Nanjing, China, with his Chinese counterpart, Zhang Zhijun of TAO. The meeting represented the first formal encounter between these two government bodies in charge of cross-strait relations. Previously, the MAC and TAO had dealt with each other indirectly and through the semi-official entities SEF and ARATS discussed earlier. During their meeting, Wang and Zhang addressed each other by their official titles, opening up a precedent of interactions for the

[73] "Xi Meets KMT's Lien, Stresses Cross-Strait Ties," *The Xinhua News Agency* (Feb 25, 2013), accessible at: http://news.xinhuanet.com/english/china/2013-02/25/c_132191064.htm.

[74] "Talk of the Day: KMT Honorary Chairman Meets Top Chinese Communist," *Focus Taiwan News Channel* (Feb 26, 2013), accessible at: http://focustaiwan.tw/ShowNews/WebNews_Detail.aspx?ID=201302260039&Type=aTOD. Emphasis added.

[75] "China's Xi to Tread Peaceful Patient Path on Taiwan," *The Chicago Tribune* (Feb 25, 2013), accessible at: http://www.chicagotribune.com/news/sns-rt-us-china-taiwanbre-91o0cc-20130225,0,2667391.story.

[76] "One China Is Republic of China: Taiwan," *Focus Taiwan News* (June 14, 2013), accessible at: http://focustaiwan.tw/news/acs/201306140017.aspx.

[77] "Xi Meets with KMT Honorary Chairman, Calling National Rejuvenation a Common Goal," *The Xinhua News Agency* (June 13, 2013), accessible at: http://news.xinhuanet.com/english/china/2013-06/13/c_132453077.htm.

ROC and PRC governments.[78] Wang visited Sun Yat-sen's mausoleum in Nanjing, expressing that "the first democratic republic in Asia—the Republic of China—was founded by Dr. Sun Yat-sen 103 years ago, and that he was very happy and moved to be able to pay homage to Dr. Sun in person today in his capacity as Minister of the MAC."[79] The MAC and TAO also promised to further and deepen the institutionalization channel between their respective agencies in order to jointly manage various socioeconomic issues in cross-strait relations. We have discussed the Xi–Ma meeting on November 7, 2015, and that encounter certainly could be interpreted in line with Beijing's more pragmatic response with respect to cross-strait relations. As a follow-up to the Xi–Ma summit, a "hotline" was also set up in late 2015 to facilitate immediate communication between the MAC and TAO should any contingencies or crises occur across the Taiwan Strait.[80]

These exchanges between the CCP and KMT suggest Xi's inclination to follow Hu Jintao's more flexible position on "one China" and the role of the ROC. Certainly, Xi Jinping's message was clear, that is, the "1992 consensus" and its "one-China" core would be the non-negotiable foundation of peaceful development across the Taiwan Strait, irrespective of which political party governs Taiwan. Yet, given the ROC's embodiment of that "one-China" principle, Beijing seems to be willing to give some leeway for that regime.

The "one China" will remain a complex and difficult issue for both the mainland and Taiwan. Indeed, the Ma administration refrained from any political and peace talks with Beijing given the domestic political constraint in Taiwan. After the KMT's poor performance in both the 2014 and 2016 elections, cross-strait exchanges have faced greater obstacles and stalemate. For its part, Beijing has persisted in restricting the ROC's

[78] "Heads of Competent Authorities for Cross-Strait Affairs Successfully Holds First Meeting, Setting an Important Milestone for Benign Development, Pragmatism, and Progress of Cross-Strait Relations," News Release of the Mainland Affairs Council, ROC (Taiwan), February 11, 2014, accessible at: http://www.mac.gov.tw/ct.asp?xItem=107565&ctNode=6337&mp=3&xq_xCat=2014.

[79] "MAC Minister Wang Yu-chi Leads Delegation to Sun Yat-sen Mausoleum in Nanjing to Pay Homage to Dr. Sun Yat-sen," News Release of the Mainland Affairs Council, ROC (Taiwan), February 12, 2014, accessible at: http://www.mac.gov.tw/ct.asp?xItem=107573&ctNode=6337&mp=3&xq_xCat=2014.

[80] "China, Taiwan Open First Hotline in Tension Reducing Measure," *Reuters* (December 29, 2015), accessible at: http://www.reuters.com/article/us-china-taiwan-hotline-id USKBN0UD07020151230.

international space and refused to renounce the use of force in dealing with the island. The Xi Jinping government has pressed Taipei to at least start political discussions at the non-governmental level, that is, through academic seminars and think-tank conferences, expressing that "political issues should never be artificially categorized as a restricted area."[81] In 2013, Xi stated, "The Chinese mainland and Taiwan should jointly push cross-strait economic cooperation to a new level by strengthening cross-strait *high level dialogue and coordination*."[82] Xi suggested that cross-strait economic ties and benefits-sharing cannot be carried out in the absence of greater strides on the political front. Furthermore, the Chinese leader emphasized that "the issue of political disagreements that exist between the two sides must reach a final solution, step by step, and these issues cannot be passed on from generation to generation."[83]

In the wake of her and the DPP's huge victory in January 2016, Tsai Ing-wen, in an interview with Taiwan's *Liberty Times*, reiterated her pledge throughout the campaign season that she would maintain cross-strait status quo, peace, and stability on the "established political basis." While refraining from accepting the "1992 consensus," the DPP president mentioned that her definition of the "established political basis" would comprise the following components: (1) that there was a bilateral summit in 1992 as a matter of historical fact and a mutual cognizance of "seeking common ground while shelving differences"; (2) the ROC Constitutional institution as it exists now; (3) the results of 20 years of bilateral negotiations and exchanges; and (4) Taiwan's democratic principle and democratic will.[84] Tsai's "ROC Constitutional order," in the view of Richard Bush, is "at least interesting" and perhaps creates "a basis for common ground" between the DPP and CCP.[85] On February 25,

[81] See "Zhang Zhijun, China's New Taiwan Affairs Head, Outlines Agenda," *South China Morning Post* (March 23, 2013), accessible at: http://www.scmp.com/news/china/article/1197552/zhang-zhijun-chinas-new-taiwan-affairs-head-outlines-agenda.

[82] "President Xi Meets Taiwan Politician," *Taiwan Affairs Office of the State Council PRC* (April 8, 2013), accessible at: http://www.gwytb.gov.cn/en/imgnews/201304/t20130409_4055165.htm. Emphasis added.

[83] "China's Xi Says Political Solution for Taiwan Can't Wait Forever," *Reuters* (October 6, 2013), accessible at: http://www.reuters.com/article/us-asia-apec-china-taiwan-id USBRE99503Q20131006.

[84] "Interview: Tsai's Cross-Strait Policy to Rest on Democratic Will," *Taipei Times* (January 22, 2016), accessible at: http://www.taipeitimes.com/News/front/archives/2016/01/22/2003637766.

[85] This author's interview with Richard Bush.

2016, Wang Yi, the PRC foreign minister, responded to the query regarding Tsai's election and the future of cross-strait relations at the end of his speech at the CSIS:

> We do not care that much who is in power in the Taiwan region of China. What we care about is, once someone has come into power, how he or she handles the cross-strait relationship, whether he or she will maintain the peaceful development of cross-strait relations, whether he or she will recommit to the political foundation of cross-strait relations. The one-China principle [is] what we care about.... I hope and expect that [Tsai] will indicate that she wants to pursue the peaceful development of cross-strait relations, and that she will accept the provision in Taiwan's own constitution that the mainland and Taiwan belong to one, the same China. She is elected on the basis of the current constitution of Taiwan, which still recognizes the mainland and Taiwan as one, the same China. It will be difficult to imagine that someone who is elected on the basis of that constitution should try to do anything in violation of Taiwan's own constitution.[86]

Wang's "constitution" remarks inevitably generated some speculation from observers and experts on cross-strait relations. Some noted China's "goodwill" and that Beijing may be moving away from the "1992 consensus" to create common talking points with Tsai Ing-wen.[87] Others, however, were more skeptical, pointing out how Chinese officials had sought to downplay Wang Yi's assertion and reiterated Beijing's insistence on the "1992 consensus" and its "one-China" principle.[88] Zhang Zhijun, the TAO head, for instance, urged the public not to "misread" Wang Yi's remarks, stating that "the core message of the foreign minister is that both sides belong to one China."[89] In March 2016, during the annual two-sessions meeting of the NPC and the Chinese People's Political Consultative Conference, Xi Jinping stressed, "Our policy towards Taiwan is clear and consistent, and it will not change along with the change in Taiwan's

---

[86] "Statesmen's Forum: Wang Yi, Minister of Foreign Affairs, PRC," The Center of Strategic and International Studies (February 25, 2016), accessible at: http://csis.org/files/attachments/160225_statesmen_forum_wang_yi.pdf.

[87] "Taiwan Responds Positively to China's remarks on Cross-Strait Ties," *The Focus Taiwan News* (Feb 26, 2016), accessible at: http://focustaiwan.tw/news/acs/201602260016.aspx.

[88] This author's interview with Douglas Paal.

[89] "Don't Misread China's External Affairs Head's Remarks on the ROC," *The China Post* (March 2, 2016), accessible at: http://www.chinapost.com.tw/taiwan/china-taiwan-relations/2016/03/02/459655/Dont-misread.htm.

political situation.... We will adhere to the '1992 consensus' as a political foundation, and continuously advance the peaceful development of cross-strait relations.... Only by accepting the '1992 consensus' and recognizing its core implications can the two sides have a common political foundation and maintain good interactions."[90]

It remains to be seen whether the Tsai administration and the PRC can reach some accommodation to manage cross-strait relations. Beijing's attitude on the "ROC constitutional order" is ambiguous since Tsai has not given much substance to what the ROC means to assure the mainland that her administration would abide by the "one-China" rubric. The essential point for Beijing, therefore, is whether Taiwan's leaders would accept that both Taiwan and the mainland are parts of China's territory. Based on the analysis of this chapter, if the DPP would unequivocally define the ROC in the same manner as the KMT, then the Chinese decision-makers would probably not worry too much about it. If the ROC, however, is merely utilized as a means of convenience to camouflage Taiwanese independence then the PRC would certainly oppose that. Bush wrote, "Tsai did not reject Xi's requirements out of hand, but she framed them in her own way." And that prevented the Chinese leadership from truly trusting Tsai's basic intentions.[91] As will be noted in Chap. 6, cross-strait negotiations between the MAC and TAO or between SEF and ARATS have reached a stalemate since Tsai's inauguration in May 2016. In addition to the DPP administration's unwillingness to accept the "1992 consensus," Beijing's corresponding hostile attitude is also a reason behind that inactive interaction. The hotline set up between the MAC and TAO in December 2015 is also on "hiatus," but the closing of communication would not be conducive to peace and stability between the two sides, especially since crisis situations have erupted in the first few months (i.e., the deportation of arrested Taiwanese phone scammers by foreign nations like Kenya, Malaysia, and Cambodia to China, the dangerous misfiring of anti-ship missiles from the Taiwanese Navy toward mainland China, the tragic tour bus fire that killed all mainland Chinese tourists aboard;

---

[90] "President Xi Warned against 'Taiwan Independence' in Any Form," *The China Daily* (March 6, 2016), accessible at: http://www.chinadaily.com.cn/china/2016twosession/2016-03/06/content_23755476.htm.

[91] Richard Bush, "Decoding Xi Jinping's Latest Remarks on Taiwan," The Brookings Institute (March 17, 2016), accessible at: http://www.brookings.edu/blogs/order-from-chaos/posts/2016/03/17-xi-jinping-speech-taiwan-bush.

and Taiwan's exclusion from the International Civil Aviation Organization (ICAO) meeting in fall 2016 after Tsai became president.

In any event, despite their ambivalence, Chinese officials may come to terms with the KMT's argument of "one China, respective interpretations" and "one China means the ROC." Essentially, the DPP's pro-independence policies have taught the PRC leaders that (1) there is a rising Taiwanese consciousness or collective identity that is different from being "Chinese"; (2) unification under the PRC has no support on the island; and (3) a substantial proportion of the Taiwanese public supports maintaining the status quo, that is, neither unification nor independence.[92] Thus, in order to better its relations with Taiwan, Beijing must reconstitute a new set of identities and interests that would simultaneously satisfy its "one-China" principle and soothe the Taiwanese public. The ROC, at least, is supported by most Taiwanese people despite their increasing qualms about being identified as Chinese. And, for the CCP officials, the ROC also retains the "Chinese" connection, however flimsy, between the mainland and Taiwan. The following chapter will examine the KMT's OCRI and nation-building efforts to reconstruct the ROC.

References

Association for Relations across the Taiwan Strait (ed.). 2005. *Jiuer Gongshi Lishi Cunzheng [The Historical Documents of the 1992 Consensus]*. Beijing: Jiuzhou Press.

Blackwill, Robert, and Kurt Campbell. 2016. *Xi Jinping on the Global Stage*. New York: Council on Foreign Relations, Special Report No. 74.

Chai, Winberg. 2015. Xi Jinping and Ma Ying-jeou's Historic 2015 Meeting in Singapore. *Asian Affairs: An American Review* 42(4): 195–202.

Chen, Qimao. 2011. The Taiwan Straits Situation since Ma Came to Office and Conditions for Cross-Straits Political Negotiations. *Journal of Contemporary China* 20(68): 153–160.

Chen, Chien-Kai. 2012. Comparing Jiang Zemin's Impatience with Hu Jintao's Patience Regarding the Taiwan Issue, 1989–2012. *Journal of Contemporary China* 21(78): 1–18.

Chen, Dean. 2014. Constructing Peaceful Development: The Changing Interpretations of 'One China' and Beijing's Taiwan Strait Policy. *Asian Security* 10(1): 22–46.

---

[92] Rigger, *Why Taiwan Matters*, especially Ch. 7.

Christensen, Thomas. 2001. Posing Problems without Catching Up. *International Security* 25(4): 5–40.
Foot, Rosemary. 2006. Chinese Strategies in a U.S. Hegemonic Global Order. *International Affairs* 82(1): 77–94.
Friedberg, Aaron. 2012. *A Contest for Supremacy*. New York: W. W. Norton.
Gill, Bates. 2010. *Rising Star*. Washington, DC: Brookings Institution Press.
Goldstein, Avery. 2005. *Rising to the Challenge*. Stanford: Stanford University Press.
Hickey, Dennis. 2007. *Foreign Policy Making in Taiwan*. New York: Routledge.
———. 2013. Waking Up to Reality. *Journal of Chinese Political Science* 18(1): 1–20.
Huang, Nian. 2013. *Liangan Da Jiagou: Da Wuding Xia De Zhongguo [The Cross-Strait Framework: A One China Roof]*. Taipei: Tianxia Wenhua Publishers.
Ikenberry, John, G. 2013. The Rise of China, the United States, and the Future of the Liberal International Order. In *Tangled Titans*, ed. David Shambaugh, 53–73. Lanham: Rowman & Littlefield.
Kang, David. 2010. *China Rising*. New York: Columbia University Press.
Katzenstein, Peter, ed. 1996. *The Culture of National Security*. New York: Columbia University Press.
Krasner, Stephen. 2004. Sharing Sovereignty: New Institutions for Collapsed and Failing States. *International Security* 29(2): 85–120.
Krebs, Ronald, and Patrick Jackson. 2007. Twisting Tongues and Twisting Arms. *European Journal of International Relations* 13(1): 35–66.
Lam, Willy. 2015. *Chinese Politics in the Era of Xi Jinping*. New York: Routledge.
Lampton, David. 2013. A New Type of Major -Power Relationship: Seeking a Durable Foundation for U.S.-China Ties. *Asia Policy* 16: 51–68.
———. 2014. *Following the Leader: Ruling China, from Deng Xiaoping to Xi Jinping*. Berkeley: University of California Press.
Lynch, Marc. 2002. Why Engage? China and the Logic of Communicative Engagement. *European Journal of International Relations* 8(2): 187–230.
Medeiros, Evan. 2009. *China's International Behavior*. Santa Monica: RAND.
Mitter, Rana. 2011. 1911: The Unanchored Chinese Revolution. *The China Quarterly* 208: 1009–1020.
Nathan, Andrew, and Andrew Scobell. 2012. *China's Search for Security*. New York: Columbia University Press.
Norrin, Ripsman, Jeffrey Taliaferro, and Steven Lobell. 2016. *Neoclassical Realist Theory of International Politics*. New York: Oxford University Press.
Qiang, Xin. 2010. Beyond Power Politics. *Journal of Contemporary China* 19(65): 525–539.
Rigger, Shelley. 2011. *Why Taiwan Matters*. Lanham: Rowman & Littlefield.

———. 2013. Taiwan in U.S. China Relations. In *Tangled Titans*, ed. David Shambaugh, 293–311. Lanham: Rowman & Littlefield.
Risse, Thomas. 2000. 'Let's Argue!' Communicative Action in World Politics. *International Organization* 54(1): 1–39.
Romberg, Alan. 2003. *Rein In at the Brink of the Precipice*. Washington, DC: The Henry L. Stimson Center.
Rose, Gideon. 1998. Neoclassical Realism and Theories of Foreign Policy. *World Politics* 51(1): 144–172.
Ross, Robert. 2000. The 1995–96 Taiwan Strait Confrontation: Coercion, Credibility, and the Use of Force. *International Security* 25(2): 87–123.
Shirk, Susan. 2008. *China: Fragile Superpower*. New York: Oxford University Press.
Su, Chi. 2009. *Taiwan's Relations with Mainland China*. New York: Routledge.
Sutter, Robert. 2013. *U.S.-Chinese Relations*. Lanham: Rowman & Littlefield.
———. 2016. *Chinese Foreign Relations*. Lanham: Rowman & Littlefield.
Swaine, Michael. 2001. Decision-Making Regarding Taiwan, 1979–2000. In *The Making of Chinese Foreign and Security Policy in the Era of Reform*, ed. David Lampton, 289–336. Stanford: Stanford University Press.
Swaine, Michael, and Ashley Tellis. 2000. *Interpreting China's Grand Strategy*. Santa Monica: RAND.
Taylor, Jay. 2009. *The Generalissimo: Chiang Kai-shek and the Struggle for Modern China*. Cambridge, MA: Harvard University Press.
Tucker, Nancy. 2009. *Strait Talk*. Cambridge, MA: Harvard University Press.
Weldes, Jutta. 1999. *Constructing National Interests*. Minneapolis: University of Minnesota Press.
Wendt, Alexander. 1992. Anarchy Is What States Make of It. *International Organization* 46(2): 391–425.
Wu, Chung-li. 2016a. Games without Frontiers, War without Tears? The Process of Campaigning in the 2016 Taiwanese General Elections. *American Journal of Chinese Studies* 23(1): 25–41.
Wu, Yu-shan. 2016b. Heading towards Troubled Waters? The Impact of Taiwan's 2016 Elections on Cross-Strait Relations. *American Journal of Chinese Studies* 23(1): 59–76.
Zhao, Suisheng. 2000a. Chinese Nationalism and Beijing's Taiwan Policy. *Issues & Studies* 36(1): 76–99.
———. 2000b. Military Coercion and Peaceful Offense: Beijing's Strategy of National Unification with Taiwan. *Pacific Affairs* 72(4): 495–512.
———. 2013. Foreign Policy Implications of Chinese Nationalism Revisited: The Strident Turn. *Journal of Contemporary China* 22(82): 535–553.
Zheng, Bijian. 2005. China's 'Peaceful Rise' to Great Power Status. *Foreign Affairs* 84(5): 18–24.

Author's Interviews

Interview with Richard Bush, Director for the Center for East Asia Policy Studies at the Brookings Institute, February 25, 2016 at Washington DC, USA. He was Chairman of the Board and Managing Director of the American Institute in Taiwan (AIT), from 1997 to 2002.

Interview with Douglas Paal, Vice-President for Studies and Director of the Asia Program at the Carnegie Endowment for International Peace, March 16, 2016 at Washington DC, USA. He previously served as the Director of the AIT, from 2002 to 2006.

CHAPTER 4

The KMT Rebuilds the ROC: Useful Foreign Foes and Enemies from Within

In this chapter, we will discuss how fragmented partisanship and political elites' divergent nation-building visions at Taiwan's domestic level contributed to the KMT administration's mainland policy from 2008 to 2016. Notwithstanding Ma Ying-jeou's successful elections in 2008 and 2012, the fierce domestic partisan rivalry between the KMT and DPP and their polarizing nation-building projects accentuated.[1] President Ma's Sino-centric agenda, to a great extent, alienated some mainstream voters on the island who were skeptical about closer cross-strait ties and, more significantly, the KMT–CCP's joint commitment to place Taiwan under a "one-China" national framework.

As Taiwan's democracy consolidates, its national identity is rooted more deeply in shared common civic values predicated on preserving a democratic polity with free markets and secure property rights. This civic culture (or civic nationalism) is participatory and inclusive because it is based more on "legal and territorial definitions and subjective loyalty than it is on pre-determined culture, blood-line or origins."[2] It has "replaced both the Chinese identity that had been imposed by the KMT and the exclusively ethnic identity that some Taiwanese nationalists were trying to establish." Thus, Taiwan's primary goal is to defend "its vibrant market

[1] Chang Bi-yu, *Place, Identity and National Imagination in Postwar Taiwan* (New York: Routledge, 2015), p. 2.
[2] Hughes 2011, p. 21.

democracy and the institutions and lifestyles associated with it, especially when the 'other' (China) does not believe in the same values."[3] It would be an oversimplification, then, to describe Taiwan's collective identity as "anti-Chinese," as it is just "non-Chinese" or not "exclusively Chinese." People in Taiwan today see no contradiction between being Taiwanese, opposing unification, and supporting cross-strait economic liberalization.[4] Cherishing their democratic "way of life," they find the PRC authoritarianism unappealing. Indeed, the more Taiwan has integrated with China socially and economically, the more consolidated Taiwanese identity has become.[5]

Nevertheless, when political elites engage in identity and nation-building politics, Taiwanese citizens tend to push back against and penalize them electorally as demonstrated in 2008, 2012, 2014, and 2016. Ma Ying-jeou, to be sure, is not anti-democratic or supporting exclusionary policies. Indeed, under Ma, the "KMT's new or revived Chinese nationalism is officially aimed at anchoring Taiwan in the Chinese nation, bridging the gap with the PRC and, last but not least, favouring the mainland's democratization."[6] His commitment to unification with China under the umbrella of future democratization "has thus moved a long way from the ideology of a party that once imprisoned people for speaking non-Mandarin dialects."[7] Yet, in the pursuit of better relations with mainland China, Ma failed to address the popular demands for greater transparency and oversight. For example, the massive Sunflower protest movement of March 2014 broke out against the KMT's attempt to rapidly push a new Cross-Strait Service Trade Agreement through the Legislative Yuan. As the agreement had already been negotiated with Beijing, Ma was hoping for a quick approval process without first securing public support and supervision.[8]

Furthermore, on the political and security front, Ma wanted to rectify the ROC-delegitimizing policies fostered by the previous Chen Shui-bian administration. The KMT government, in turn, promoted a more

---

[3] Shirley Lin 2016, p. 31.
[4] Ibid.
[5] Ibid., p. 210.
[6] Jean-Pierre Cabestan, "Cross-Strait Integration and Taiwan's New Security Challenges." In Gunter Schubert, (ed.), *Taiwan and the "China Impact"* (New York: Routledge, 2016), p. 293.
[7] Hughes 2011, pp. 18–19.
[8] Wang Chi 2015, p. 201.

China-centric political, economic, and ideational campaign in numerous venues, through bilateral cross-strait economic integration, revisions of school textbooks, name rectifications in official proclamations and documents, and linking Taiwan–China's shared historical memory and cultural heritage.[9] While emphasizing his Taiwanese roots, Ma was doubtlessly pushing for an assimilation approach to reintegrate Taiwan into the Chinese nation on the basis of the "1992 consensus." Particularly in Ma's second term, the KMT saw a sharp and precipitous plunge in its public support. Although the KMT's weakening popularity was partly the consequence of the administration's ineffective handling of a series of socioeconomic policies, its mainland policy had doubtlessly inflicted great political and social tensions.[10] "The Ma administration's lack of concern about growing Chinese influence in all aspects of Taiwanese life has already made national identity a salient issue again."[11] Critics and those in opposition were skeptical of Ma's rapprochement policy, raising questions on whether more intimate cross-strait relations could endanger Taiwan's sovereignty and economic autonomy. Benefits from the deepening of Taiwan–China economic integration accrued mainly in the hands of wealthy and powerful political and business interests having privileged connections with the top KMT and CCP echelons.[12] All in all, these concerns—the perceived unequal distribution of economic profits from cross-strait economic integration, widening of the income gap between the rich and poor, and the potential political dominance of China over Taiwan—eventually led to the KMT's crushing electoral defeats in November 2014 and January 2016.

1 The International and Domestic Settings Behind Ma Ying-jeou's Mainland Policy

As discussed in Chap. 2, international structural context is essential for understanding the overarching perimeter of a state's strategic options even though the specific choice of the policy instrument is then decided by the domestic political conditions. The strong momentum enjoyed by Ma Ying-jeou in the wake of his election in March 2008 was, to a great extent,

---

[9] Hughes 2014.
[10] John Hsieh, "Taiwan in 2014: A Besieged President amid Political Turmoil," *Asian Survey* 55, no. 1 (2015), pp. 142–147.
[11] Shirley Lin 2016, p. 220.
[12] Wu Chung-li 2016, p. 33.

the result of American support and confidence in the new KMT government to repair relations with mainland China.

US–China–Taiwan Relations on the Eve of Ma's Election in 2008

In the words of Su Chi, the foremost external structural constraint for Taiwan comes from Sino–American interactions. This can also be conceived of as a "big triangle relationship," comprising the United States, the PRC, and Taiwan.[13] Indeed, while Taiwan's security is threatened by the mainland, it is guaranteed by the United States, and no leader in Taiwan can afford to dismiss these two cardinal facts. As noted, Beijing aims for the ultimate reunification with Taiwan and would use military force if peaceful means cannot accomplish the task. The PRC's National People's Congress passed the Anti-Secession Law in 2005 to provide the legal basis for the PRC to resort to military action if Taiwan declares de jure independence or indefinitely procrastinates on the issue of national reunification. On the contrary, Washington has been Taiwan's chief security protector since the early 1950s, and such commitment has persisted under America's Taiwan Relations Act (TRA) of 1979 (see Chaps. 1 and 5).

Though friendly toward Taiwan, the George W. Bush administration repudiated Chen Shui-bian's revisionist referendum initiatives. With China's premier Wen Jiabao standing by his side, Bush, in December 2003, maintained that "the U.S. government's policy is one China, based upon the three communiqués and the Taiwan Relations Act. We oppose any unilateral decision by either China or Taiwan to change the status quo. And the comments and actions made by the leader of Taiwan indicate that he may be willing to make decisions unilaterally to change the status quo, which we oppose."[14] As the Bush administration was restraining Taipei from overstepping the red line, Chen remained unyielding after winning his second term by a razor-thin margin in March 2004. In February 2006,

---

[13] This author's interview with Dr. Su Chi on July 16 2014, Taipei, Taiwan. Dr. Su was minister of the ROC's MAC from 1999 to 2000, Taiwan's legislator from 2005 to 2008, and secretary general of the ROC's National Security Council for President Ma Ying-jeou from 2008 to 2010. He is now the chairman of the Taipei Forum Foundation.

[14] "President Bush and Premier Wen Jiabao Remarks to the Press," *The White House News & Policies* (December 9, 2003), accessible at: http://georgewbush-whitehouse.archives.gov/news/releases/2003/12/20031209-2.html.

the Chen government effectively backtracked from its "five no's" promise[15] by declaring that the National Unification Guideline would "cease to apply," and the NUC would "cease to operate."[16] Though the Taiwanese leader justified his actions by citing China's Anti-Secession Law and the People's Liberation Army (PLA)'s increasing deployment of short- and medium-range missiles across the strait, Washington expressed frustration over what it viewed as Taipei's callousness and irresponsibility.[17]

After failing to get Taipei to retract its announcement, the US State Department issued a statement, expressing American "understanding" that the "announcement did not abolish the council, did not change the status quo, and that Chen's previous assurance remains intact."[18] When Chen sought to call for a referendum on Taiwan's membership to the UN, the Bush administration called that "a step toward a declaration of independence."[19] Deputy Undersecretary of State Richard Armitage admonished that the Taiwan Relations Act did not require the United States to defend Taiwan.[20] In September 2007, Thomas Christensen, the deputy assistant secretary of state for East Asian and Pacific Affairs, commented that a "strong and moderate Taiwan" is in the interests of US security as well as peace and stability across the strait. Describing Chen as pushing the UN referendum merely for "short-term political gain," which would be "fundamentally harmful to Taiwan's external relations,"

---

[15] In Chen's first inaugural address on May 20, 2000, the new president, to maintain a moderate standing, announced his "five nos" pledge. As long as Beijing has no intention to use military force against Taiwan, the DPP government will not (1) declare independence; (2) change the national title; (3) push forth the inclusion of the so-called state-to-state description in the ROC Constitution; and (4) promote a referendum to change the status quo in regard to the question of independence or unification. For the "fifth no," Chen affirmed that the abolition of the NUC or the National Unification Guidelines (two institutional arrangements in the ROC that have great constitutional and symbolic meaning for a future reunification with mainland China) will not be an issue. See Su Chi, *Taiwan's Relations with Mainland China* (New York: Routledge, 2009), pp. 92–93. For the full text of President Chen's first inaugural address, see Chen Shui-bian, "Taiwan Stands Up: Presidential Inaugural Address," (May 20, 2000), accessible at: http://china.usc.edu/(S(vp0nss55wvfm1kbu11v2nn45)A(cFcf0oy-zAEkAAAANThhZWE5OWItMzg0MS00N2E0LTg1ZTgtYTY0NWM3ZmYyNDAxsqzE6IN5ymmiSuRACVYt93gM_-41))/ShowArticle.aspx?articleID=1302.

[16] Susan Shirk, *China: Fragile Superpower*, pp. 209–210.

[17] Nancy Tucker, *Strait Talk*, p. 278.

[18] Quote taken from Susan Shirk, *China: Fragile Superpower*, p. 209.

[19] Quote taken from Dennis Hickey, "Rapprochement between Taiwan and the Chinese Mainland," p. 235.

[20] Nancy Tucker, *Strait Talk*, p. 271.

Christensen stated that "as much as we [the U.S.] oppose Beijing's threat to use force, we also take it very seriously, and Taipei cannot afford to do otherwise. It's for this reason that Taiwan's security is inextricably linked to the avoidance of needlessly provocative behavior. That does not mean that Taipei should or can be passive in the face of the PRC pressure. But it means that responsible leadership in Taipei has to anticipate potential Chinese red lines and reactions and avoid unnecessary and unproductive provocations."[21]

Taiwan's unruly behavior, accordingly, placed the United States and the PRC in a rare united front on the Taiwan Strait issue. President Chen apparently paid a heavy political price in the end, not only at the cost of DPP's defeat in the 2008 elections but also causing a severe rupture in Taipei–Washington relationship.[22] In addition to Taipei's excessive anti-China policy maneuvering, the Chen administration and the first family's corruption scandals further tarnished the image of the DPP. It was against this backdrop that the KMT's Ma Ying-jeou was elected Taiwan's president in March 2008, winning a resounding victory by garnering 58 percent of the popular vote. Both Bush and Hu Jintao supported Ma's pledge to ameliorate cross-strait tensions, as stability across the Taiwan Strait would resonate with their respective national interests.[23]

The Ma Administration's Rehabilitation of the ROC as the Central Chinese State

In addition to international systemic pressures exerted by Washington and Beijing, Taiwan's mainland strategy is also a product of its highly contentious domestic politics, characterized by the absence of consensus among elites, political parties, and societal forces. The national identity issue and debates over Taiwan's political status vis-à-vis mainland China have been the long-standing domestic division between the KMT and

---

[21] Thomas Christensen, "A Strong and Moderate Taiwan," *A Speech to the U.S.-Taiwan Business Council at the Defense Industry Conference, Annapolis, Maryland* (September 11, 2007), accessible at: http://2001-2009.state.gov/p/eap/rls/rm/2007/91979.htm.

[22] S. Philip Hsu, "Between Identity Quest and Risk Aversion," pp. 715–716. This viewpoint was also expressed by the DPP party official during interview with this author.

[23] This author's interview with Su Chi. This point was also confirmed by an official in Taiwan's Mainland Affairs Council, who requested to remain anonymous during an interview with this author on August 7, 2014, Taipei, Taiwan.

DPP political elites.[24] Thus, on the one hand, there are Chinese nationalists "promoting a unified China [under the ROC] and identifying themselves as Chinese." These ROC advocates are more inclined to support Ma Ying-jeou, his pro-China faction within the KMT, and close partisan allies such as the New Party and James Soong's PFP On the other hand, "Taiwanese nationalists hope for a fully independent Taiwan where its citizens identify themselves as Taiwanese rather than Chinese."[25] They are determined to jettison the Sino-centric campaign propagated by the KMT since 1945 (stressing the "great Chinese nationalism" and peripheralization of Taiwan as merely an outpost of China), and believe that the Taiwanese people must "cultivate a sense of Taiwanese subjectivity—the conviction that Taiwan is every bit as much a subject in history as other nation-states are and enjoys the right to determine its own future autonomously, free of Chinese pressure."[26] These Taiwanese nationalists are more predisposed to vote for the DPP and its affiliated political candidates who have championed a "cultural reconstruction" movement including initiatives such as rectifying the name of many agencies and organizations to stress "Taiwan," promoting islander dialects in language policy, revising the official policy toward the mass media to reverse the previous KMT domination of outlets, and changing the focus from Chinese to Taiwanese history, literature, and arts in the education system.[27] Accordingly, the specific contours of Taiwan's mainland policy are dictated and constrained by its political leaders' nationalistic orientations and identity affiliation. In the process of nation building, Taiwan's political elites attempt to "mold common identification among citizens with the nation-state."[28]

As a mainlander politician, Ma Ying-jeou knew the importance of gaining trust from the Taiwanese people, and he walked a tightrope during both the 2008 and 2012 presidential campaigns by reaffirming his status quo policy of "no unification, no independence, and no use of force."[29] Emphasizing his "new Taiwanese identity,"[30] Ma expressed his

---

[24] Fu-Kuo Liu, "Ma Ying-jeou's Rapprochement Policy: Cross-Strait Progress and Domestic Constraints," in Jean-Pierre Cabestan and Jacques deLisle eds., *Political Changes in Taiwan under Ma Ying-jeou*, pp. 139–155.
[25] Fell, *Government and Politics in Taiwan*, p. 134.
[26] Daniel Lynch, "Taiwan's Self-Conscious Nation-Building Project," p. 517.
[27] Ibid., pp. 521–526.
[28] Fell, p. 134.
[29] Hughes, "Revisiting Identity Politics under Ma Ying-jeou," p. 122.
[30] Fell, p. 135.

firm support of Taiwanese sovereignty, culture, and values, and promised that Taiwan's future would be determined by the 23 million people on the island.[31] Nevertheless, the KMT leader also insisted, on numerous occasions, that he would improve and deepen cross-strait relations on the basis of "one China, respective interpretations" or the "1992 consensus" that has been dismissed by the DPP counterparts as well as the nativists' faction within the KMT.[32] After President Chiang Ching-kuo's death in 1987, the KMT immediately descended into a party riven by the pro-China (non-mainstream) and the pro-Taiwan or nativists (also known as the mainstream or localized, *bentupai*) factions. The latter group was led by the then president and KMT chairman Lee Teng-hui. However, after the KMT's first loss of power in the March 2000 presidential election, the party underwent a reshuffling or "purge." According to Clark and Tan:

> Lee Teng-hui's [expulsion] from the KMT [in the wake of that party's defeat in 2000] changed the nature of the KMT significantly. With the triumph of Lee and his mainstream faction in the party during the 1990s, the old KMT of the authoritarian era and 'White Terror' had clearly been supplanted. The post-Lee Kuomintang, in contrast, seemed much more compatible, especially to DPP supporters, with the old China-centric paradigm. Indeed, Lee's departure brought the return to power of many pro-China members of the anti-mainstream faction.[33]

Furthermore, following the then KMT chairman Lien Chan's ice-breaking visit to mainland China in April 2005, the pro-China wing of the KMT won the dominant position, culminating in Ma's successful bid for the party's chairmanship in July 2005 that defeated the localized faction of the Legislative Yuan Speaker Wang Jin-pyng.[34] Traditional Chinese nationalist icons such as Sun Yat-sen, Chiang Kai-shek, and Chiang Ching-Kuo also resurfaced in the KMT campaign propaganda and discourses. Under

---

[31] Ibid., pp. 223–224. See also Frank Muyard, "Midterm Analysis of the Ma Ying-jeou Administration," *China Perspective* (2010), p. 19.

[32] See "A Conversation with Ma Ying-jeou," The Council on Foreign Relations (March 20, 2006), accessible at: http://www.cfr.org/china/conversation-ma-ying-jeou-rush-transcript-federal-news-service-inc/p10217. See also "Ma Reaffirms '1992 Consensus and '3Nos,'" *The China Post* (August 29, 2011), accessible at: http://www.chinapost.com.tw/taiwan/china-taiwan-relations/2011/08/29/314938/Ma-reaffirms.htm.

[33] Clark and Tan, *Taiwan's Political Economy*, p. 142.

[34] Hughes, "Revisiting Identity Politics under Ma Ying-jeou," p. 122. See also Fell, *Government and Politics in Taiwan*, pp. 96–97.

Ma, the KMT scored an overwhelming victory over the DPP in the local elections of December 2005, leading to his ultimate ascendancy to the presidential office.[35]

Cross-Strait Relations under the "1992 Consensus"
From 2008 to 2016, President Ma had justified the term "one China" to encompass both Taiwan and the mainland regions, although that "China" means squarely the ROC, in accordance with the ROC's Constitution, the NUC's "Definition of One China Resolution," and the "Act Governing Relations between the People of the Taiwan Area and the Mainland Area."[36] As examined in Chap. 3, the NUC "one-China" Resolution of August 1991, which designated cross-strait relations as essentially "one ROC, two areas," furnished the basis for negotiations between Taiwan's SEF and the PRC'sARATS[37] in Hong Kong in November 1992. The meeting, in turn, led essentially to a "verbal consensus" in which both Taipei and Beijing would agree to disagree on the meaning of "one China."[38]

[35] Ibid., pp. 219–220.
[36] Interview with Dr. Chao Chun-shan, on July 8, 2014, Taipei, Taiwan. Dr. Chao was appointed by the Ma administration as chairman of Taiwan's Prospect Foundation and the Foundation on Asia-Pacific Peace Studies. Dr. Chao is a close brain trust for President Ma Ying-jeou on cross-strait relations. The ROC Constitution (1947), NUC Resolution (1991), and the Act Governing Relations between the People of the Taiwan Area and the Mainland Area (1992) all stipulate that Taiwan and the mainland are "areas" or "regions" under the sovereignty of the Republic of China. For the full text of the Act Governing Relations between the People of the Taiwan Area and the Mainland Area, see http://www.mac.gov.tw/ct.asp?xItem=106120&ctNode=5914&mp=3. See also, Office of the President, Republic of China, "Zongtong Chuxi Zhonghua Minguo Shinxian 60 Nian Yantao Hui"[President Ma Attending the Conference on the 60th Anniversary of the ROC Constitution], (December 21, 2008); accessible at: http://www.president.gov.tw/Default.aspx?tabid=131&itemid=14549&rmid=514&sd=2008/12/21&ed=2008/12/25.
[37] SEF and ARATS are semi-government organizations (also known colloquially as the "white gloves") representing Taipei and Beijing, respectively, to negotiate socio-economic, technical, and functional issues between the two sides. The official government organizations—ROC's MAC and the PRC's TAO—are responsible for managing cross-strait relations but did not meet directly. It was not until 2014 did the chiefs of MAC and TAO (Wang Yu-chi and Zhang Zhijun, respectively) met directly and formally opened up the "official channel."
[38] "President Ma Delivers Address at Symposium on 1992 Consensus," (November 9, 2012), accessible at: http://english.president.gov.tw/Default.aspx?tabid=1124&itemid=28549&rmid=3048. For more substantive discussions of the "1992 consensus" or the OCRI policy, both the views from the KMT government and the People's Republic of China, see Su Chi and Cheng An-guo eds., *Yige Zhongguo Gezi Biaoshu Gongshi De Shishi [One China,*

Thus, the Hong Kong meeting of 1992 constructed the notion of OCRI, thereby paving the way for the upcoming meeting between Koo Chen-fu, chairman of SEF, and Wang Daohan, head of ARATS, in Singapore in April 1993.

As noted earlier, Beijing has neither accepted nor opposed the OCRI. While the PRC emphasizes the part that "both sides of the strait uphold the principle of one China," Taipei, especially the KMT, has construed that both Taiwan and the mainland belong to the ROC. In other words, Beijing focuses on "one China" whereas the KMT government focuses on "respective interpretations."[39] At any rate, "one China" is the common denominator for both the KMT and CCP. To be sure, the term "1992 consensus" was not even used until April 2000, when Su Chi created the term in order to "mask over" the sensitive term "one China," in the OCRI formulation. Su maintained that he was hoping that the then incoming Chen Shui-bian administration would accept the language and continue discussions with Beijing on that foundation.[40] In the future, he stressed, the CCP, KMT, and DPP could all refer simply to the "1992 consensus" and "simultaneously maintain their own distinct interpretations."[41] Such "creative ambiguity" would be beneficial to the peace and stability of cross-strait relations. However, under President Chen, the "1992 consensus" was essentially tossed away and the SEF-ARATS talks ran into a hiatus.[42] Beijing began to use the term more widely after the meeting between the then KMT chairman Lien Chan and

Respective Interpretations: A Historical Account of the Consensus] (Taipei: National Policy Foundation, 2003); Association for Relations Across the Taiwan Strait (ARATS) eds., *Jiuer Gongshi Lishi Cunzheng [The Historical Documentations of the 1992 Consensus]* (Beijing: Jiuzhou Press, 2005); Su Chi, *Taiwan's Relations with Mainland China*, especially Chapter 1; and Arthur Ding and Lin Join-sane eds., *Jiuer Gongshi Ershi Zhounian Xueshu Yantao Huiyi Shilu [The 1992 Consensus: The 20th Anniversary Academic Conference Records]* (Taipei: The Strait Exchange Foundation and National Chengchi University's Institute of International Relations, 2012).

[39] This author's interview with Chao Chun-shan.

[40] Interview with Dr. Su Chi. This was also confirmed by this author's interview with the MAC official.

[41] Interview with Dr. Su Chi. He further elaborated that on the "one-China" issue, the CCP's position is "yes", KMT "yes, but…" and the DPP "no." While both the KMT and CCP could agree on the "yes" part, there is no room for any compromise between the CCP and DPP. Hence, he thought, the "1992 consensus" could serve as a useful terminology especially for the DPP, which rejects "one China." Nonetheless, the DPP has refused to accept the "1992 consensus."

[42] Interview with the MAC official.

the CCP general secretary Hu Jintao in April 2005. The "1992 consensus" formally appeared in Hu's 18th Party Congress report in November 2012.[43] After taking office in 2008, the Ma administration resurrected the "1992 consensus," calling it the bedrock foundation for a sturdy cross-strait relationship.[44]

In addition, President Ma endeavored to use the "1992 consensus" to bring back the ROC's "one-China" legitimacy over Taiwan in order to reconstitute people's national consciousness and weaken the DPP's pro-independence advocacy.[45] Though he was neither pushing for Taiwan's unification with the PRC nor accepting Beijing's "one country, two systems," the president sought to redress Lee Teng-hui and Chen Shui-bian's more extremist de-Sinification policies and to re-institute the ROC's centrality in Taiwan. For him, "one China" being the ROC must always be stressed in order to promote the legitimacy of the republic. Such a course of action, in the view of the Ma administration, would also help to stabilize Taiwan's political system and its relations with mainland China.[46] As discussed earlier, in his second inaugural address on May 20, 2012, Ma explicitly proclaimed the idea of "one ROC, two areas," in which he construed the relationship between mainland China and Taiwan as "not one between two states but rather a special relationship between two regions that are politically equal to each other."[47]

Ma's moves, observed Jacques deLisle, are reminiscent of the Chiang Kai-shek and Chiang Ching-kuo eras, with the "long untenable claim that the ROC was the sole government of the state of China, temporarily limited to the territory of Taiwan by an illegitimate revolutionary regime exercising de facto control over the mainland and having no right to rule over

---

[43] Interview with the MAC official, who requested to remain anonymous. See also "Full Text of Hu Jintao's Report at 18th Party Congress," (November 17, 2012), accessible at: http://news.xinhuanet.com/english/special/18cpcnc/2012-11/17/c_131981259_11.htm.

[44] Ma Ying-jeou, "Building National Security for the Republic of China," *Videoconference with the Center for Strategic & International Studies* (May 12, 2011), p. 2, accessible at: csis.org/files/attachments/110512_President_Ma_CSIS.pdf.

[45] In my interviews with Chao Chun-shan and Su Chi, they both noted that President Ma had aimed to create a balance between the ROC and Taiwan. But, clearly, Ma viewed the ROC, rather than Taiwan, as the central Chinese state, established in 1912 and continuing to exert independent sovereignty even after the government retreated from mainland China in 1949. Ma's emphasis on the ROC set him apart from the DPP.

[46] Interview with the MAC official who requested to remain anonymous.

[47] Baohui Zhang, "Taiwan's New Grand Strategy," p. 273.

Taiwan."[48] In his National Day address on October 10, 2013, President Ma stated that "cross-strait relations are not international relations."[49] He suggested that both sides are "mutually not denying each other's effective governance in their respective territorial jurisdictions" even though, based on the ROC and PRC Constitutions, neither party can "recognize each other's legal sovereignty."[50]

President Ma also framed his OCRI in terms of economic benefits, noting that by accepting the "1992 consensus," cross-strait economic ties would be strengthened, which, in turn, would fix Taiwan's economic problems.[51] Having good relations with Beijing was seen as indispensable to "ending the island's economic isolation of the Chen era and to recover its international standing."[52] The cross-strait détente under the Ma administration led to a series of cross-strait socioeconomic accords such as the opening of the "three links" (postal, transportation, and trade) and 23 agreements signed between the SEF and ARATS which included ECFA and various collaborations over transportation, health, education, tourism, food safety, science, agriculture, and mutual judicial assistance. In 2015, total bilateral trade between Taiwan and mainland China was about $129 billion and Taiwan's investment in the mainland was roughly $11 billion.[53] The PRC has become Taiwan's primary economic partner, although the relationship has been asymmetrical, with Taiwan more dependent on China than vice versa. In the words of Dittmer, "Taiwan's

---

[48] Jacques deLisle, "Taiwan and Soft Power," p. 279.

[49] See "President Ma's National Day Address," *Office of the President, Republic of China* (October 10, 2013), accessible at: http://english.president.gov.tw/Default.aspx?tabid=491&itemid=30933&rmid=2355.

[50] Interview with Chao Chun-shan. This confusion results from the fact that both the ROC and PRC Constitutions are "one China" based. Hence, Taipei's and Beijing's sovereignty claims are essentially identical and overlapping.

[51] Dafydd Fell, *Government and Politics in Taiwan*, p. 224. See also Gunter Schubert, "Between Strategic Change and Ideological Adjustment: The DPP's China Policy Debate in the Aftermath of the 2012 National Elections," *Taiwan Political Science Review* 16, no. 2 (2012), pp. 250–251.

[52] Elena Atanassova-Cornelis, "Shifting Domestic Politics and Security Policy in Japan and Taiwan: The Search for a Balancing Strategy between China and the U.S.," *Asian Pacific Review* 20, no. 1 (2013), p 65.

[53] Bilateral trade was at around $134 billion in 2014 whereas Taiwan's investment in China was $14.6 billion in 2010. See "Cross-Strait Economic Statistics Monthly No. 279," the Mainland Affairs Council, Republic of China (Taiwan), July 28, 2016, accessible at: http://www.mac.gov.tw/ct.asp?xItem=115183&ctNode=5934&mp=3.

trade dependency ratio is 70 percent, some 40 percent of which is with the PRC (up from 29 percent in 2010), while 80 percent of Taiwan's FDI goes to China (vs. 50 percent in 2003). The corresponding figures for the mainland are much smaller."[54] As noted, Taiwan's greater economic reliance on the PRC sparked the island's increasing suspicion about Beijing's intention and also led to people's distrust toward the KMT government throughout the 2014–16 electoral cycles.

Nevertheless, from the Ma administration's perspective, Chao Chun-shan said, it is about "survival politics." Taiwan must befriend China in order to expand its international space, as well as to integrate economically into the growing networks of free-trade agreements across the Asia Pacific, or Taiwan could soon be marginalized and suffocated.[55] Ma's reelection in 2012 was, according to Chao, attributed partly to the DPP's refusal to accept the "1992 consensus," as many Taiwanese business elites came out on the eve of the polling day to openly endorse the continuation of the KMT's policy stance.

Naming China

Naming China is a key nation-building mechanism of constituting and reconstituting Taiwan's national identity and political relations with the mainland. According to Hui-Ching Chang and Richard Holt, "name changes reshuffle power, altering ideological and political configurations, as names are assigned and appropriated in political agendas, mobilizing action while being resisted, disputed and contested."[56] In other words, people in Taiwan "negotiate their identities through how they view China."[57] Political leaders and elites, therefore, have incentives to shape how China is perceived and called. Unlike the DPP, which used "China" or the "People's Republic of China" in order to single out the latter as a separate and different state from an independent Taiwan, the Ma government had, in February 2011, instructed all government organizations and agencies that Taiwan should not name China "China" or the "PRC," but call it "mainland" *dalu* or "opposite side" *duian*. Such designation was important for Ma because cross-strait relations are not state-to-state but

---

[54] Lowell Dittmer, "Taiwan's Narrowing Strait," pp. 15–16.
[55] Interview with Chao Chun-shan.
[56] Chang Hui-Ching, and Richard Holt, *Language, Politics and Identity in Taiwan* (New York: Routledge, 2015), p. 3.
[57] Ibid., p. 5.

predicated upon the "one-China" rubric that positions Taiwan and the mainland as regions within a single country.[58] In a similar vein, the Ma government has required Taiwan's embassies and overseas representative offices to describe foreigners coming to Taiwan as *fan hua* (or coming to China) rather than *fan tai* (coming to Taiwan).[59]

History Curriculum Reform
In any serious nation-building project, history education plays an indispensable role. The perspective adopted by the history curriculum and textbooks will inevitably shape and socialize how youths view and imagine their national identity. This will have a long-lasting effect on the ideological orientations and behaviors of future voters, activists, and, possibly, political leaders. Indeed, Taiwan's education reform is an ongoing wrestling battleground between the KMT and DPP, each seeking to "hegemonize" its political interpretations of China–Taiwan relations into the history narratives of Taiwan. In this author's interview with Ma Wei-min, he succinctly put it: "While the DPP made revision towards more independence-leaning, the KMT under President Ma wanted to change the textbooks back on a more China-centric perspective." Though the president embraces a "strong Chinese nationalistic consciousness," he is not enthusiastic about reunifying Taiwan and the mainland under the PRC system. His vision is a united democratic China based on the ROC Constitution. Yet, even such a formulation proves to be "too extremist" for the DPP and its supporters.[60]

As early as 1997, the Lee Teng-hui administration commenced the task of putting in place a Taiwanese-centered history and social studies curriculum, known as "Knowing Taiwan" (or *renshi* Taiwan). The objective is to sweep away the KMT's Sino-centric worldview, "replacing it with a Taiwan-focused curriculum that, among other things, discussed the Japanese colonial period (1895–1945) objectively and gave Malayo-Polynesian aboriginals a more exalted place in Taiwanese history."[61] In addition, these revised textbooks assert that Taiwan's ethnic pluralism has produced a "distinctive 'Taiwanese consciousness' and that the Taiwanese people have repeatedly demonstrated heroism over the centu-

[58] Ibid., p. 9.
[59] Hughes, "Revising Identity Politics under Ma Ying-jeou," pp. 123–124.
[60] Interview with Ma (Jesse) Wei-min on July 14, 2016, Taipei, Taiwan. Ma is the editor-in-chief of the Apple Daily Newspaper in Taiwan. The Apple Daily has the largest readership and circulation in Taiwan.
[61] Lynch, pp. 515–516.

ries by resisting the imposition of authoritarian rule from abroad, especially from China."[62] Then, in 2006, the Chen Shui-bian government began to formally separate Taiwanese and Chinese history as distinct topics. The obvious implication was that Chinese history should be taught as "foreign history" to Taiwanese students.

After coming to power in 2008, the Ma government began to change some of his predecessors' education initiatives by elevating the importance of China.[63] The links between Taiwan and mainland China should be more strongly emphasized. In doing so, he hoped to reintegrate Taiwan and the mainland under a greater "one-China" framework, although that China is the ROC. In 2007, Ma published a monograph entitled *Original Native Spirit: the Model Story of Taiwan*.[64] In it, he emphasized the positive contributions made by China to Taiwan's economic and political development. According to Christopher Hughes:

> [Ma] thus challenges the narrative of the '400 years of tragedy' under foreign occupation that is promoted by the pro-independence movement by describing the achievements of figures from China from the reforming Qing Dynasty governor Liu Mingchuan, through key political actors in the Republican period, such as the philosopher and cultural commentator Hu Shi, the early critic of the KMT dictatorship in Taiwan, Lei Chen (Lei Zhen), and Chiang Kai-shek's son, Chiang Ching-kuo. He also tackles the existence of a distinctive Taiwanese consciousness before 1945 by pointing out that many natives of the island joined the Chinese in the resistance against Japan, both in Taiwan and the mainland. He also disputes the accusation that the Taiwanese were not consulted about their future status after World War Two by observing that the island sent delegates to take part in the National People's Congress in Nanjing when it drew up and promulgated the 1947 ROC Constitution.[65]

In 2013, the president set up a history curriculum task force headed by Wang Hsiao-po, a professor of Chinese Philosophy at the Shih Hsin

---

[62] Ibid.

[63] The DPP calls Ma's behaviors "authoritarian" and intending to push for "de-Taiwanization." See Chris Wang, "Historians Insist Ma Should Leave Textbooks Alone," *Taipei Times* (July 12, 2012), accessible at: http://www.taipeitimes.com/News/front/archives/2012/07/17/2003537940.

[64] Ma Ying-jeou, *Original Native Spirit: the Model Story of Taiwan [Yuanxiang jingshen: Taiwan de dianfan gushi]* (Taipei, Taiwan: Tianxia Publishers, 2007).

[65] Hughes 2011, p. 18.

University and also a staunch supporter of "one China," to review and "fine-tune" Taiwan's high school history program.⁶⁶ Wang noted in 2015 that "in all countries, history textbooks represent the national stance.... In our opinion, the textbook [sanctioned] by the Republic of China's Ministry of Education should conform to the principles and spirit of the Republic of China's constitution, in which de-Sinification is impossible. Without China, how could the Republic of China exist?"⁶⁷ At one point, the curriculum chair contended that "the ROC capital is Nanjing, but Taipei is the current capital of the Taiwan area." Furthermore, he stressed that the previous textbooks under Presidents Lee and Chen contain much inaccurate information such as describing "Taiwanese who were enlisted to serve in the Imperial Japanese Army during WWII as willingly joining the Japanese Army out of patriotism." Comfort women were painted as "having volunteered to work in wartime brothels in Japan."⁶⁸ The then KMT presidential candidate Hung Hsiu-chu also remarked, "Today, we are restoring [history textbooks] to the right track...at least under the constitution of the Republic of China."⁶⁹

In February 2014, the committee announced that some amendments to the textbooks will start effectively in August 2015. Though many KMT supporters had complained that Ma was too timid and conciliatory to the DPP and Taiwanese nationalists,⁷⁰ critics of the president accused that over 60 percent of all text relating to Taiwan history will be revised, with most alterations relating to the period after 1949.⁷¹ For instance, the KMT's rule on Taiwan would be depicted in a much more favorable light even though the government's authoritarianism would still be underscored. Many of the KMT's repressive policies (including the February 28, 1947 incident and White Terror era) would be justified by the national emergency circumstances of the time (i.e., the Chinese Civil War and the Cold War) whereas the KMT's economic development has

---

⁶⁶ Grace Tsoi, "Taiwan Has Its Own Textbook Controversy Brewing," *Foreign Policy* (July 21, 2015), accessible at: http://foreignpolicy.com/2015/07/21/taiwan-textbook-controversy-china-independence-history/.
⁶⁷ Ibid.
⁶⁸ "Curriculum Academic Sparks Fury," *Taipei Times* (August 2, 2015), accessible at: http://www.taipeitimes.com/News/front/archives/2015/08/02/2003624442.
⁶⁹ Grace Tsoi, "Taiwan Has Its Own Textbook Controversy Brewing."
⁷⁰ This author's interview with Chou Chih-wei on July 28, 2016, Taipei, Taiwan. Chou is the chairperson of the KMT's Culture and Communications Committee.
⁷¹ Grace Tsoi, "Taiwan Has Its Own Textbook Controversy Brewing."

benefited Taiwan's modernization and the island's eventual democratization. The Japanese period on Taiwan is portrayed as a "colonial rule" in terms of "aggressive invasion" and "forcible occupation." The negative impacts of the Japanese colonization on Taiwan are treated in greater length than the previous textbook versions. On the other hand, Taiwan was "retroceded" to, rather than "taken over" by, the ROC government after the war ended in 1945.[72] Clearly, the Ma administration attempted to use the textbook reform to "rebuild the KMT legitimacy among Taiwanese youth, an important block of new and future voters often suspicious of Beijing."[73]

Nonetheless, the Ma government's textbook reform did not go very far given the administration's low approval rating and persisting anti-KMT sentiment among young people and students throughout 2014 and 2015. In June 2016, the new Tsai Ing-wen administration put a halt to the textbook controversy and declared that they would repeal the KMT's "fine-tuning" initiative.[74]

Shared Chinese Roots

At the same time, President Ma described that people on both sides of the Taiwan Strait are rooted in the *Zhonghua minzu*, meaning a "shared Chineseness based on the idea of racial and cultural unity." During his presidency, Ma restarted the rituals of celebrating the birthday of Confucius and the ceremonies to pay respect to the Yellow Emperor. Both Taiwan and mainland China, according to the president, have the historical mission to rejuvenate *Zhonghua wenhua*, or Chinese culture and heritage.[75] Chapter 1 notes that a similar position was stated during the Xi–Ma summit of November 2015. On the National Day, October 10, 2011, marking the centennial celebration of the 1911 Xinhai Revolution, President Ma recounted the ROC's major historical sacrifices and accomplishments on the mainland as well as Taiwan. He said, "Since the inception of the republic 100 years ago, countless numbers of our citizens have perished amid the travails of the Northern Expedition, the War of Resistance against Japan,

---

[72] Ibid.
[73] Ibid.
[74] "Taiwan's New Government Drops 'China-Centric' Curriculum after Widespread Protests," *HKFP* (June 1, 2016), accessible at: https://www.hongkongfp.com/2016/06/01/taiwans-new-govt-drops-china-centric-curriculum-after-widespread-protests/.
[75] Hughes, "pp. 124–125, p. 129.

government action to end the Communist rebellion, and the defense of Taiwan and its outlying islands against invasion by Communist forces."[76]

While constantly commemorating the ROC's founder, Dr. Sun Yat-sen, Ma pushed back against the DPP's dismissal of the ROC, by asserting that "the Republic of China's existence is referred to not in the past tense, but in the present. For the republic has continued to flourish in Taiwan for more than six decades." Noting the interconnectedness between the ROC and Taiwan and that people on both sides of the Taiwan Strait are ethnic Chinese, the KMT leader wished to call up people's historical memories and Chinese patriotism toward the republic:

> It was the sacrifice of 20 million soldiers and civilians of the Republic during the War of Resistance against Japan that enabled Taiwan to end Japan's colonial rule. And, had it not been for the retrocession of Taiwan from Japan to the Republic, the setbacks encountered by ROC armed forces in the civil war against the Communists in mainland China might have spelled the death of the Republic more than six decades ago.... Today, the people of Taiwan enjoy freedom, democracy, and affluence. They have come to identify solidly with their nation, the Republic of China, and the ROC Constitution has long served as the bedrock of a society-wide consensus. The ideals that Dr. Sun Yat-sen sought in establishing the Republic were not achieved in the mainland during his lifetime, but they have come to fruition here in Taiwan.[77]

By the same token, on December 3, 2013, celebrating the 70th anniversary of the Cairo Declaration, Ma took up the controversy surrounding Taiwan's post-WWII status, as some Taiwan independence supporters have long contended that the island was never formally returned by Japan to the ROC and, therefore, its status has remained "indeterminate." The president refuted these accusations by stressing: "In fact, the [Cairo] Declaration is a treaty.... From the perspective of international law, any concrete promise made by an official of a country in their capacity as head of state, prime minister, or foreign affairs is legally binding." In 1943, Chiang Kai-shek, Winston Churchill, and Franklin D. Roosevelt met in Cairo, Egypt, and

---

[76] President Ma Ying-jeou's National Day Address 2011, "A Century of Struggle, a Democratic Taiwan," Office of the President, Republic of China (Taiwan), October 10, 2011, accessible at: http://english.president.gov.tw/Default.aspx?tabid=1124&itemid=25533&rmid=3048.

[77] Ibid.

agreed to the "return of territories stolen by Japan, including Taiwan, to the ROC." This is the legal basis on which the ROC exercises legitimate sovereign claim over Taiwan.[78] It's beyond the scope of this book to substantively discuss the merits and demerits of the Cairo Declaration.[79] Suffice it to note that the KMT leader strived to recentralize the role of the ROC in Taiwan's history, identity, and national consciousness.

Furthermore, August 15, 2015 marked the 70th anniversary of the end of the War of Resistance against Japan in World War II, and, as a result, the Ma administration used the opportunity to remember the KMT's contribution and courageous acts. Military parades, archival exhibitions, and commemoration events were held by Taipei throughout the year. First, the president challenged Beijing's official line, which overwhelmingly focuses on the heroics of the CCP army during the fight against Japanese invasion. In fact, the Xi Jinping government was also organizing its own military parade on September 3rd to remember the Chinese struggle during the war. In spite of the amelioration of KMT–CCP relations since 2005, the PRC has continued to downplay the role of the KMT government, stating that Chiang Kai-shek was, at best, only passively resisting Japanese aggression while devoting most of his energy to combating the Chinese Communists. Ma, on the other hand, asserted, "In the face of history, there is only one truth.... The victory of the war of resistance was the result of our entire citizenry's heroic struggle led by Generalissimo Chiang Kai-shek. No one should tamper or distort it."[80] As a fervent Chinese nationalist, the KMT leader also mentioned firmly, "Some believe that the atomic bombs that were dropped in Hiroshima and Nagasaki by the United States were the main reason the ROC was able to win the war. But, in fact, the ROC forces fought alone, without outside help, during the initial stages of war. That kept 800,000 Japanese military personnel tied up in the Chinese Theater, which turned out to be a key factor that

---

[78] "Ma Reaffirms Validity of Cairo Declaration," *Taiwan Today* (December 3, 2013), accessible at: http://taiwantoday.tw/ct.asp?xitem=212265&CtNode=414.

[79] On the controversies surrounding Taiwan's postwar legal status, see Edward Dreyer, "The Myth of 'One China,'" in Peter Chow, ed., *The One China Dilemma*, pp. 19–36; and also in the same volume, J Bruce Jacobs, "Taiwan's Colonial History and Postcolonial Nationalism," pp. 37–56; and Huang-chih Chiang and Jau-yuan Huang, "On the Statehood of Taiwan: A Legal Reappraisal," pp. 57–80.

[80] "Taiwan President Remembers Nationalist Victory in Sino-Japanese War," *Reuters* (July 4, 2015), accessible at: http://www.reuters.com/article/us-taiwan-military-id USKCN0PE0HS20150704.

allowed the Allied forces to ultimately win World War II."[81] Ma backed up his stances by citing the works of American and British historians such as Lloyd Eastman and Rana Mitter.[82]

Second, responding to those in Taiwan who perceived the Japanese rule from 1895 to 1945 as favorable to the island's economic modernization and development, Ma concentrated on the Taiwanese people's own anti-Japanese resistance movement during that "colonial era." He stated:

> Anti-Japanese movements continued unabated after the Qing court (1644–1911) was defeated in the First Sino-Japanese War (1894–95), and signed the Treaty of Shimonoseki in 1895, ceding Taiwan and the Pescadores (Penghu) to Japan. Early on, heroes such as Chiu Feng-chia, Wu Tang-hsing, Chiang Shao-tsu, Chien Ta-shih, Yu Ching-fang, Luo Fu-hsing, Lin Tsu-mi, and Mona Rudao led armed resistance. Then Lin Hsien-tang, Chiang Wei-shui, Liao Chin-ping, Weng Chun-ming and others engaged in non-violent resistance in a bid to gain autonomy and democracy. During the War of Resistance Against Japan, General Li Yu-bang organized volunteer Taiwanese partisan fighters to carry out guerilla operations against Japan in the coastal provinces of Fujian and Zhejiang. Li Wan-chu participated in the Institute of International Studies. Chiu Nien-tai led the Guangdong eastern regional service corps against Japan. Lin Cheng-heng joined the Chinese Expeditionary Force to Burma. More than 50,000 people including Hsieh Tung-min, Huang Chao-chin, and Lien Chen-tung made contributions to Taiwan's retrocession. The historical facts reveal that during the Japanese colonial era, the Taiwanese people showed strong determination to resist Japan, a concrete demonstration of Taiwan's solidarity.[83]

Though underscoring the importance of the ROC and Japan's "special partnership," President Ma urged Tokyo to "continue to face up to history and adopt a more sincere, more forward-looking, and responsible attitude, along with taking concrete action to forge true reconciliation and

---

[81] "President Ma Attends Opening Ceremonies for Exhibits Commemorating the 70th Anniversary of Victory in War of Resistance and Taiwan Retrocession," Office of the President, Republic of China (Taiwan), July 3, 2015, accessible at: http://english.president.gov.tw/Default.aspx?tabid=491&itemid=35152&rmid=2355.

[82] See Lloyd Eastman, *Seeds of Destruction* (Stanford University Press, 1984) and Rana Mitter, *Forgotten Ally* (First Mariner books, 2013).

[83] "President Ma Attends Opening of Exhibit Commemorating 70th Anniversary of ROC's Victory in War Against Japan and Taiwan's Retrocession," Office of the President, Republic of China (Taiwan), August 15, 2015, accessible at: http://english.president.gov.tw/Default.aspx?tabid=491&itemid=35468&rmid=2355.

develop friendly and cooperative relations with neighboring countries."[84] Critics see Ma's representation as too China-leaning and hostile against Japan and even the United States.[85]

2 Elite Fragmentations Between the KMT and DPP and Societal Discontent

The DPP's Position

Notwithstanding Tsai Ing-wen's pledge to maintain the cross-strait status quo after becoming Taiwan's president in May 2016 (see Chaps. 5 and 6), the DPP has remained largely committed to a "one-China, one-Taiwan" policy stance, even though there is a sizable faction within the party that emphasizes taking a more "pragmatist" approach to build a constructive relationship with Beijing.[86] The party remains skeptical about the existence of the "1992 consensus," pointing out that while SEF and ARATS met in Hong Kong in late 1992, there was no concrete consensus on the definition of "one China." At best, the 1992 meeting itself was only a historical fact. Since Beijing's "one China" is clearly the PRC, the DPP contends that the KMT's interpretation could be sustained only if the mainland were to openly accept the ROC. Otherwise, the notion of OCRI is merely based on naivety or "wishful thinking."[87] More importantly, in an interview with this author, the DPP official stated that the Communist Party wished to use the "1992 consensus" to forge a "united front" with the KMT to combat the DPP and drive a wedge in Taiwanese domestic politics.[88] The DPP and critics voiced similar concerns in the wake of the Xi–Ma summit, asserting that, in their opening remarks, President Ma "left out the standard add-on to Taipei's version of 'one China' that has been the basis of his cross-strait policy since 2008: he did not mention [the ROC] or 'respective interpretations,' under which Beijing and Taipei 'agree to disagree.'"[89]

[84] Ibid.
[85] Interview with a DPP party official in the Department of China Affairs, who requested to remain anonymous, Taipei, Taiwan, July 22, 2014.
[86] Gunter Schubert, "Between Strategic Change and Ideological Adjustment," pp. 233–270.
[87] Interview with DPP party official.
[88] Ibid.
[89] J. Michael Cole, "Ma and Xi Hold 'Historic' Meeting in Singapore," Thinking Taiwan (November 7, 2015), accessible at: http://thinking-taiwan.com/ma-xi-historic-meeting-singapore/.

When running for Taiwan's presidency in 2012, Tsai Ing-wen called the "1992 consensus" "invented" and "non-existent." Instead, she proposed a "Taiwan consensus" in which democracy and popular will are the solid foundations in dealing with Beijing. Taipei can only negotiate with the PRC when there is internal unity and agreement.[90] Furthermore, the party continues to adhere to its "Resolution on Taiwan's Future," passed in 1999 (which, to some extent, supersedes the DPP's more extreme "Taiwan Independence Clause" passed in 1991).[91] Essentially, the resolution states:

> Taiwan is a sovereign and independent country. In accordance with international laws, Taiwan's jurisdiction covers Taiwan, Penghu, Jinmen, and Mazu, its affiliated islands and territorial waters. Taiwan, although named the Republic of China under its current constitution, is not subject to the jurisdiction of the People's Republic of China. Any change in the independent status quo must be decided by all residents of Taiwan by means of plebiscite.[92]

Significantly, while accepting the ROC as Taiwan's existing official title, the resolution recognizes that Taiwan is a sovereign independent state and that, unlike the KMT's definition, the ROC Constitution only pertains to Taiwan, Penghu, Jinmen, Mazu, offshore islands, and territorial waters, but not to mainland China.

The "ROC" is only a present tense, not a permanent status, as the title can be amended if allowed by changing circumstances.[93] Living with the ROC, in other words, is merely for the sake of political pragmatism or expediency.[94] Indeed, the resolution further expresses:

---

[90] Gunter Schubert, "Between Strategic Change and Ideological Adjustment," p. 246.

[91] The DPP's "Taiwan Independent Clause" calls for the creation of the Republic of Taiwan. The "Resolution," on the other hand, was ratified in May 1998 to moderate the DPP's pro-independence position and to strengthen the electoral prospects of Chen Shui-bian for the coming presidential election in March 2000. See Gunter Schubert, "Between Strategic Change and Ideological Adjustment," p. 239. See also Su Chi, *Taiwan's Relations with Mainland China*, pp. 98–99.

[92] DPP, "Resolutions Regarding Taiwan's Future," (May 1999), accessible at: http://dpptaiwan.blogspot.tw/2011/03/1999-resolution-regarding-taiwans.html.

[93] Gunter Schubert, "Between Strategic Change and Ideological Adjustment," p. 240.

[94] Interview with Dr. Su Chi. He commented that the DPP obviously dislikes the ROC but could use it for pragmatism.

Under the current social consensus, externally, Taiwan no longer insists on using the "Republic of China" as the sole national name to participate in various governmental and non-governmental organizations. Domestically, after breaking the KMT's mythical claim of being the "sole legitimate government of all China," we pushed for constitutional and political reforms.... In developing a new national identity, we promoted the Taiwanization of public education to rebuild awareness of Taiwanese history and culture...and the government announced lifting the restriction on using the title "Taiwan" in national organizations. The principle of Taiwan's sovereign independence has comprehensively demonstrated its superiority and legitimacy in application.[95]

Consequently, the DPP seeks to sever the ties between Taiwan and China. The party has urged the "renunciation of the one China principle" because it could create "international confusions and provide the pretext for [the PRC's] forceful annexation."[96] This notion also applies to the ROC, which upholds Taiwan's connection to China even though it is a "China that was not recognized by Beijing and many other nations in the world."[97] Thus, the ROC may stand on an equal footing with Taiwan or be subordinated to Taiwan, but it can no longer subsume Taiwan.[98] In July 2014, Tsai described that "robust Taiwanese consciousness, which identifies with Taiwan and holds strong to the values of independence and autonomy [and] which for the emerging new generations, has already become as natural as the air that they breathe."[99]

Rising Societal Taiwan-Centric Sentiments

Meanwhile, Taiwan's indigenous nationalism continues to increase unabated. Though a strong majority of the Taiwanese people (80 percent), according to a public opinion poll by the MAC in March 2016, endorses the "ROC's constitutional framework,"[100] it is unclear how the general

---

[95] DPP, "Resolutions Regarding Taiwan's Future."
[96] Ibid.
[97] Chang and Holt, "Taiwan and ROC," p. 312.
[98] Ibid., p. 313.
[99] "DPP's Chair Tsai Ing-wen's Comments on Proposed Freeze on Independence Platform," (July 22, 2014), accessible at: http://dpptaiwan.blogspot.tw/2014/07/dpp-chair-tsai-ing-wens-comments-on.html.
[100] "Public Views on Current Cross-Strait Relations," the Mainland Affairs Council, Republic of China (Taiwan), March 29, 2016, accessible at: http://www.mac.gov.tw/public/Attachment/651313484572.pdf.

public really defines the ROC. When asked whether they identify with the "1992 consensus" in which "one China" refers to the ROC, those supporting that position becomes 60 percent (still a majority).[101] However, close to 73 percent of respondents oppose the statement that "both sides belong to one China."[102] Such ambivalence probably reveals the deep-seated complexity of cross-strait relations and people's uncertainty about the phrase "one China." To be sure, many Taiwanese people have long been disenchanted with the ROC, viewing the regime as China-centric, authoritarian, and illegitimate. Hence, they are not entirely supportive of the ROC state. To them, the KMT's ROC and CCP's PRC both symbolize an undemocratic China that seeks to dominate Taiwan.[103] Moreover, the DPP party official interviewed by this author added that many people in Taiwan today, especially the younger generation, view the ROC and Taiwan synonymously. "The ROC is Taiwan, and Taiwan is ROC." It is about Taiwan's democracy and freedom and has nothing to do with mainland China. When Taiwanese people cheer for Taiwan's sports teams, for example, they often bring along the ROC national flag with them. But, to them, this flag is the Taiwanese national flag.[104]

Since the early 1990s, people who identify themselves as Taiwanese have continued to increase whereas those who perceive themselves as Chinese have steadily declined. In 2004, for instance, 41 percent identified themselves as Taiwanese, 6.2 percent as Chinese, and 47 percent as both Chinese and Taiwanese. Yet, in 2014, those numbers changed to 60, 3.5, and 33 percent, respectively[105] (see Fig. 4.1 below).

As Fig. 4.2 further illustrates, over the past 20 years, a consistent overwhelming majority of the Taiwanese public—more than 80 percent—has supported maintaining the status quo that is neither independence nor unification. Yet, interestingly, those who opt for "the maintenance of status quo now and independence later" steadily increased from roughly 8 percent in 1994 to about 18 percent in 2014. In contrast, those who

---

[101] "Public Views on Current Cross-Strait Relations," the Mainland Affairs Council, ROC (Taiwan), November 11, 2015, accessible at: http://www.mac.gov.tw/public/Attachment/5122916242137.pdf.

[102] "Public Views on Current Cross-Strait Relations," March 29, 2016.

[103] Chang and Holt, "Taiwan and ROC," p. 302.

[104] Interview with the DPP official.

[105] "Changes in the Taiwanese/Chinese Identity of Taiwanese as Tracked in Surveys by the Election Study Center, National Chengchi University (NCCU), 1992–June 2014," accessible at http://esc.nccu.edu.tw/course/news.php?Sn=166.

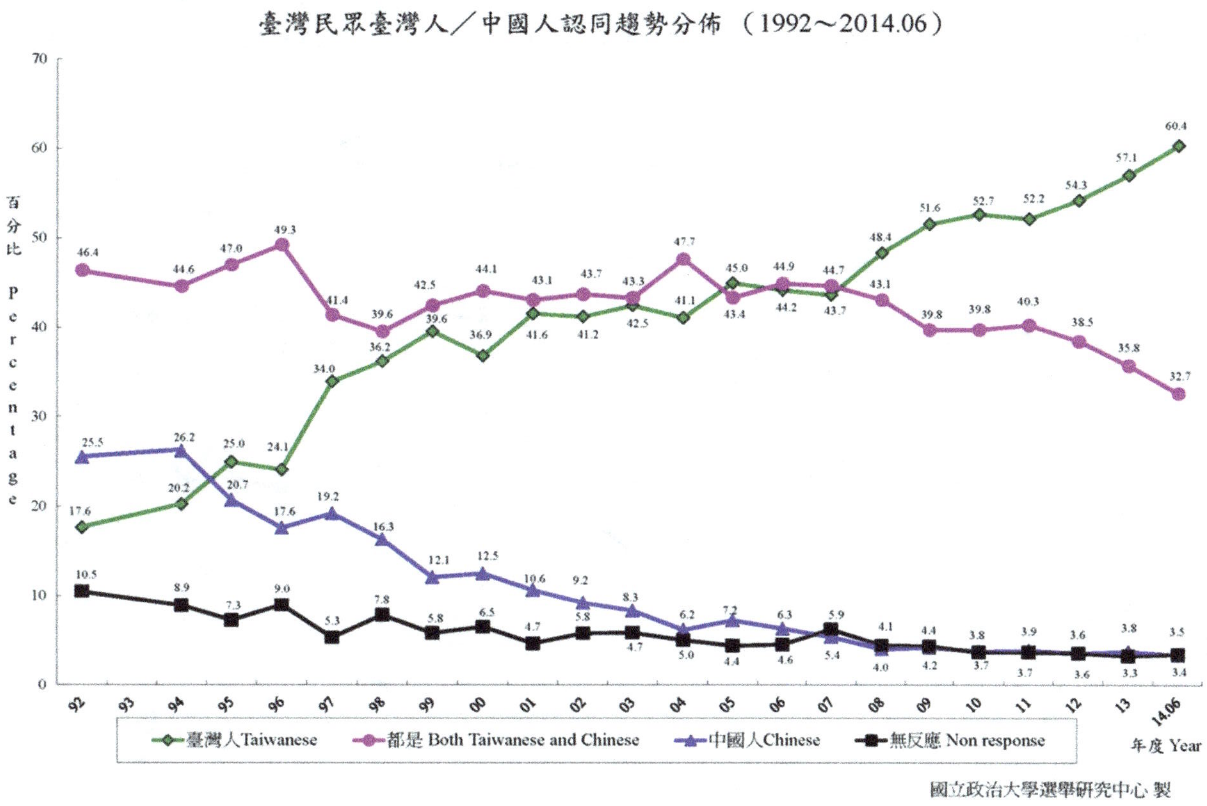

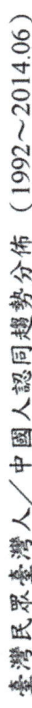

Fig. 4.1 Changes in the Taiwanese/Chinese identity of Taiwanese as tracked in the surveys by the Election Study Center, NCCU (1992–2014.06) (*Source*: The Election Study Center, National Chengchi University, Taipei, Taiwan)

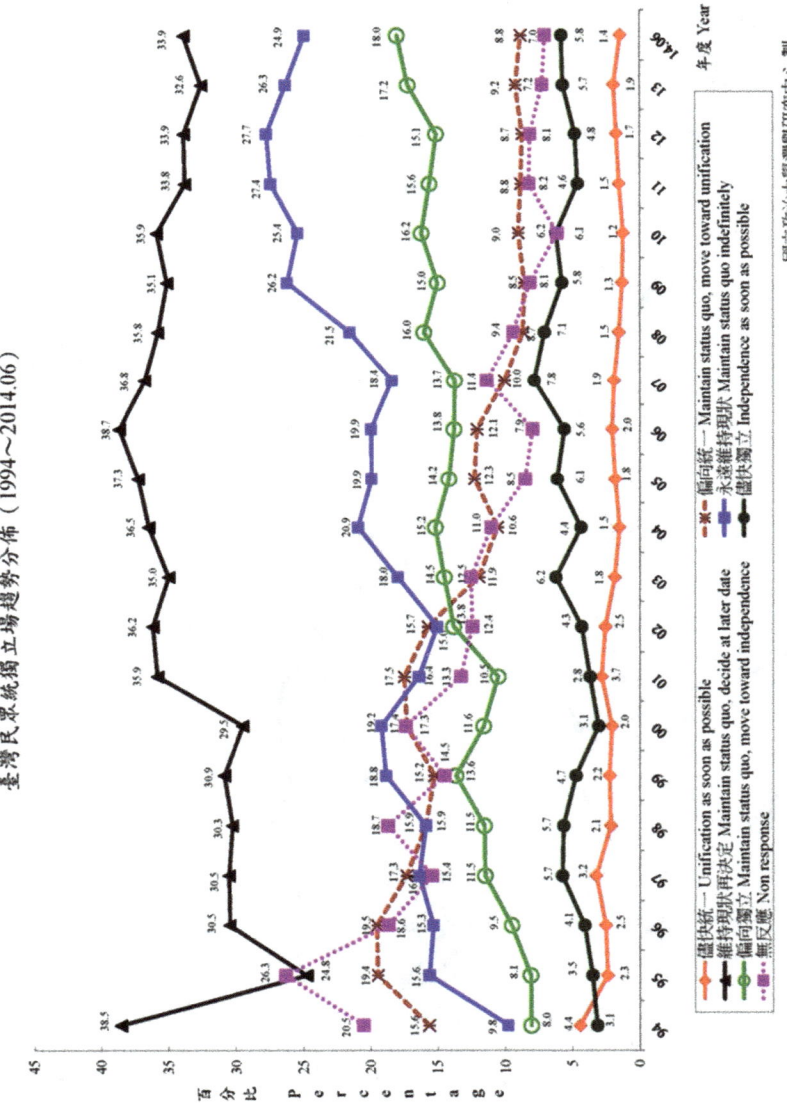

Fig. 4.2 Changes in the unification–independence stances of Taiwanese as tracked in surveys by the Election Study Center, NCCU (1994–2014.06) (*Source*: The Election Study Center, National Chengchi University, Taipei, Taiwan)

desire to maintain the "status quo now and unification later" dropped from 19 percent in 1995 to 9 percent in 2014. Close to 60 percent simply wants "status quo indefinitely" (34 percent) or "status quo but to decide later" (25 percent). Outright unification is the least appealing option, ranging no higher than 2 percent of the total population, and even those advocating for immediate independence ranks higher, at about 6 percent. It is clear, then, that while Taiwanese-centered consciousness and identity rise, the general Taiwanese public's desire to unite with mainland China continues to dwindle. A not so insignificant minority—about a quarter (25 percent)—actually wants independence whether now or later.

The bulk of the status quo advocates, however, seem to have reservations and doubts about their future intentions. According to Brett Benson and Emerson Niou, a reasonable explanation accounting for the public's indecision may be their "uncertainty about the U.S. commitment to defend Taiwan. This, in turn, gives reason for the Taiwanese to worry about China's threat to retaliate if Taiwan moves toward independence."[106] Another scholar observed that people in Taiwan support the deepening of Taiwanization and identity, but their "risk aversion" has also restrained them from endorsing formal Taiwan independence.[107]

Several reasons may explain Taiwan's rising identity. First, in spite of cross-strait peaceful development, Beijing has never renounced the use of force to take back Taiwan if necessary. Indeed, the PRC continues to position intermediate and short-range missiles targeting the island.[108] Unlike the Ma government,[109] most Taiwanese people perceive the PRC as "hostile" toward Taiwan. In the March 2016 poll released by the MAC, about 60 percent of Taiwanese citizens considered the PRC's attitude toward the ROC government "unfriendly" whereas 21 percent felt otherwise. On Beijing's attitude toward the Taiwanese people, though more respondents took a positive view, at 34 percent, a simple majority—51 percent—suggested it was unfriendly.[110]

Second, China has not given up on restricting and suppressing Taiwan's international space even though some minor concessions have been made

---

[106] Brett Benson and Emerson Niou, "Public Opinion, Foreign Policy, and the Security Balance in the Taiwan Strait," *Security Studies* 14, no. 2 (2005), p. 286.

[107] S. Philip Hsu, "Between Identity Quest and Risk Aversion," pp. 715–716.

[108] Interview with the MAC official.

[109] "Ma Warns against Exaggerations on Cross-Strait Ties," Overseas Office of the Republic of China (Taiwan) (April 2014), accessible at: http://www.taiwanembassy.org/ca/yvr/ct.asp?xItem=494792&ctNode=2237&mp=2.

[110] "Public Views on Current Cross-Strait Relations," March 29, 2016.

since 2009.[111] This is illustrated by Beijing's stern warning in 2013, for instance, to the new Pope to not give too much leeway to Taiwan.[112] Furthermore, as discussed earlier, whenever Taiwan is allowed to participate in any NGOs, international events, and agencies, the island is always required to use the title "Chinese Taipei" instead of the ROC. A case in point isBeijing's initial insistence during the 2008 Summer Olympics that Taiwan be represented as "China Taiwan". Strong protests from Taipei eventually forced the PRC to settle with "Chinese Taipei," which is more acceptable to the Taiwanese than the clearly PRC-dominant "China Taiwan."

Third, the maturing of Taiwan's younger generation, who has been aware of the PRC's saber rattling toward Taiwan (i.e., missile exercises and military threats in the late 1990s) and Beijing's human rights repressions and undemocratic practices, and who has been socialized under a Taiwan-centric education system, also contributes to the decline of Chinese identity.[113] In spring 2014, Taiwan's Sunflower students' movement was composed primarily of these youth who felt deeply perturbed by the Ma administration's close dealings with mainland China, and especially the alleged KMT majority tyranny in pushing through the passage of the Cross-Straits Agreement on Trade in Services[114] in

[111] Interview with the DPP party official. The MAC official also concurred on this point, commenting that, in recent years, Beijing has relaxed somewhat when Taipei asserts "one China" is the ROC. But, internationally, Beijing never concedes on the fact that "one China" is the PRC.

[112] "China to New Pope: Welcome, But Stay Away from Taiwan," *The Washington Times* (March 14, 2013), accessible at: http://www.washingtontimes.com/news/2013/mar/14/china-new-pope-welcome-stay-away-taiwan/.

[113] Liao Da-chi et al., "The Decline of 'Chinese Identity in Taiwan?!—An Analysis of Survey Data from 1992 to 2012," *East Asia* 30 (2013), pp. 273–290. These growing trends were also confirmed during this author's interview with Dr. Liao Da-chi, July 17, 2014, Kaohsiung, Taiwan. She is a professor and director of the Institute of Political Science at the National Sun-Yat-sen University.

[114] This agreement, signed by SEF and ARATS in June 2013, is a follow-up to ECFA. The purpose is to reduce restrictions on trade in services and expand the scope of market and business for service suppliers. The KMT government has tried to assure the Taiwanese service sectors that the pact would provide preferential treatments for Taiwanese service suppliers in mainland China and that stringent regulations would be implemented to make sure that liberalization would not compromise Taiwan's economy. See "ECFA: Q &A about the Cross-Straits Agreement on Trade in Services," (Taipei: Ministry of Economic Affairs, ROC, 2014). However, according to critics, the government's lack of sufficient communication

Table 4.1 The Taiwanese public's views on the pace of cross-strait exchanges

Average % from each year	Too fast	Just right	Too slow	Sum of just right and too slow	No opinion/ Don't know
2008	33.4%	44.1%	16.0%	60.1%	6.6%
2009	33.4%	42.7%	12.4%	55.1%	11.7%
2010	37.0%	41.6%	12.5%	54.1%	8.8%
2011	29.3%	46.9%	13.4%	60.3%	10.4%
2012	31.0%	42.4%	15.4%	57.8%	11.1%
2013	34.1%	41.3%	13.5%	54.8%	11.2%
2014	32.2%	39.7%	15.2%	54.9%	12.9%
2015	28.4%	41.6%	18.1%	59.7%	11.9%
2016	17.1%	42.4%	27.4%	69.8%	13.3%

Source: The Mainland Affairs Council, Republic of China, Taiwan; August 2008 to July 2016

the Legislative Yuan.[115] Their three-week-long occupation of the legislature aimed at giving people a greater role in supervising cross-strait economic pacts.[116]

Table 4.1 displays the average of the public attitudes, per year, toward the speed of cross-strait exchanges since the election of the KMT administration in May 2008. Throughout the Ma Ying-jeou presidency, the general views regarding China–Taiwan interactions have been quite positive, hovering between 54 and 60 percent. Nonetheless, the two highest points were reached in 2008 and 2011 with 60.1 and 60.3 percent, respectively, which coincided with Ma's first election and reelection. Then, there were notable declines in support in the midst of political storms over the signing of ECFA in 2010 (54.1 percent) and the Cross-Straits Service Trade Agreement and the Sunflower movement in 2013 (54.8 percent) and 2014 (54.9 percent). In the MAC poll of December 2014, for instance, the proportions of those finding the pace of cross-strait exchanges "just right" and "too fast" are 37.8 and 28.6 percent, respectively, whereas those believing them to be "too slow" or with "no opinion" are 16.8 and 16.8 percent, respectively. Thus, 54.6 percent

and information-sharing has galvanized enormous skepticism from Taiwan's public, who remain confused over the specific implications of the agreement.

[115] Interview with Ma Wei-ming.
[116] "Sunflower Sutra," The Economist (April 8, 2014), accessible at: http://www.economist.com/blogs/banyan/2014/04/politics-taiwan.

perceived cross-strait exchanges as either at the right pace or that they should move forward more rapidly.[117] However, if we compare the similar MAC poll from August 2008, when the KMT had just returned to power, we may find some changes in attitudes. Back then, those who felt that the pace of exchange was "just right" and "too fast" were 40.6 and 29.5 percent, respectively, while "too slow" or "no opinion" were 17.5 and 12.4 percent, respectively.[118] The total of those believing the speed of interactions was either just right or too slow combined to 58.1 percent. Consequently, between 2008 and 2014, there has been a decrease of almost 4 percent in people's feeling that cross-strait exchanges are on the right track.

The interesting observation, moreover, pertains to the year 2016. The average result shows that close to 70 percent finds cross-strait interchanges as either too slow or just right whereas about 17 percent sees them as too fast. The latter represents the lowest manifestation in that category when compared to those in President Ma's tenure. For example, in the MAC poll of July 2016, roughly 74 percent sees that cross-strait economic exchanges are either just right or too slow whereas 13 percent views the pace as too fast.[119] This reversal of attitude should probably be read in light of Taiwan's changing political dynamics—that the Tsai administration, since her inauguration in May 2016, has assumed a more circumspect policy stance on cross-strait interactions. The new president's refusal to accept the "1992 consensus" has also led to suspension of cross-strait negotiations and slowdown of socio-commercial interactions. As a result, the people may find Tsai more conservative in her handling of cross-strait affairs when compared to her predecessor. Indeed, as discussed in Chap. 2, the Taiwanese people, while rejecting unification with mainland China, still support economic liberalization with the PRC as long as these exchanges would not compromise Taiwan's security, democracy, and autonomy.

---

[117] "Public's Views on Current Cross-Strait Relations," the Mainland Affairs Council Republic of China (Taiwan), December 25, 2014, http://www.mac.gov.tw/public/Attachment/52514151258.pdf.

[118] "Public's Views on Current Cross-Strait Relations," the Mainland Affairs Council Republic of China (Taiwan), (August 2008), accessible at: http://www.mac.gov.tw/public/Attachment/96315264474.pdf.

[119] "Public's Views on Current Cross-Strait Relations," MAC, August 9, 2016, accessible at: http://www.mac.gov.tw/ct.asp?xItem=115356&ctNode=5649&mp=1.

3 Conclusion

Given the PRC's ultimate aim to unify with Taiwan, the CCP leaders have an incentive to forge a "united front" with the KMT and its like-minded allies to jointly oppose the DPP and Taiwan independence.[120] For its part, the Ma administration, in order to reinstate the ROC's "one-China" nationalism, also found it conducive to side with Beijing to deepen cross-strait political and socioeconomic cooperation. Unlike the KMT, political leaders of the DPP have generally disputed the ROC's ruling legitimacy over Taiwan after the end of WWII, pointing out Taiwan's indeterminate legal status following Japan's surrender in 1945 and that the defeated ROC that retreated to Taipei after 1949 was simply a "government in exile."[121] Moreover, the DPP and its supporters have viewed the notion of "one China" or the "1992 consensus" as antithetical to Taiwan's freedom and democracy. For many Taiwanese people, even the ROC is a symbol of KMT dictatorship. They accused the Ma administration of surrendering Taiwan's political autonomy and sovereignty to Beijing. To be sure, President Ma's China-friendly policy cannot account entirely for his low popular approval rating (9 percent at one point in early 2014),[122] yet it is probably fair to say that, in light of these public opinion ratings and increasing mass movements, there is a widening disconnect between his mainland policy and the mainstream Taiwanese identity and preferences. Though Taiwan's new president Tsai Ing-wen has promised to abide by the ROC's constitutional order, she has refrained from explicitly accepting the "1992 consensus" and the "one-China" principle underlying the ROC Constitution.[123]

---

[120] Cabestan 2016, pp. 295–296.

[121] "Tsai Blasted for 'Government-in-Exile' Remark," *Taipei Times* (May 27, 2010), accessible at: http://www.taipeitimes.com/News/front/archives/2010/05/27/2003473982.

[122] "On the Antlers of a Dilemma: The Ambitions of Ma Ying-jeou, Taiwan's President, Collide with Popular Suspicion of China," *The Economist* (March 29, 2014), accessible at: http://www.economist.com/news/asia/21599812-ambitions-ma-ying-jeou-taiwans-president-collide-popular-suspicion-china. For instance, Ma's offensives against the Legislative Yuan Speaker Wang Jin-pyng in September 2013 also triggered backlashes against the president. See "Politics in Taiwan: Daggers Down," *The Economist* (September 21, 2013), accessible at: http://www.economist.com/news/asia/21586546-struggle-between-president-and-ruling-party-heavyweight-has-consequences-islands.

[123] Richard Bush, "Cross-Strait Relations: Not a One-Way Street," The Brookings Institution (April 22, 2016), accessible at: http://www.brookings.edu/blogs/order-from-chaos/posts/2016/04/22-cross-strait-relations-bush.

Accordingly, for a deeply internally divided polity like Taiwan, the presence of an external challenge (the PRC) could widen that political polarization through the latter's intentional or strategic promotion and assistance of like-minded domestic interests and elites in their quest to propagate certain ideological or nation-building initiatives. More often than not, domestic actors disagree over whether the foreign power even constitutes a genuine national security challenge. Consequently, in line with neoclassical realism, when elites have incoherent views regarding national security, it is highly unlikely that the state will be able to construct an effective grand strategy in response. Some leaders or factions will want to balance against one threat, whereas others will want to balance against another. Certain segments of political elites and societal forces may actually find it expedient and conducive to ally with that foreign power to subdue and undermine their political rivals.

Chapter 5 will concentrate on how Ma's China-leaning policy has generated some discrepancies between Taiwan and America's national security interests, especially on the KMT's similar maritime territorial claims, with Beijing, on the East and South China Sea disputes. This should demonstrate how domestic nation building can undermine a polity's foreign policy stance.

References

Association for Relations Across the Taiwan Strait, (ed.). 2005. *Jiuer Gongshi Lishi Cunzheng [The Historical Documents of the 1992 Consensus]*. Beijing: Jiuzhou Press.

Atanassova-Cornelis, Elena. 2013. Shifting Domestic Politics and Security Policy in Japan and Taiwan: The Search for a Balancing Strategy between China and the U.S. *Asian Pacific Review* 20(1): 55–78.

Brett, Benson, and Emerson Niou. 2005. Public Opinion, Foreign Policy, and the Security Balance in the Taiwan Strait. *Security Studies* 14(2): 274–289.

Cabestan, Jean-Pierre. 2016. Cross-Strait Integration and Taiwan's New Security Challenges. In *Taiwan and the "China Impact."*, ed. Gunter Schubert, 282–300. New York: Routledge.

Chang, Bi-yu. 2015. *Place, Identity and National Imagination in Postwar Taiwan*. New York: Routledge.

Chang, Hui-Ching, and Rich Holt. 2009. Taiwan and ROC: A Critical Analysis of President Chen Shui-bian's Construction of Taiwan Identities in National Speeches. *National Identities* 11(3): 301–330.

———. 2015. *Language, Politics and Identity in Taiwan*. New York: Routledge.

Chiang, Huang-chih, and Jau-yuan Huang. 2008. On the Statehood of Taiwan: A Legal Reappraisal. In *The One China Dilemma*, ed. Peter Chow, 57–80. New York: Palgrave Macmillan.

Clark, Cal, and Alexander Tan. 2012. *Taiwan Political Economy*. Boulder: Lynne Rienner Publishers.

deLisle, Jacques. 2014. Taiwan and Soft Power. In *Political Changes in Taiwan under Ma Ying-jeou*, ed. Jean-Pierre Cabestan and Jacques deLisle, 265–295. New York: Routledge.

Ding, Arthur, and Join-sane Lin, ed. 2012. *Jiuer Gongshi Ershi Zhounian Xueshu Yantao Huiyi Shilu [The 1992 Consensus: The 20th Anniversary Academic Conference Records]*. Taipei: The Strait Exchange Foundation and National Chengchi University's Institute of International Relations.

Dittmer, Lowell. 2014. Taiwan's Narrowing Strait: A Triangular Analysis of Taiwan's Security since 2008. In *The U.S. Strategic Pivot to Asia and Cross-Strait Relations*, ed. Peter Chow, 15–29. New York: Palgrave Macmillan.

Dreyer, Edward. 2008. The Myth of 'One China. In *The One China Dilemma*, ed. Peter Chow, 19–36. New York: Palgrave Macmillan.

Eastman, Lloyd. 1984. *Seeds of Destruction*. Stanford: Stanford University Press.

Fell, Dafydd. 2012. *Government and Politics in Taiwan*. New York: Routledge.

Hickey, Dennis. 2011. Rapprochement between Taiwan and the Chinese Mainland: Implications for American Foreign Policy. *Journal of Contemporary China* 20(69): 231–247.

Hsieh, John. 2015. Taiwan in 2014: A Besieged President amid Political Turmoil. *Asian Survey* 55(1): 142–147.

Hsu, Philip. 2010. Between Identity Quest and Risk Aversion: Lessons from the Chen Shui-bian Presidency for Maintaining Cross-Strait Stability. *Journal of Contemporary China* 19(66): 693–717.

Hughes, Christopher. 2011. Negotiating National Identity in Taiwan: Between Nativization and De-Sinicization. In *Taiwan's Democracy*, ed. Robert Ash, John Garver, and Penelope Prime, 1–21. New York: Routledge.

———. 2014. Revisiting Identity Politics under Ma Ying-jeou. In *Political Changes in Taiwan under Ma Ying-jeou*, ed. Jean-Pierre Cabestan and Jacques deLisle, 120–136. New York: Routledge.

Jacobs, Bruce. 2008. Taiwan's Colonial History and Postcolonial Nationalism. In *The One China Dilemma*, ed. Peter Chow, 37–56. New York: Palgrave Macmillan.

Liao, Da-chi, et al. 2013. The Decline of 'Chinese Identity in Taiwan?!—An Analysis of Survey Data from 1992 to 2012. *East Asia* 30: 273–290.

Lin, Shirley. 2016. *Taiwan's China Dilemma*. Stanford: Stanford University Press.

Liu, Fu-kuo. 2014. Ma Ying-jeou's Rapprochement Policy: Cross-Strait Progress and Domestic Constraints. In *Political Changes in Taiwan under Ma Ying-jeou*, ed. Jean-Pierre Cabestan and Jacques deLisle, 139–155. New York: Routledge.

Lynch, Daniel. 2004. Taiwan's Self-Conscious Nation Building Project. *Asian Survey* 44(4): 513–533.
Ma, Ying-jeou. 2007. *Yuanxiang jingshen: Taiwan de dianfan gushi [Original Native Spirit: the Model Story of Taiwan]*. Taipei: Tianxia Publishers.
Mitter, Rana. 2013. *Forgotten Ally*. New York: First Mariner books.
Muyard, Frank. 2010. Midterm Analysis of the Ma Ying-jeou Administration. *China Perspective*: 1–21.
Schubert, Gunter. 2012. Between Strategic Change and Ideological Adjustment: The DPP's China Policy Debate in the Aftermath of the 2012 National Elections. *Taiwan Political Science Review* 16(2): 233–270.
Shirk, Susan. 2008. *China: Fragile Superpower*. New York: Oxford University Press.
Su, Chi. 2009. *Taiwan's Relations with Mainland China*. New York: Routledge.
Su, Chi, and Cheng An-guo, (eds.). 2003. *Yige Zhongguo Gezi Biaoshu Gongshi De Shishi [One China, Respective Interpretations: A Historical Account of the Consensus]*. Taipei: National Policy Foundation.
Tucker, Nancy. 2009. *Strait Talk*. Cambridge, MA: Harvard University Press.
Wang, Chi. 2015. *Obama's Challenge to China*. Burlington: Ashgate.
Wu, Chung-li. 2016. Games without Frontiers, War without Tears? The Process of Campaigning in the 2016 Taiwanese General Elections. *American Journal of Chinese Studies* 23(1): 25–41.
Zhang, Baohui. 2011. Taiwan's New Grand Strategy. *Journal of Contemporary China* 20(69): 269–285.

Author's Interviews

Interview with Chao Chun-shan, July 8, 2014, Taipei, Taiwan. Chao served as Chairman of Taiwan's Prospect Foundation and the Foundation on Asia-Pacific Peace Studies during the Ma Ying-jeou administration.
Interview with Su Chi, July 16 2014, Taipei, Taiwan. Su was Minister of Taiwan's Mainland Affairs Council (MAC) from 1999 to 2000, Taiwan's legislator from 2005 to 2008, and Secretary General of the ROC's National Security Council for President Ma Ying-jeou from 2008 to 2010. He is now the chairman of the Taipei Forum Foundation.
Interview with Liao Da-chi, July 17, 2014, Kaohsiung, Taiwan. Liao is Professor and Director of the Institute of Political Science at the National Sun-Yat-sen University.
Interview with an official from the DPP's Department of China Affairs, who requested to remain anonymous, July 22, 2014, Taipei, Taiwan.
Interview with an official in Taiwan's Mainland Affairs Council, who requested to remain anonymous, August 7, 2014, Taipei, Taiwan.

Interview with Ma (Jesse) Wei-min, July 14, 2016, Taipei, Taiwan. Ma is the editor-in-chief of the Apple Daily Newspaper in Taiwan.
Interview with Chou Chih-wei, July 28, 2016, Taipei, Taiwan. Chou was the Chairperson of the KMT's Culture and Communications Committee from April 2016 to October 2016.

CHAPTER 5

US Strategic Ambiguity, Rising China, and Taiwan's Security

When the KMT regained political power in Taiwan, in March 2008, America's strategic relations with the PRC were much more benign and cooperative than they have been since 2010. As discussed in Chap. 4, Taiwan's President Ma Ying-jeou initially enjoyed strong US support in shaping and deepening cross-strait socioeconomic ties on the basis of the "1992 consensus." Recall that shortly after Ma's electoral victory on March 22, 2008, China's leader Hu Jintao, in a telephone conversation with President George W. Bush, expressed that both China and Taiwan should "restore consultation and talks on the basis of the '1992 consensus,' which sees both sides recognize there is only one China, but agree to differ on its definition."[1] President Bush, according to his national security adviser Stephen Hadley, welcomed the Chinese leader's flexibility.[2] This chapter,[3] therefore, will discuss America's changing attitude toward the

[1] "Chinese, U.S. Presidents Hold Telephone Talks on Taiwan, Tibet," *The Xinhua News Agency* (March 27, 2008), accessible at: http://news.xinhuanet.com/english/2008-03/27/content_7865209.htm. In this author's interview with Richard Bush, however, he noted that although the Xinhua website did display this news article, it was immediately taken down and never appeared again in the Chinese media. Thus, Beijing probably felt "it was a mistake" to give any official credence to the so-called "one China," respective interpretations.
[2] David G. Brown, "Taiwan Voters Set a New Course," *Comparative Connections*, 10, no. 1, (April 2008), p. 4.
[3] This chapter has been expanded, revised, and updated from an article written by this author. See Dean P. Chen, "U.S.–China Rivalry and the Weakening of the KMT's '1992

KMT's "1992 consensus" policy as Taiwan, under Ma, became too closely aligned with Beijing on the East and South China Sea maritime disputes. Though Washington has remained consistent in its long-standing strategic ambiguity policy to maintain peace and stability across the Taiwan Strait, the Ma government's China-leaning policy contradicted, to some extent, America's policy. The incongruity between Taiwan's cross-strait position and US security imperatives was due to the KMT administration's preoccupation with rebuilding the ROC central legitimacy within Taiwan (explained in Chap. 4), hence illustrating how domestic politics can affect national security calculations.

1   US Position on the Taiwan Issue Since 2008: An Overview

In his visit to mainland China in November 2009, President Barack Obama declared, "I am very pleased with the reduction of tensions and improvement in cross-strait relations, and it is my deep desire and hope that we will continue to see great improvement between Taiwan and the People's Republic in resolving many of these issues."[4] On October 4, 2011, testifying before the US House Foreign Affairs Committee, Kurt Campbell, the then assistant secretary of state of East Asian and Pacific Affairs, praised President Ma's "1992 consensus" in helping to stabilize cross-strait relations. He remarked,

> One of the dominant issues affecting peace and stability in the East Asia and Pacific region—especially between the United States and China—is the potential for conflict across the Taiwan Strait. Over the past three years, we have witnessed remarkable progress in cross-strait relations. In his inaugural address, Taiwan President Ma called on the PRC "to seize this historic opportunity to achieve peace and co-prosperity." He pledged that there would be "no reunification, no independence, and no war" during his tenure. President Ma also proposed that talks with the PRC resume on the basis of the "1992 consensus," by which both sides agree that there is only

Consensus' Policy: Second-Image Reversed, Revisited," *Asian Survey* 56, no. 4 (2016), pp. 754–778.

[4] "Remarks by President Barack Obama at Town Hall Meeting with Future Chinese Leaders," The White House Office of the Press Secretary (November 16, 2009), accessible at: https://www.whitehouse.gov/the-press-office/remarks-president-barack-obama-town-hall-meeting-with-future-chinese-leaders.

one China, but essentially agree to disagree on what the term "one China" means ... These overall developments helped produce a generally positive atmosphere for the resumption of semi-official talks between Taiwan's Straits Exchange Foundation (SEF) and the PRC's Association for Relations across the Taiwan Strait (ARATS).[5]

Thus, for Taiwan, whose security, autonomy, and democracy have long depended so heavily upon Washington's support and defense commitments, US interests and attitudes toward Beijing are vital determinants of Taiwan's relations with the mainland.[6] Indeed, the cross-strait relationship, in the words of Hu Weixing, is never a "purely bilateral relationship between Beijing and Taipei"; rather, it is "overshadowed by the competitive and cooperative relations between the United States and China."[7]

In recent years, however, the PRC's increasingly assertive foreign policy behaviors have triggered heightened anxiety among its regional neighbors and promoted Washington's "rebalancing" policy toward the Asia-Pacific.[8] Beijing's determined drive to advance claims in disputed maritime territories in the East and South China Seas suggests that the Chinese leadership may be forsaking its peaceful development grand strategy in favor of nationalistic expansionism, thereby raising the chances of confrontation in Asia and involving America in the conflict.[9] Consequently, the intensified Sino-American competition raises an important question on whether the KMT's China-friendly policy was

---

[5] "Why Taiwan Matters, Part II: Testimony by Kurt Campbell, Assistant Secretary, Bureau of East Asian and Pacific Affairs, Testimony before the House Foreign Affairs Committee," The US Department of State (October 4, 2011), accessible at: http://www.state.gov/p/eap/rls/rm/2011/10/174980.htm.

[6] Brett Benson and Emerson Niou, "Public Opinion, Foreign Policy, and the Security Balance in the Taiwan Strait," *Security Studies* 14, no. 2 (2005), pp. 274–289. See also Philip Hsu, "Between Identity Quest and Risk Aversion: Lessons from the Chen Shui-bian Presidency for Maintaining Cross-Strait Stability," *Journal of Contemporary China* 19, no. 66 (2010), pp. 693–717.

[7] Weixing Hu, "Introduction," in Weixing Hu ed., *New Dynamics in Cross-Strait Relations: How Far can the Rapprochement Go?* (New York: Routledge, 2013), p 8 and p. 3.

[8] David Shambaugh, *China Goes Global* (New York: Oxford University Press, 2013), pp. 77–78.

[9] Robert Sutter, "More American Attention to Taiwan amid Heightened Competition with China," *American Journal of Chinese Studies* 22, no. 1 (April 2015), p. 5. See also "Xi's History Lessons," *The Economist* (August 15, 2015), accessible at: http://www.economist.com/news/leaders/21660977-communist-party-plundering-history-justify-its-present-day-ambitions-xis-history.

compatible with Washington's security interests in East Asia and toward the Taiwan Strait. After all, the friend or working partner of a potential competitor may become a menace as well.[10]

Hence, as cross-strait relations improved under Ma Ying-jeou, a major debate had been sparked within America's policymaking circle regarding whether or not the United States should distance itself from Taiwan in order to protect US interests.[11] There are two reasons behind those advocating for "abandoning" Taiwan. First, a Taiwan choosing to bandwagon with an autocratic and belligerent China could undermine US democratic values as well as its strategic and economic interests across the Asia-Pacific.[12] Second, as cross-strait relations warm up, Taiwan would cease to become a stumbling block between the United States and China, hence ameliorating the security dilemma between them. Thus, Washington should disengage from Taiwan in order to solidify its ties with Beijing.[13] On the other hand, the dissenters have stressed that appeasing Beijing over Taiwan would serve only to embolden China's appetite and aggressive impulse. This could endanger the security of America and its allies in the Pacific, with the latter losing faith in Washington's resolve and credibility.[14] Therefore, an array of US congressional representatives, specialists, and commentators were urging the Obama White House to step up America's security, diplomatic, and economic relations with Taiwan in order to more forcefully balance against China's rise and to frustrate Beijing's territorial

---

[10] On this realist power-politics logic, see Hans Morgenthau, *Politics among Nations* (New York: McGraw-Hill, 1985) and Kenneth Waltz, *Theory of International Politics* (New York: McGraw-Hill, 1979).

[11] For a good summary of this so-called abandonment debate, see Richard Bush, "U.S.–Taiwan Relations since 2008," in Jean-Pierre Cabestan and Jacques deLisle eds., *Political Changes in Taiwan under Ma Ying-jeou* (New York: Routledge, 2014), pp. 221–224.

[12] Nadia Tsao, "Rohrabacher to Leave Taiwan Caucus Position," *Taipei Times* (March 15, 2009), accessible at: http://www.taipeitimes.com/News/taiwan/archives/2009/03/15/2003438534.

[13] See Bruce Gilley, "Not So Dire Straits: How Finlandization of Taiwan Benefits U.S. Security," *Foreign Affairs* (Jan/Feb 2010), pp. 44–60; Charles Glaser, "Will China's Rise Lead to War: Why Realism Does Not Mean Pessimism," *Foreign Affairs* (March/April 2011), pp. 80–91. See also Charles Glaser, "A U.S.–China Grand Bargain?: The Hard Choice between Military Competition and Accommodation," *International Security* 39, no. 4 (2015), pp. 49–90.

[14] Nancy Tucker and Bonnie Glaser, "Should the United States Abandon Taiwan?" *The Washington Quarterly* 34, no 4 (2011), pp. 23–37.

ambitions in the East and South China Seas.[15] From the perspective of these critics, the Obama administration had been too timid in the face of China's rising assertiveness. Thus, the United States should cultivate stronger ties with Taiwan to "balance against China's expansionism" or to show "negative costs for China's interests if it pursues its salami slicing in nearby disputed territories."[16] Taiwan, in other words, is the "cork in the bottle" if the "United States needs to shore up radars, defenses, and other anti-China military preparations along the first island chain running from Japan through Taiwan to the Philippines."[17]

The Obama administration, nevertheless, repeatedly reaffirmed its staunch commitment to cross-strait peace and stability and endorsement of Ma Ying-jeou's détente policy, effectively dispelling any speculations that Washington would sacrifice Taiwan as Taipei strengthened relations with Beijing or to use the island in a strategic counterbalancing or deterrence against the PRC.[18] In November 2014, President Obama spoke about cross-strait relations in Beijing:

> I reaffirmed my strong commitment to our one-China policy based on the three Joint Communiqués and the Taiwan Relations Act. And we encourage further progress by both sides of the Taiwan Strait towards building ties, reducing tensions, and promoting stability on the basis of dignity and respect, which is in the interests of both sides, as well as the regions and the United States.[19]

Obama reiterated these lines of thinking at the White House Rose Garden with President Xi Jinping during the latter's state visit in September

---

[15] Robert Sutter, "More American Attention to Taiwan amid Heightened Competition with China," pp. 8–9.

[16] Ibid., p. 10.

[17] Ibid., pp. 10–11.

[18] "Why Taiwan Matters, Part II: Testimony by Kurt Campbell, Assistant Secretary, Bureau of East Asian and Pacific Affairs, Testimony before the House Foreign Affairs Committee." See also Richard Bush, "U.S.–Taiwan Relations since 2008," p. 224; and Dennis Hickey, "Parallel Progress: U.S. Taiwan Relations during An Era of Rapprochement," *Journal of Chinese Political Science* (2015), online access DOI 10. 1007/s11366-015-9355-1.

[19] "Remarks by President Obama and President Xi Jinping in Joint Press Conference," The White House Office of the Press Secretary (November 12, 2014), accessible at: http://www.whitehouse.gov/the-press-office/2014/11/12/remarks-president-obama-and-president-xi-jinping-joint-press-conference.

2015.[20] Calling Taiwan a "vital partner for the United States in Asia," Susan Thornton, the deputy assistant secretary of state for the Bureau of East Asian and Pacific Affairs, noted in May 2015 that "an important ingredient of that close relationship [between Washington and Taipei] in recent years has been the stable management of cross-strait ties."[21] The US government, according to Robert Sutter, seems to "treat Taiwan matters in ways that do not undermine the framework that has been established since Ma Ying-jeou's presidency that serves to reassure China and avoid bringing the Taiwan issue to the top of the American policy agenda with China once again. Disrupting or destroying this framework would cause major problems for U.S. policymakers dealing with China on a day-to-day basis."[22]

In light of this logic, the Obama government, therefore, also refrained from explicitly mentioning Taiwan in its rebalancing to Asia strategy to prevent provoking China's ire and generating serious frictions in the Sino-American relationship.[23] Indeed, since the 1950s, Taiwan has been a sensitive issue in America's China policy. Knowing that reunification with Taiwan plays an essential role in the Chinese quest for national unity and territorial integrity, US policymakers have preferred to support the island through less obtrusive means, fearing that unequivocal positions would instigate Chinese anti-Americanism, encourage Taiwan's unilateral behaviors, and jeopardize US–China relations.[24] The Obama administration, accordingly, inherited this same set of considerations.[25]

This chapter, nonetheless, argues that although the Obama administration had, in general, applauded and encouraged cross-strait rapprochement since 2008, its support was not without reservations. Indeed, as the Ma Ying-jeou government became too closely attached to Beijing and polarized, through the KMT's attempts to rehabilitate a Sino-centric

[20] "Remarks by President Obama and President Xi of the People's Republic of China in Joint Press Conference," The White House Office of the Press Secretary (September 25, 2015), accessible at: https://www.whitehouse.gov/the-press-office/2015/09/25/remarks-president-obama-and-president-xi-peoples-republic-china-joint.

[21] "Taiwan: A Vital Partner in East Asia" The US Department of State (May 21, 2015), accessible at: http://www.state.gov/p/eap/rls/rm/2015/05/242705.htm.

[22] Robert Sutter, "More American Attention to Taiwan amid Heightened Competition with China," p. 15.

[23] Ibid., p. 9.

[24] Nancy Tucker, *Strait Talk*, pp. 11–16.

[25] Robert Sutter et al., "Balancing Acts: The U.S. Rebalance and Asian Pacific Stability," Sigur Center for Asian Studies, The George Washington University (August 2013), p. 21.

nationalist paradigm, Taiwan's democratic politics domestically (see Chap. 4), Taipei actually deviated away from the cross-strait equilibrium maintained under Washington's strategic ambiguity framework that has been the US Taiwan Strait policy since the onset of the Cold War.[26] Under this policy, as discussed in Chap. 1, which was institutionalized by the three Sino-American Joint Communiqués of 1972, 1978, and 1982, the Taiwan Relations Act (TRA) of 1979, and President Ronald Reagan's Six Assurances of 1982, the United States aims at deterring both parties from unilaterally upsetting cross-strait peace and stability (such as Taipei declaring de jure independence or Beijing coercing reunification) in order to sustain Taiwan's self-defense and freedom without impinging upon Beijing's "one-China" principle.[27] America respects the decision of any resolution between Taiwan and the PRC as long as the process of reaching that outcome is peaceful, consensual, and without coercion.[28] In addition, because Taiwan has become a full-fledged liberal democracy, the US

[26] Nancy Tucker, *Strait Talk: United States–Taiwan Relations and the Crisis with China* (Cambridge, MA: Harvard University Press, 2009); and Richard Bush and Alan Romberg, "Cross-Strait Moderation and the United States—A Response to Robert Sutter," *PACNET* no. 17A (March 12, 2009), p. 1.

[27] In addition to the references given in Chap. 1, it is important to stress again that numerous studies have already examined the three Sino-American Communiqués, the TRA, and President Ronald Reagan's Six Assurances. It is beyond the scope of the present chapter to treat these topics substantively, but suffice it to note that while the communiqués stressed on the normalization of US–PRC diplomatic relations, Washington's "acknowledgment" of Beijing's "one-China" principle in which Taiwan is part of the mainland, and that America would eventually end arms sales to Taiwan, the TRA and the Six Assurances actually committed the United States to ensure Taiwan's security, the maintenance of unofficial US–Taiwan ties, and that America would not push Taipei into any political negotiations with Beijing. These contradictions generate perplexities and ambiguities that serve to prevent either side from recklessly instigating tension and confrontation. See Robert Ross, "The 1995–96 Taiwan Strait Confrontation: Coercion, Credibility, and the Use of Force," *International Security* 25, no. 2 (2000), pp. 87–123; Thomas Christensen, "The Contemporary Security Dilemma: Deterring a Taiwan Conflict," *The Washington Quarterly* 25, no. 4 (2002), pp. 7–21; Alan Romberg, *Rein In at the Brink of Precipice: American Policy toward Taiwan and U.S.-PRC Relations* (Washington DC: The Henry L. Stimson Center, 2003); Richard Bush, *At Cross Purposes: U.S.-Taiwan Relations since 1942* (New York: M.E. Sharpe, 2004); Nancy Tucker, *Strait Talk: United States-Taiwan Relations and the Crisis with China* (Cambridge, MA: Harvard University Press, 2009).

[28] See Nancy Tucker, "If Taiwan Chooses Unification, Should the United States Care?" *Washington Quarterly* 25 no. 3 (2002), pp. 15–28; Nancy Tucker and Bonnie Glaser, "Should the United States Abandon Taiwan?"; and Shelley Rigger, *Why Taiwan Matters* (Lanham, MD: Rowman & Littlefield, 2011).

government also has emphasized that the Taiwanese people's preferences should be taken seriously prior to reaching any cross-strait agreements. While satisfying Washington's security imperatives, strategic ambiguity, as a result, strives to fulfill the United States' fundamental liberal objective in preserving the de facto autonomy and security of Taiwan, a successful ethnically Chinese democracy, whose experience—transitioning from a Leninist party-state to a multiparty democratic system—may bring a transformative effect on promoting political change in the PRC. As the United States opposes Beijing's coercive reunification, it also does not support formal Taiwanese independence since it would "retard the hope for political reform on the mainland because democracy would be associated with the breakup of the nation, and political reforms would seem like dupes or even agents of the United States and the Taiwan traitors who declared independence."[29] Strategic ambiguity, in short, is an ambiguous *means* toward the unambiguous *ends* of fostering China's political and economic liberalization and creating a peaceful and consensual resolution of cross-strait impasse.

This author posits that there were signs of increasing qualms in the Obama administration toward the KMT's "1992 consensus" policy. In light of that, the KMT–CCP's common identification with a Chinese nation, whether the ROC or PRC, has put Taiwan in a "pan-Chinese union" with the mainland and placed some of the island's strategic and economic interests at odds with those of the United States and its allies in Asia. The KMT and CCP have more or less relied on the similar historical claims to defend Chinese sovereignty over contested island territories in the East China and South China Seas.

Moreover, the Ma administration's emphasis on closer economic integration enhanced Beijing's leverage over Taiwan and caused an erosion of the island's democracy. As cross-strait military and economic balances shift toward China's favor, Taiwan's freedom of action has become diminished. Such a scenario has threatened to constrain Taipei to follow a path leading to accommodation of and eventual unification with China.[30] This, as a result, contradicted American interests in a peaceful and consensual resolution of the Taiwan Strait tension since the Ma administration's

---

[29] Thomas Christensen, "The Contemporary Security Dilemma," *The Washington Quarterly* 25, no. 4 (2002), p. 19.

[30] Robert Sutter, "More American Attention to Taiwan amid Heightened Competition with China," pp. 6–7.

pro-mainland initiatives were "moving against" the "trajectory of mainstream Taiwanese public opinion" which is "moving away from identification with China and support for unification."[31] Many societal actors in Taiwan, as noted in Chap. 4, asserted that the KMT administration entered into these economic agreements without allowing for much public scrutiny, and that many of the so-called peace dividends only benefited the rich business tycoons and entrepreneurs instead of accruing in the general increase of wealth or income for the average middle- and lower-income citizens.

Domestic political oppositions and civil-societal groups in Taiwan gained ascending momentum to challenge Ma's pro-China policy, as demonstrated by the Sunflower students' movement in March 2014 to occupy Taiwan's Legislative Yuan to block the Cross-Strait Service Trade Agreement and the KMT's devastating losses in the local elections of November 2014.[32] In August 2015, hundreds of high school students stormed the Ministry of Education to protest the government's initiatives of "fine-tuning" history textbooks and curriculum (see Chap. 4). The youth accused the KMT of attempting to "brainwash" them into accepting a "one-China" view of history.[33] Chapter 1 has discussed that the historic summit between Xi Jinping and Ma Ying-jeou, the first ever top leadership meeting between the two sides since 1949, in November 2015 sought to further consolidate the "one-China" core of the "1992 consensus" and rally the electoral prospect of the failing KMT. Yet, the Xi–Ma meeting did not enhance the prospects of the New Taipei City mayor, the then KMT chairman and also presidential candidate, Eric Chu. Despite replacing the less popular Hung Hsiu-chu (who was chosen initially by the KMT primary in July 2015 to run for the presidency) as the ultimate presidential contender, Chu was soundly defeated by the DPP Tsai Ing-wen in January 2016. The DPP has also won a decisive majority in the Legislative Yuan, ushering in an age of the DPP-controlled unified government over both the executive and legislative branches.

---

[31] Christopher Hughes, "Revisiting Identity Politics under Ma Ying-jeou," in Jean-Pierre Cabestan and Jacques deLisle eds., *Political Changes in Taiwan under Ma Ying-jeou* (New York: Routledge, 2014), pp. 130–131.

[32] Jonathan Sullivan, "The Battle for Taiwan's Soul: The 2016 Presidential Election," *The National Interest* (May 3, 2015), accessible at: http://nationalinterest.org/feature/the-battle-taiwans-soul-the-2016-presidential-election-12790.

[33] "Taiwan School Textbook Row Highlights Antipathy to 'One China,'" *The Reuters* (August 3, 2015), accessible at: http://www.reuters.com/article/2015/08/03/us-taiwan-politics-education-idUSKCN0Q806820150803.

Meanwhile, America's attitude toward the Xi–Ma summit, though welcoming, was based on a note of caution. The closeness manifested by the KMT and CCP inevitably created an impression that both leaders were attempting to create a "united front" on various issues that may contradict American interests and Taiwan's security. Writing in 2014, Lowell Dittmer stated, "[Though] a stabilization of cross-strait relations has been welcomed by Washington, the prospect of anything approaching a Taiwan-China 'marriage' would be highly detrimental to Taiwan's defense prospects against the country that is still its foremost national security threat while jeopardizing its security relations with the sole guarantor of its survival as a sovereign entity."[34] Richard Bush also aptly described, in early 2015, the delicate position the Ma government had presented to the United States:

> A Taiwan that, on the one hand, acts toward Beijing in a manner consistent with U.S. interests (by reassuring Beijing that it has no intention of challenging China's fundamental goals and by seeking to broaden the scope of cross-strait cooperation), yet, on the other, remains *skeptical of Beijing's unification formula remains worthy of American support* because it will be significant element in America's effort constructively to address the rise of China.[35]

Hence, just as the United States took the side of Beijing in 2007–08 to "temper provocative Democratic Progressive Party's moves toward formal independence,"[36] Washington, to stem the KMT's "tilt" toward Beijing, would find it imperative to strategically embrace Taiwanese nationalists in order to recalibrate cross-strait security balance. Although the United States reiterated its neutrality in Taiwan's 2016 presidential election, Washington's high-profile treatment of the DPP presidential candidate, Tsai Ing-wen, during her visit to America in June 2015 raised eyebrows in China and among the KMT leadership.[37] This, to be sure, does not

---

[34] Lowell Dittmer, "Taiwan's Narrowing Strait," pp. 26–27.

[35] Richard Bush, "U.S.–Taiwan Relations since 2008," p. 229. *Emphasis added*.

[36] Lowell Dittmer, "Taiwan's Narrowing Strait," p. 19.

[37] Eric Chu of the KMT also visited the United States in mid-November 2015, despite the compressed campaign timeframe resulted from his late declaration of candidacy. Like Tsai in June, Chu was also warmly greeted and accommodated by ranking Obama administration officials from the Department of State, Department of Defense, and the National Security Council. The KMT candidate held a closed-door meeting with prominent think-tank experts and specialists at the Brookings Institution. However, since Chu's visit followed immediately after the Xi–Ma meeting, his trip created the impression that he needed to reassure the

suggest that Washington is eschewing its enduring strategic ambiguity policy. Rather, pulling Taiwan away from the PRC orbit would be more compatible with US interests in continuing with that long-standing policy framework and sustaining its rebalance toward the Asia-Pacific.

2 INCREASING US WARINESS OF THE KMT'S "ONE-CHINA" POLICY

On numerous occasions, the United States has officially proclaimed that it does not interfere in Taiwan's internal political process or seek to influence Taiwanese democratic preferences. In the words of Daniel Russel, the US assistant secretary of state for East Asian and Far Eastern Affairs,

> Taiwan is a thriving democracy. And I think that is one of the things that American people love the best about Taiwan. We certainly respect that democracy, and we respect the right of the voters on Taiwan to make their own choices. For that reason, we don't take sides and we don't take actions that would imply that we are taking sides in any election. We respect the people of Taiwan and we respect their ability to select their own leaders.[38]

Nonetheless, to safeguard and promote its national interests, Washington has attempted to shape the domestic political arrangements and decision-making of its allies and adversaries. Indeed, all great powers have done this, as supported by the second-image reversed theory noted in Chap. 1, wishing to mold others' policies toward their liking.[39] Given Taiwan's vital position in US–China relations, it would come as no surprise if America

---

United States that the KMT's cross-strait policy had not deviated away from America's security interests. See Alison Hsiao, "Chu Has Messages from Ma for US: KMT Lawmaker," *Taipei Times* (November 12, 2015), accessible at: http://www.taipeitimes.com/News/front/archives/2015/11/12/2003632253. See also Debra Ma, "Why the Road to Taiwan's Presidency Runs through Washington," *Bloomberg Business* (November 13, 2015), accessible at: http://www.bloomberg.com/news/articles/2015-11-13/why-the-road-to-the-taiwan-presidency-runs-through-washington. "Chu Held Talks with U.S. Officials on Visit to Washington," *The Focus Taiwan News* (November 13, 2015), accessible at: http://focustaiwan.tw/news/aipl/201511130003.aspx.

[38] "Readout of Secretary Kerry's Travel to Beijing, Seoul, and Seattle, by Daniel Russel, Assistant Secretary, Bureau of East Asian and Far Eastern Affairs," The US Department of State (May 21, 2015), accessible at: http://fpc.state.gov/242635.htm.

[39] On how international power politics and economic relations shape states' domestic interests, institutions, and preferences, consult literatures on the "second-image reversed" theory discussed in Chap. 1.

were to voice its concerns when the island is making crucial choices regarding future association with Beijing. Richard Bush, the former chairman of the AIT and a seasoned observer on US–China–Taiwan relations, stated in September 2014 that the United States "has not been quiet on Taiwan's past presidential elections and will express its views on Taiwan's 2016 presidential election." "This is something we do. We feel there is a need for us to express our views on how our interests will be affected by Taiwan's elections. To say nothing, which some in Taiwan might want us to do, is actually meant as a statement as well," he remarked.[40] Though Bush's representations were immediately refuted by US officials as merely his personal and unofficial views,[41] one cannot entirely dismiss them. Recall that the George W. Bush administration rebuked Chen Shui-bian's referendum initiatives in the late 2000s and sternly cautioned Taipei against making any moves that would jeopardize its security relations with China and the United States.[42] The Hu–Bush conversations in March 2008 were repeatedly cited by President Ma Ying-jeou to underscore US–PRC's joint endorsement of the "1992 consensus."[43]

When the DPP presidential candidate Tsai Ing-wen traveled to the United States in September 2011 to campaign for her election bid in 2012, an anonymous senior-ranking Obama administration official told the *Financial Times* that Tsai's election "could raise tensions with China," adding that "she left us with distinct doubts about whether she is both willing and able to continue the stability in cross-strait relations the region has enjoyed in recent years."[44] Washington's "vote of no confidence," although

[40] "U.S. To Have Voice in Taiwan's 2016 Presidential Election: Bush," *Focus Taiwan News* (September 13, 2014), accessible at: http://m.focustaiwan.tw/news/aipl/201409130014.aspx. See also Richard Bush, "Taiwan's January 2016 Election and Their Implications for Relations with China and the United States," p. 19.

[41] "Washington Says Bush's Taiwan Remarks His Own," *Taipei Times* (September 18, 2014), accessible at: http://www.taipeitimes.com/News/taiwan/archives/2014/09/18/2003599986.

[42] "A Strong and Moderate Taiwan, by Thomas Christensen, Deputy Assistant Secretary for East Asian and Pacific Affairs," The US Department of State (September 11, 2007), accessible at: http://2001-2009.state.gov/p/eap/rls/rm/2007/91979.htm.

[43] "1992 Consensus Verified by History: Ma," *The China Post* (May 15, 2015), accessible at: http://www.chinapost.com.tw/taiwan/china-taiwan-relations/2015/05/15/436072/1992-Consensus.htm.

[44] "U.S. Concerned about Taiwan Candidate," *The Financial Times* (September 15, 2011), accessible at: http://www.ft.com/intl/cms/s/0/f926fd14-df93-11e0-845a-00144feabdc0.html#axzz3bm75hK48.

indirect, clearly played a significant part in the DPP's defeat in 2012 by sending the message that a Tsai administration would derail cross-strait peace and stability. These incidents took place when Sino-American relations were much more benign and cross-strait rapprochement on the basis of the "1992 consensus" did not contradict America's national interests.

KMT's "One China" and US Interests

Nevertheless, international power relations between Washington (as well as Tokyo, being America's staunchest security ally in Asia) and Beijing have transformed in recent years, particularly after tensions spiked over territorial disputes in the East and South China Seas. And, given the KMT's almost identical sovereign claims with Beijing over these areas, Taiwan's role in these disputes also had become complicated.

The Deterioration of Sino-Japanese Relations since Shinzo Abe's Reemergence in 2012

Five years of unstable leadership and political paralysis in Tokyo between 2007 and 2012 contributed to a slowdown in Japan's security policy reform (which has aimed at moving away from its pacific and defensive-oriented military posture imposed by the United States after WWII) and put a halt to some US–Japan defense initiatives that started after the end of the Cold War.[45] After the Liberal Democratic Party's resounding victory in the December 2012 election, however, Prime Minister Shinzo Abe (who briefly held that position as well in 2006–07) proposed the removal of important constitutional constraints on Japan's military and a revision of the educational system to encourage a stronger sense of patriotism among the country's young people.[46] Abe defended his policies by claiming that the country needed to respond to a series of missile provocations

---

[45] For a good overview of Japan's foreign and security affairs after WWII, see Roberto Bendini, *In-Depth Analysis: Japan Foreign and Security Policy at a Crossroads* (European Union: Directorate-General for External Policies Policy Department, August 2015), accessible at http://www.europarl.europa.eu/RegData/etudes/IDAN/2015/549065/EXPO_IDA(2015)549065_EN.pdf. See also Dennis Hickey and Lilly Kelan Lu, "Japan's Military Modernization: The Chinese Perspective," in James Hsiung ed., *China and Japan at Odds* (New York: Palgrave Macmillan, 2007); pp. 95–112; and Emma Chanlett-Avery and Ian Rinehart, *The U.S.–Japan Alliance* (Washington DC, Congressional Research Service, Feb 9, 2016), p. 2, accessible at https://www.fas.org/sgp/crs/row/RL33740.pdf.

[46] Roberto Bendini, *Japan Foreign and Security Policy at a Crossroads*, p. 12.

by Pyongyang and increasingly aggressive maritime advances and operations by Beijing in the East and South China Seas. He claimed that Japan must strengthen its military power in order to meet these new security challenges in the Asia-Pacific.[47] With respect to China, the prime minister stressed,

> We have an immediate neighbor [the PRC] whose military expenditure is at least twice as large as Japan's and second only to the U.S. defense budget. The country has increased its military expenditures, hardly transparent by more than 10 percent annually for more than 20 years since 1989. And then my government has increased its defense budget only by zero point eight percent. So call me, if you want, a right-wing militarist.[48]

In short, Abe now seeks to turn Japan into a more "normal" country by increasing the flexibility and capabilities of the Self Defense Forces (SDF).

In order to realize the goal of becoming a more "normal" country, the Abe administration made some meaningful modifications to Tokyo's security policy during 2014 and 2015. These changes include the following: (1) reinterpret Article 9 of the Constitution to allow for the exercise of the right of collective self-defense; (2) pass a package of security legislation that provides a new legal framework for the new interpretation; (3) modestly increase Japan's military budget; (4) relax Japan's previous bans on arms exports; (5) establish a National Security Council to facilitate decision-making on foreign policy; (6) pass a "state secrets" bill permitting more intelligence-sharing with the United States; and (7) commit political capital and resources to advance the US–Japan agreement to relocate a controversial marine airbase in Okinawa.[49]

In April 2015, the Obama and Abe governments both agreed to yet another revision of the US–Japan Military Defense Guidelines (the last was in September 1997). The new pact deepens alliance cooperation in a way that "more intricately intertwines U.S. and Japanese security, making it difficult to avoid involvement in each other's military engagements."[50] Advances in SDF capabilities gave Japan a potent deterrent power that complements the US forces, and both sides have deepened their bilat-

---

[47] Emma Chanlett-Avery and Ian Rinehart, *The U.S.-Japan Alliance*, p. 6.
[48] Quoted from Sheila Smith, *Intimate Rivals: Japanese Domestic Politics and a Rising China* (New York: Columbia University Press, 2016), p. 6.
[49] Emma Chanlett-Avery and Ian Rinehart, *The U.S.-Japan Alliance*, pp. 14–15.
[50] Ibid.

eral cooperation in areas like ballistic missile defense, cyber-security, and military use of space. With a more liberal interpretation of the Japanese Constitution, Tokyo will now more easily exercise the right of collective self-defense and come to the defense of the United States if its military and/or territories are under attack.[51] The PRC's rising global/regional influence and more assertive behavior in the East and South China Seas have served as a major impetus behind this closer security union.[52] For example, during his April 2014 visit to Japan, President Obama affirmed that the United States regards the Senkaku/Diaoyu Islands as falling under the purview of Article 5 in the US–Japan Security Treaty and promised that Washington would oppose any attempt to undermine Japan's control of the islands.[53] It is also noteworthy that Japan is one of the 12 active members of the American-proposed Trans-Pacific Partnership (TPP) free trade pact that, if enacted, will further solidify US economic connections with the Asia-Pacific.

These recent changes in US–Japan security and economic ties are transforming the strategic environment of the entire Asia-Pacific region, particularly in the face of a more powerful and influential China. However, to be sure, the Abe administration has confronted numerous difficulties in its quest to "come out" and become a "normal country." Japan's imperialist past (and its efforts to whitewash or glorify atrocities committed during the imperialist era) continues to drive a wedge between Tokyo and its neighbors. Both mainland China and South Korea view Abe's defense agenda with deep suspicion. Beijing and Seoul both contend that Japanese political elites have not learned and accepted the lessons of Japan's troubled past and that their apologies lack sincerity. Given that America's rebalancing or "pivot" policy to Asia depends, to a great extent, on more coordination between Tokyo and Seoul, such a gulf of mistrust will not be conducive to their strategic interests. Moreover, domestic political considerations in Japan pose another obstacle. While the Japanese people have felt the increasing sense of uncertainty and vulnerability in response to

---

[51] Ibid., p. 4.
[52] Ibid., pp. 9–10.
[53] Ankit Panda, "Obama: Senkakus Covered under U.S.–Japan Security Treaty," *The Diplomat* (April 24, 2014), at http://thediplomat.com/2014/04/obama-senkakus-covered-under-us-japan-security-treaty/. While backing Tokyo's effective administration over the Senkaku/Diaoyu Islands since 1971, the United States has refrained from taking a stance on the sovereignty issue, hence leaving China, Japan, and Taiwan asserting their respective sovereignty claims over these island territories.

China's rising military and economic clout, they have also voiced strong opposition to Abe's plan to pursue a more muscular foreign policy.[54] For example, Japan was rocked by protests and turmoil in 2015 when the Japanese Diet passed the Security Bills that helped to undergird the reinterpretation of Japan's pacifist constitution.

To mollify these sentiments, Abe now claims that Japan's exercise of its collective self-defense will be constitutional only when meeting three conditions: (1) when an armed attack against a foreign country that is in a close relationship with Japan occurs and as a result threatens Japan's survival and poses a clear danger to fundamentally overturn people's right to life, liberty, and pursuit of happiness; (2) when there is no other appropriate means available to repel the attack and ensure Japan's survival and protect its people; and (3) if Japan limits the use of force to the minimum extent necessary.[55] Although the language of these conditions appears ambiguous and seems to be crafted to allow flexibility when different security contingencies arise, it appears that institutional and domestic roadblocks could inhibit full implementation at least in the foreseeable future. In January 2016, Abe further reassured that Japan would not take part in America's campaign against the Islamic State of Iraq and Syria in the Middle East.[56]

In sum, Japan is now in a difficult position in world affairs. Despite Tokyo's declared intent to move forward with stronger defense capabilities and closer ties with the United States, the baggage of history continues to prevent it from making greater strides. This was perhaps best illustrated by President Obama's visit to Hiroshima in May 2016. (Abe also visited the Pearl Harbor in December 2016 to pay his respect and offered repentance for Japan's attack on December 7, 1941). On the one hand, it was unprecedented for an incumbent American president to pay tribute to the site where US warplanes dropped atomic bombs to end the Pacific War 71 years ago. Obama's gesture may have symbolized a new chapter in US–Japan relations and his commitment to eliminate nuclear weapons. On the other hand, the memories of the war cannot be so easily dispelled, as the president, knowing full well the feelings of other Asian countries, reiterated that he "was not going to apologize" but merely to

---

[54] Sheila Smith, *Intimate Rivals,* pp. 18–19.
[55] Emma Chanlett-Avery and Ian Rinehart, *The U.S.-Japan Alliance,* p. 4.
[56] Vladimir Terehov, "Japan's Foreign Policy Message of Early 2016," *New Eastern Outlook* (Feb 9, 2016), at http://journal-neo.org/2016/02/09/japan-s-foreign-policy-messages-of-early-2016/.

"pay respect to the Japanese people" and to bolster a very important alliance in the Asia-Pacific.[57]

The Senkaku/Diaoyu Islands in the East China Sea
Nevertheless, in spite of Tokyo's challenging tasks to balance between domestic political concerns, historical feuds, and coping with a rising China, Sino-Japanese relations have worsened in the East China Sea. Situations have turned more adversarial between both countries which have contested sovereignty over the Senkaku/Diaoyu Islands. In September 2010, after the Japanese Coastal Guard detained a Chinese fishing boat along with its captain and crew, for the latter's trawler struck two Japanese Coast Guard vessels near one of the Senkaku/Diaoyu Islands, Beijing reacted sharply to the standoff.[58] The Japanese authority released all the crew except the captain, announcing he would be subject to a judicial proceeding. The PRC retaliated by arresting four Japanese businessmen in western China and banned exporting to Japan rare-earth minerals, which are vital for the Japanese electronics and digital product assembly.[59] Although Tokyo relented and released the captain, this showdown not only rekindled Sino-Japanese rivalry over the Senkaku/Diaoyu Islands but also, in the words of Jeffrey Bader, demonstrated to the world that Beijing would be ready to "upend global trading arrangements and practices (regarding rare earths) in retaliation for what looked like a bilateral dispute and to give it international consequences."[60]

The KMT government of Ma Ying-jeou also took up anti-Japanese position on the issue, even though Taiwan's official stance was to remain neutral in between these great power rivalries. Indeed, starting in 2012, China and Japan have deepened their clashes over their respective sovereign claims on the Senkaku/Diaoyu Islands, sometimes edging close to military conflicts. Although, through his "East China Sea Peace Initiative," President Ma openly rejected teaming up with Beijing

---

[57] Gardiner Harris, "In Obama's Visit to Hiroshima, a Complex Calculus of Asian Politics," *The New York Times* (May 26, 2016), at http://www.nytimes.com/2016/05/26/world/asia/obama-hiroshima-visit.html.

[58] "Amid Tension, China's Blocks Vital Exports to Japan," The New York Times (September 22, 2010), accessible at: http://www.nytimes.com/2010/09/23/business/global/23rare.html.

[59] Jeffrey Bader, *Obama and China's Rise*, pp. 106–107.

[60] Ibid., p. 108.

to counter Tokyo's claim over these territories,[61] the ROC government unequivocally reaffirmed its "sovereignty" over the island islets and their nearby waters, thereby revealing Taipei's determination to not "cede even an inch of territory" and implicitly buttressing the Chinese position.[62] The KMT, as discussed in Chap. 1, has asserted the similar maritime claims as the CCP over the East and South China Seas.[63]

Hence, Taipei and Beijing are actually "on the same side" in dealing with these territorial issues.[64] In September 2012, after Japan's Noda government nationalized three of the eight Senkaku/Diaoyu Island islets, the ROC government lodged a strong protest and recalled its chief representative to Tokyo to return to Taiwan immediately. President Ma even flew out to the Pengjia Island in the vicinity of the Senkaku/Diaoyu Island chains to declare that Taipei would back up its commitment to defend the ROC sovereignty as well as to safeguard the security of fishermen. Taiwan's Coast Guard vessels were even dispatched to escort several Taiwanese fishing boats and, on several occasions, faced minor standoffs with the Japanese Coast Guard, resulting in a few hours of firing water cannons.[65]

---

[61] Interview with the MAC official, who requested to remain anonymous. President Ma, on August 5, 2012, broached the idea of an "East China Sea Peace Initiative," suggesting that all parties should "refrain from antagonistic conduct" and "shelve controversies," by establishing a mechanism for cooperation on jointly exploring and developing the region. See Tsai Zheng-jia, "ROC Takes Lead with East China Sea Peace Initiative," *Taiwan Today* (August 13, 2012); accessible at: http://taiwantoday.tw/ct.asp?xItem=194661&ctNode=426.

[62] Tuan Cheng, "Taiwan-U.S. Relations: Close but Uncertain," *China Report* 49, no. 4 (2013), p. 381.

[63] Bill Hayton, *The South China Sea* (New Haven: Yale University Press, 2014), pp. 97–98. See also Stein Tonnesson, "The South China Sea: Law Trumps Power," *Asian Survey* 55, no. 3 (May/June 2015), p. 462.

[64] Lowell Dittmer, "Taiwan's Narrowing Straits," p. 23. Chien-peng Chung, *Domestic Politics, International Bargaining and China's Territorial Disputes* (New York: Routledge, 2004), pp. 28–31. This point was also confirmed by a DPP official who requested to remain anonymous during my interview. The official mentioned that Ma's policy has been quite hostile toward Japan.

[65] For a good sketch of the Senkaku/Diaoyu contentions between the PRC, Taiwan, and Japan after 2012, see Wei-chin Lee, "A Quartet in Disharmony: Taiwan, Japan, China, and the U.S. in the Diaoyu(Tai)/Senkaku Islands Disputes in the 2010s," *American Journal of Chinese Studies* (Special Issue, 2014), pp. 95–109; and Chong-Pin Lin, "Behind Rising East Asian Maritime Tensions with China: Struggle without Breaking," *Asian Survey* 55, no. 3 (May/June 2015), pp. 480–483.

Obviously, Beijing "welcomed Taiwan's assertiveness, not only because it supported China's historically based claims to the territory in question but because of the potential merger of Chinese and Taiwanese national identities [a pan-Chinese solidarity]."[66] Ma's "one-China" stance has created such an impression even though the president was keenly aware that "any explicit move or coordination with China would put Taiwan awkwardly between China's hope of using the dispute as opportunity to mold its 'one China' principle into Taiwan's policy discourses on the one side and the U.S.-Japan anxiety of Taiwan's drifting inches closer to China's embrace on the other side."[67] In order to prevent Taiwan from bandwagoning with the PRC, Japan negotiated a fisheries agreement with Taipei in April 2013 to accord benefits and protections to Taiwan's fishermen.[68] Though Washington had persistently claimed that it did not take any position on the question of sovereignty, the Obama administration stated that the Senkaku/Diaoyu Islands would fall under Article 5 of the US–Japanese Security Treaty, which authorizes the United States to help defend areas and territories under Japanese administration.[69] As tensions mounted in 2013, the Ma government refrained from getting involved. For instance, in November 2013, Taipei, while expressing "serious concern" about Beijing's recently imposed air defense identification zone, issued only a relatively mild condemnation. Both Washington and Tokyo were disappointed by Taiwan's lack of stronger reaction toward Beijing's unilateral behavior.[70] Taiwan's actions "were perceived as deviating from

[66] Lowell Dittmer, "Taiwan's Narrowing Straits," p. 24.

[67] Wei-chin Lee, "A Quartet in Disharmony," p. 105.

[68] Ryo Sahashi, "Japan–Taiwan Relations since 2008: An Evolving practical, Non-Strategic Partnership," in Jean-Pierre Cabestan and Jacques deLisle, eds., *Political Changes in Taiwan under Ma Ying-jeou,* pp. 232–246. See also Katherine Tseng Hui-Yi, "New Challenges to the New Leadership: The Deterioration of the Diaoyu Island Dispute," in Zheng Yongnian and Lance Gore, eds., *China Entering the Xi Jinping Era* (New York: Routledge, 2015), pp. 285–302.

[69] Tuan Cheng, "Taiwan–U.S. Relations," p. 381. See also "Joint Press Conference with President Obama and Prime Minister Abe of Japan," *The White House* (April 24, 2014), accessible at: http://www.whitehouse.gov/photos-and-video/video/2014/04/24/president-obama-holds-press-conference-prime-minister-abe-japan#transcript.

[70] J. Michael Cole, "China's ADIZ: Taiwan's Dilemma," *The Diplomat* (November 28, 2013), accessible at: http://thediplomat.com/2013/11/chinas-adiz-taiwans-dilemma/. See also Shannon Tiezzi, "Why China's Air Defense Identification Zone Is Terrible for Cross-Strait Relations," *The Diplomat* (November 28, 2013), accessible at: http://thediplomat.com/2013/11/why-chinas-air-defense-identification-zone-is-terrible-for-cross-strait-relations/.

American interest in East Asia."[71] Dittmer aptly summed up the complex relationships:

> Taiwan is increasingly integrated with the mainland in economic and commercial terms while its security interests are underwritten by the United States with the indispensable logistical support of Japan. Ma's longstanding [ideological] convictions have brought him into support of China's territorial claims, to the dismay of both Tokyo and Washington. Taipei has been trying to reinterpret its position on sovereignty issues in more innocuous and conciliatory terms while reaffirming its security commitments. But, it is a delicate balance.[72]

The South China Sea Contentions: The "Nine-Dashed Line" versus Freedom of Navigation

In the early and mid-2000s, Beijing wished to assure the regional and international communities that its rise is peaceful and cooperative, conducive to stability and economic "win-win" for all while seeking to dampen suspicions incurred from China's aggressive behaviors in the Taiwan Strait and South China Sea territorial competitions during the mid-1990s.[73] The crisis of Mischief Reef (located just west of Palawan and claimed by the Philippines), for instance, was instigated by Beijing in late 1994 as it unilaterally occupied and built living structures on it. The incident pitted China against the Association of Southeast Asian Nations (ASEAN), which was in the process of expanding its membership to include Vietnam, Laos, Myanmar, and Cambodia. Nonetheless, as both parties decided to de-escalate, the Mischief Reef contention was actually, in the words of one observer, followed by the "most constructive of all periods in South China Sea diplomacy." Indeed, Beijing and Hanoi reached agreement on their land border (1999) as well as on their maritime boundary in the Gulf of Tonkin (2000). China and ASEAN agreed in 2002 on a Declaration of Conduct, which included a pledge to "refrain from action of inhabiting on the presently uninhabited islands, reefs, shoals, cays, and other features."[74]

However, probably due to its renewed confidence after emerging relatively unharmed from the 2008 global financial crisis and its successful hosting of the Summer Olympics, Beijing has begun to talk about

---

[71] Tuan Cheng, "Taiwan-U.S. Relations," p. 381.
[72] Lowell Dittmer, "Taiwan's Narrowing Straits," pp. 27–28.
[73] Bill Hayton, *The South China Sea*, pp. 86–89.
[74] Stein Tonnesson, "The South China Sea," p. 469.

America's "declining power." The Chinese leadership felt that the PRC "did not need to suppress its ambitions. It should assume a leadership role. It should use the leverage provided by its wealth, not least in relation to the United States, which owed it over a trillion dollars. It should utilize the military assets it had begun to develop in the past two decades to project Chinese strength abroad and to undercut American influence."[75] The increasingly contentious US–Chinese relations and a spike in tensions in Asia after 2010 raised questions about whether an ascending China would continue its peaceful development policy or embrace a more confrontation approach toward regional and international affairs.[76] The Obama administration was wary of Beijing's reluctance to more actively cooperate with Washington in addressing their economic policy disagreements, Iran and North Korea's nuclear ambitions, climate change, and humanitarian crises in Libya and Syria. Both Washington and Seoul, for instance, were dismayed by Beijing's inaction in pressuring North Korea to account for its provocations in March and November 2010, which were, respectively, the sinking of the South Korean ship *Cheonan* and firing artillery shells at the Yeonpyeong Island. These episodes resulted in South Korean military and civilian casualties.[77]

With respect to the South China Sea, in March 2009, Chinese vessels "shadowed and aggressively maneuvered" in dangerously close proximity to the *USNS Impeccable* to harass the American oceanic surveillance ship while it was conducting routine operations in China's EEZ off Hainan Island.[78] Washington maintained the legality of this mission under the UNCLOS, whereas Beijing challenged that US naval activities clearly violated the PRC sovereignty. Similar dangerously near-colliding encounters have persisted ever since as US naval ships have continued their operations in the vicinity of the South China Sea. Beijing also took up more restrictive and belligerent actions against fishing boats from Vietnam and other nearby states in the region.[79] In May 2009, for the first time, the PRC attached to an official diplomatic communication to the UN its map with the

---

[75] Jeffrey Bader, *Obama and China's Rise*, p. 81.
[76] Avery Goldstein, "U.S.-China Interactions in Asia," in David Shambaugh ed., *Tangled Titans* (Lanham, MD: Rowman & Littlefield, 2013), pp. 263–264.
[77] Ibid., p. 270.
[78] "U.S. Accuses the Chinese of Harassing Naval Vessel," *The New York Times* (March 9, 2009), accessible at: http://www.nytimes.com/2009/03/09/world/asia/09iht-ship.3.20710715.html?_r=0.
[79] Chong-Pin Lin, "Behind Rising East Asian Maritime Tensions with China," p. 485.

"Nine-Dashed Line" to promote its territorial and maritime claims over almost the entire South China Sea. This initiative generated protests from many nearby Southeast Asian countries exerting their respective claims, including Malaysia, Vietnam, Indonesia, Brunei, and the Philippines.[80]

Responding to Beijing's acts, the Obama administration opted for a more hardline position toward China. At the July 2010 ASEAN Regional Forum (ARF) meeting in Hanoi, the then Secretary of State Hillary Clinton pushed back against China's intransigence over the South China Sea conflicts by affirming America's interest in ensuring freedom of passage through international waters and peaceful resolution of sovereignty disputes. The implicit message was to warn China that "it should not assume its material advantage over smaller ASEAN states would enable it to get its way in settling the disputes bilaterally."[81]

She noted: "The United States supports a collaborative diplomatic process by all claimants for resolving the various territorial disputes without coercion. We oppose the use or threat of force by any claimant. While the United States does not take sides on the competing territorial disputes over land features in the South China Sea, we believe claimants should pursue their territorial claims and accompanying rights to maritime space in accordance with the UN Convention on the Law of the Sea [UNCLOS]. Consistent with customary international law, legitimate claims to maritime space in the South China Sea should be derived solely from legitimate claims to land features."[82]

Furthermore, on November 17, 2011, President Obama, in his speech to the Australian Parliament, announced America's rebalancing or "pivot" to the Asia Pacific after winding down the decade-long US war on terrorism in Iraq and Afghanistan. Explaining America's interests in the region's peace, stability, and prosperity, he remarked, "The United States has been, and always will be a Pacific nation. ... As the world's fastest growing region—and home to more than half the global economy—the Asia Pacific is critical to achieving my highest priority, and that's creating jobs and opportunity for the American people. With most of the world's nuclear power and some half of humanity, Asia will largely define

---

[80] Stein Tonnesson, "The South China Sea," p. 464.
[81] Avery Goldstein, "U.S.-China Interactions in Asia," p. 273.
[82] Secretary Clinton's remarks at the ARF are quoted from Bill Hayton, *The South China Sea*, p. 191.

whether the century ahead will be marked by conflict or cooperation."[83] In a *Foreign Policy* article, Secretary Clinton summarized that the Obama administration's "pivot" would proceed along "six key lines of action: strengthening bilateral security alliances; deepening [US] working relationships with emerging powers, including with China; engaging with regional multilateral institutions; expanding trade and investment; forging a broad-based military presence; and advancing democracy and human right."[84] The "pivot," then, is a multifaceted grand strategy that encompasses the security, economic, diplomatic, and normative dimensions.[85]

Without a doubt, Washington is targeting at China's emergence in the twenty-first century, which has posed greater security and economic challenges to the United States and its allies in the Asia-Pacific.[86] Given the increasingly competitive relationship between Washington and Beijing,[87] both powers naturally seek to gain greater power and security relative to each other. As a response, Washington has resorted to a balancing or hedging strategy to "protect, and whenever possible to expand, the extant U.S. advantages in relative power." A key component is to "support the rise of other Asian powers located along China's periphery."[88] Though

---

[83] "Remarks by President Obama to the Australian Parliament," The White House—Office of the Press Secretary (November 17, 2011), accessible at: http://www.whitehouse.gov/the-press-office/2011/11/17/remarks-president-obama-australian-parliament.

[84] Hillary Clinton, "America's Pacific Century," *Foreign Policy* (November 2011), accessible at: http://www.foreignpolicy.com/articles/2011/10/11/americas_pacific_century. Clinton essentially coined the term "pivot" in this article. See also Mark Manyin, et al., "Pivot to the Pacific? The Obama Administration's 'Rebalancing' toward Asia," Congressional Research Service Report for Congress (March 28, 2012), pp. 1–29.

[85] For a detailed analysis on each of these dimensions, see Robert Sutter et al., "Balancing Acts: The U.S. Rebalance and Asian Pacific Stability," Sigur Center for Asian Studies (August 2013), pp. 11–16.

[86] Chris Buckley, "Xi Jinping's Rapid Rise in China Presents Challenges to the U.S.," *The New York Times* (November 11, 2014), accessible at: http://www.nytimes.com/2014/11/12/world/asia/president-xi-jinping-makes-it-his-mission-to-empower-china.html.

[87] Aaron Friedberg, *A Contest for Supremacy*; Avery Goldstein, "First Thing First: The Pressing Danger of Crisis Instability in U.S.-China Relations," *International Security* 37, no. 4 (Spring 2013), pp. 49–89. See also John Mearsheimer, "The Gathering Storm: China's Challenge to U.S. Power in Asia," *The Chinese Journal of International Politics* 3 (2010), pp. 381–396, and Ashley Tellis, "U.S.-China Relations in a Realist World," in David Shambaugh, ed., *Tangled Titans*, pp. 75–100.

[88] Ashley Tellis, "Balancing without Containment: A U.S. Strategy for Confronting China's Rise," *The Washington Quarterly* 36, no. 4 (2013), pp. 111–112.

acting tougher on the PRC, the Obama administration had, on numerous occasions, reassured Beijing that America "does not seek the containment of China, as the case with the Soviet Union, both because of the inherent differences between those two nations and because of the hopelessness of pursuing such a policy toward a country that was much more profoundly integrated into the global system."[89]

Since Beijing's "Nine-Dashed Line" assertion of sovereignty over the South China Sea is built upon a Chinese map, entitled "Map of South China Sea Islands," published in 1947 (though it was called the "Eleven-Dashed Line" then) when Chiang Kai-shek's Kuomintang government was still ruling the mainland,[90] the PRC and ROC are actually in unison on this issue despite the Ma administration's refusal to cooperate with Beijing on exerting those rights.[91] The KMT and CCP's shared commitment to China's nationalistically historical claim can be seen by Chiang Kai-shek's Nanjing KMT regime using "national humiliation" as a unifying idea to bring the country together and to assert sovereignty over territories (whether real or imagined) lost to the Western and Japanese imperialist powers.[92] Indeed, the Ma Ying-jeou government's attitude had been quite ambivalent. On the one hand, Taipei noted that its claims are more limited than Beijing's and, which would be conforming to the UNCLOS, that is, its claims are restricted to islands and 3–12 nautical miles of their adjacent waters.[93] On the other hand, the KMT administration also suggested that Taiwan's sovereignty over the South China Sea, based on the 1947 map, is actually more expansive, covering all the islands, reefs, and shoals as well as their surrounding waters.[94] The US State Department, in a report issued in December

[89] Jeffrey Bader, *Obama and China's Rise*, p. 69.
[90] See the US Department of State, Bureau of Oceans and International Environmental and Scientific Affairs, *Limits in the Sea No. 143, China: Maritime Claims in the South China Sea* (The US Department of State Report, December 5, 2014), accessible at: http://www.state.gov/documents/organization/234936.pdf. Bill Hayton, *The South China Sea*, Chapter 2.
[91] Shannon Tiezzi, "Taiwan's South China Sea Headache," *The Diplomat* (November 4, 2015), accessible at: http://thediplomat.com/2015/11/taiwans-south-china-sea-headache/. See also Zheng Wang, "Chinese Discourse on the 'Nine-Dashed Line': Rights, Interests, and Nationalism," *Asian Survey* (May/June 2015), pp. 502–524.
[92] Bill Hayton, *The South China Sea*, p. 53.
[93] Lynn Kuok, "Tides of Change: Taiwan's Evolving Position in the South China Sea and Why Other Actors Should Take Notice," East Asia Policy Paper No. 5 (Washington DC: The Center for East Asia Policy Studies at Brookings Institution, May 2015), p. 6. See also "Joining the Dashes," *The Economist* (October 4, 2014), accessible at: http://www.economist.com/news/asia/21621844-south-china-seas-littoral-states-will-fight-museums-archives-and.
[94] Lynn Kuok, "Tides of Change," p. 7.

2014, challenged the "Nine-Dashed Line," stressing that "unless China clarifies that the dashed-line claim reflects only a claim to islands within that line and any maritime zones that are generated from those land features in accordance with the international law of the sea, [as reflected in UNCLOS], its dashed-line claim does not accord with the international law of the sea."[95]

Moreover, America refuted against Beijing (or Taipei) using history as the basis of maritime jurisdiction, except in a narrow category of near-shore "historic bays" and "historical title" in the context of territorial sea boundary delimitation.[96] Indeed, the complexity of competing historical claims (among the regional states there) over the South China Sea makes it highly unlikely that history can ever prevail over international legal arguments which must be based on concrete evidence of continuous and effective occupation of the territorial and maritime features.[97] Thus, if Taiwan would take the more restrained approach, by following the UNCLOS, it would be more in tune with Washington's interests toward the South China Sea contention, thereby de-legitimizing Beijing's open-ended position.[98] Nevertheless, while being ambiguous to avoid antagonizing Beijing and Washington,[99] President Ma did not go so far as to explicitly renounce the "Nine or Eleven-Dashed Line." Doing so would repudiate the one

---

[95] US Department of State, Bureau of Oceans and International Environmental and Scientific Affairs, *Limits in the Sea*, p. 24.

[96] Ibid., pp. 19–22.

[97] Bill Hayton, *The South China Sea*, p.99. See also the US Department of State, Bureau of Oceans and International Environmental and Scientific Affairs, *Limits in the Sea No. 143, China: Maritime Claims in the South China Sea* (The US Department of State Report, December 5, 2014), accessible at: http://www.state.gov/documents/organization/234936.pdf.

[98] "Joining the Dashes."

[99] Lynn Kuok, "Tides of Change," p. 9. Shannon Tiezzi, "Taiwan Will Not Cooperate with China in South China Sea," *The Diplomat* (May 15, 2014), accessible at: http://thediplomat.com/2014/05/taiwan-will-not-cooperate-with-china-in-south-china-sea/. To be sure, on May 26, 2015, the Ma administration issued the "South China Sea Peace Initiative," calling all claimants to shelve disputes over sovereignty and cooperate on sharing natural resources. This is based on President Ma's "East China Sea Peace Initiative" proclaimed in August 2012 to urge China and Japan to exercise restraint on the disputed Senkaku/Diaoyu Islands. See "Taiwan Offers South China Sea Peace Plan," The Reuters (May 26, 2015), accessible at: http://www.reuters.com/article/2015/05/26/us-taiwan-south-china-sea-idUSKBN0OA16420150526.

Bill Hayton, *The South China Sea*, p.99. See also the US Department of State, Bureau of Oceans and International Environmental and Scientific Affairs, *Limits in the Sea No. 143, China: Maritime Claims in the South China Sea* (The US Department of State Report, December 5, 2014), accessible at: http://www.state.gov/documents/organization/234936.pdf.

China core of the "1992 consensus" framework jointly upheld by the KMT and CCP.¹⁰⁰

In 2014 and 2015, Beijing's land reclamation initiatives on islands and reefs in the South China Sea escalated the prospect of military confrontations with claimants in the region and threatened to drag the United States into the fray.¹⁰¹ By late October 2015, less than two weeks before the Xi–Ma summit, the Obama administration dispatched a guided-missile destroyer, the *USS Lassen*, to travel within 12 nautical miles of the Chinese-controlled Subi Reef in the South China Sea on a freedom of navigation patrol to challenge the PRC's "Nine-Dashed Line" position that essentially claims the entire South China Sea within its territorial and maritime borders.¹⁰² At the same time, the PCA in The Hague also accepted the case brought forward by the Philippines to discuss and rule whether the Chinese "Nine-Dashed Line" is even legitimate under the UNCLOS. In July 2016, the PCA ruled against the Chinese (as well as the ROC's) claims over the South China Sea, and Chap. 6 will look at the responses of Taiwan's new Tsai Ing-wen government.

The Ma Ying-jeou administration staunchly stood by the "1992 consensus" as the bedrock foundation to deal with Beijing. The KMT won itself no favor from the United States by following closely to the "Dashed-Line" position. Nevertheless, the KMT also could not abandon this since it would explicitly undermine the legitimacy of any Chinese claim to the dashed line as national boundary or enclosing historic rights and put China in a bad light.¹⁰³ Against this backdrop, many American domestic actors, such as congressional elites, scholars, and commentators, wanted to "push against the White House's restraint," calling on the Obama government to "reinforce U.S. interests in Taiwan."¹⁰⁴ This have included recommendations on selling more advanced weapons to Taiwan and more vocal American support

---

¹⁰⁰ Lynn Kuok, "Tides of Change," p. 13.

¹⁰¹ "South China Sea: Try Not to Blink," *The Economist* (May 30, 2015), accessible at: http://www.economist.com/news/asia/21652348-china-asserts-itself-naval-and-air-power-and-america-responds-risks.

¹⁰² Helene Cooper, "Challenging Chinese Claims, U.S. Sends Warships near Artificial Island Chain," *The New York Times* (October 26, 2015), accessible at: http://www.nytimes.com/2015/10/27/world/asia/challenging-chinese-claims-us-sends-warship-near-artificial-island-chain.html.

¹⁰³ Christopher Hughes, "Revisiting Identity Politics under Ma Ying-jeou," p. 127. See also Lowell Dittmer, "Taiwan's Narrowing Strait," pp. 24–27.

¹⁰⁴ Robert Sutter, "Hardening Competition with China—Implications for U.S. Taiwan Policy," *China & U.S. Focus Digest* (September 5, 2014), accessible at: http://www.chinausfocus.com/foreign-policy/hardening-competition-with-china-implications-for-us-taiwan-policy/.

of the DPP and other opposition parties in Taiwan's 2016 elections.[105] The US Congress continued to pass legislation and hold hearings to urge the Obama administration in various ways to encourage Taiwan's democratization, to meet Taiwan's self-defense needs, and to assist with Taiwan's bid to participate in regional economic integration and international organizations, including the US-backed TPP free trade agreement. Furthermore, the numbers of congressional members visiting Taiwan and the stature of these member visits have increased.[106] Furthermore, in 2015, the US Congress urged the Obama administration to permit active duty US generals and flag officers to be able to visit Taiwan and step up military cooperation with Taiwanese military officials. In 2016, the House of Representatives and Senate also formally incorporated, for the first time, both the TRA and President Reagan's Six Assurances in a concurrent congressional resolution reaffirming US commitments to the defense of Taiwan's security and democracy.[107]

On the South China Sea territorial disputes, many US analysts and former government officials have called on Taiwan to behave more responsibly on the matter. Jeffrey Bader, for instance, argued that, as the original creator of the so-called Eleven/Nine-Dashed Line in the late 1940s to designate Chinese claims over most of the South China Sea, the ROC government on Taiwan should "reevaluate its position in line with existing international law." If Taiwan were to do this, it would "demonstrate the extremity and unreasonableness of China's current claim, pushing Beijing to do a similar revaluation."[108] Nonetheless, as already noted, President Ma

---

[105] Robert Sutter, "More American Attention to Taiwan amid Heightened Tension with China," p. 12.

[106] Ibid.

[107] William Lowther, "U.S. Senate Reaffirms TRA, 'Six Assurances,'" *Taipei Times* (July 9, 2016), accessible at: http://www.taipeitimes.com/News/taiwan/archives/2016/07/09/2003650668.

[108] Robert Sutter, "Hardening Competition with China—Implications for U.S. Taiwan Policy." See Jeffrey Bader, "The U.S. and China's Nine-Dash Line: Ending the Ambiguity," Brookings Institution (Feb 6, 2014), accessible at: http://www.brookings.edu/research/opinions/2014/02/06-us-china-nine-dash-line-bader. See also William Lowther, "Glaser Urges Ma to be Proactive in South China Sea," *Taipei Times* (April 17, 2014), accessible at: http://www.taipeitimes.com/News/taiwan/archives/2014/04/17/2003588239; and Bill Hayton, *The South China Sea*, p. 265. Hayton posited, "The chances of a freer debate on Chinese history are much greater in Taiwan than on the mainland. There are already a number of 'dissident' academics in rethinking aspects of twentieth-century history. Taiwan is also where the archives of the Republic of China, the government that first drew up the 'U-shaped [Dashed] line,' are stored. An open and thorough examination of the haphazard process through which the line came to be drawn might convince opinion-formers to reexamine some of the nationalist myths they have long declared to be gospel truth."

showed little interest in clarifying the ROC's "Dashed Line" position, for fear of aggravating China and compromising the KMT's own "one-China" ruling political legitimacy. In October 2015, the then KMT presidential candidate, Eric Chu, also noted that he and his party would not "stand behind the United States" on the South China Sea dispute, while Tsai Ing-wen sounded more in tune with America's position on the matter as she suggested that "all parties should put forth their proposals and state their stances based on the legal principles of the United Nations Convention on the Law of the Sea."[109] The KMT's seeming passivity and half-hearted efforts to defend against an assertive PRC disappointed some long-time American supporters of Taiwan and reinforced the notion that the island will inevitably capitulate to Beijing's economic and military power.[110]

The Obama Administration's Push Back against the "1992 Consensus"

Responding to these concerns regarding Taiwan's security and China's increasing belligerence, the Obama administration displayed greater unease on the KMT's peaceful overtures to Beijing. American officials admonished Taipei against leaning too intimately toward China at the expense of Taiwan's interests and security. Assistant Secretary Russel warned that cross-strait bilateral exchanges should be done "at a pace acceptable to people on both sides of the strait" and "free from coercion."[111] In an interview with Taiwan's *Business Weekly* in June 2014, former secretary of state Hillary Clinton noted that President Ma's push for closer cross-strait relations could "lead to Taiwan losing its economic and political independence and becoming vulnerable to overreliance on China."[112]

---

[109] "KMT, DPP Presidential Candidates Comment on South China Sea Strategy," *The Focus Taiwan News* (October 28, 2015), accessible at: http://focustaiwan.tw/news/aipl/201510280032.aspx.

[110] John J. Mearsheimer, "Taiwan's Dire Straits," *The National Interest* (March/April 2014), pp. 29–39.

[111] "Testimony of Daniel R. Russel, Assistant Secretary of State, Bureau of East Asian and Pacific Affairs, U.S. Department of State before the Senate Committee on Foreign Relations Subcommittee on East Asian and Pacific Affairs," (April 3, 2014), accessible at: http://www.foreign.senate.gov/imo/media/doc/Russel_Testimony1.pdf.

[112] Jason Pan, "Reliance on China Makes Taiwan Vulnerable: Clinton," *Taipei Times* (June 25, 2014), accessible at: http://www.taipeitimes.com/News/front/archives/2014/06/25/2003593606. For the original interview transcript, see *Business Weekly* no. 1389 (June 30, 2014–July 6, 2014), pp. 58–73.

She advised Taiwan to decide on its relations with China "carefully and smartly." President Obama expressed his support for greater cross-strait contacts but emphasized that they should be carried out "on the basis of dignity and respect."[113]

In a similar vein, commenting on Eric Chu's visit to Beijing and meeting with Xi Jinping in May 2015, the US State Department suggested that the "pace and scope of [cross-strait] interactions should be acceptable to people on both sides of the strait." The KMT and CCP leaders both promised to continue and strengthen cross-strait peaceful development and economic exchanges on the basis of the "1992 consensus."[114] In particular, Chu noted that Taiwan wishes to participate in the Beijing-led AIIB and the RCEP. He added that Taiwan aspires to "play a greater role in the global community, [and that] the two sides should cooperate to reach out to the Asia Pacific and work together on regional peace, environmental protection, and economic cooperation based on the '1992 consensus.'"[115] Following Ma Ying-jeou's cross-strait position, the KMT chairman described that under the "1992 consensus," both Taiwan and China "belong to one China but with each side ascribing different contents and definitions to the concept of one China."[116]

Xi welcomed his counterpart's adherence to the "1992 consensus" and urged both the KMT and CCP to "share the sacred responsibility to realize the revival of the Chinese nation, improve people's welfare, and safeguard peace across the strait."[117] Indeed, in March 2015, Xi Jinping warned Taiwan that failure to accept the "one-China" core of the "1992

---

[113] "Remarks by President Obama and President Xi Jinping in Joint Press Conference," The White House-Office of the Press Secretary (November 12, 2014), accessible at: http://www.whitehouse.gov/the-press-office/2014/11/12/remarks-president-obama-and-president-xi-jinping-joint-press-conference.

[114] Austin Ramzy, "Chinese Leader and Head of Taiwan's Kuomintang Discuss Economy and Disaster Response," *The New York Times* (May 4, 2015), accessible at: http://sinosphere.blogs.nytimes.com/2015/05/04/eric-chu-xi-jinping-kuomintang-china-taiwan/?_r=0. For formal KMT press release on Eric Chu's opening remarks during his meeting with Xi Jinping, see http://www.kmt.org.tw/2015/05/blog-post_78.html.

[115] "Chu, Xi, Looking Forward to Greater Cross-Strait Cooperation," *Focus Taiwan News* (May 4, 2015), accessible at: http://focustaiwan.tw/news/acs/201505040014.aspx.

[116] "KMT Chief Calls for Continued Cooperation across Taiwan Strait," *Focus Taiwan News* (May 4, 2015), accessible at: http://focustaiwan.tw/news/acs/201505040012.aspx.

[117] "Xi Calls on Building Community of Shared Destiny across the Taiwan Strait," *The Xinhua News Agency* (May 4, 2015), accessible at: http://news.xinhuanet.com/english/2015-05/04/c_134208776.htm.

consensus" would undermine mutual trust and lead back to the "old path of turbulence." He added that "it is frequently said that 'if the foundation is not sturdy, the earth will move and the mountains will shake.'"[118] At the Xi–Ma summit, the Chinese leader repeatedly talked about the importance of upholding the "1992 consensus," and such insistence would continue well after Tsai had become Taiwan's president. Although, as we discussed in Chap. 3, Beijing has tended to de-emphasize KMT's long-standing OCRI initiative to represent "one China" as the ROC, the Ma administration's acceptance of "one China" as a foundational premise for cross-strait engagements was "good enough" for the CCP authority.[119] The DPP charged that Chu was effectively plunging Taiwan into Beijing's "one-China framework" by conceding and limiting the island's sovereignty and presence on the international stage.[120]

Washington, nevertheless, declined to take a clear stance on the "1992 consensus."[121] Refuting President Ma's claim that the "1992 consensus" was recognized and agreed upon by mainland China, Taiwan, and the United States,[122] the AIT (which is America's de facto embassy in Taiwan) affirmed that "the scope and nature of cross-strait interaction is for the two sides to decide … The U.S. takes no position on the substance of such matters."[123] In her speech at the Brookings Institution on May 21, 2015, Susan Thornton responded to reporters' queries regarding the "1992 consensus" by stating that "we want to see the continued stabile foundation and continuation of stable cross-strait ties … [But] as to the name given to that foundation, I don't think it's really appropriate

---

[118] Xi's remarks on the "1992 consensus" are quoted from Alan Romberg, "Squaring the Circle: Adhering to Principle, Embracing Ambiguity," *China Leadership Monitor* (July 2015), pp. 7–8.

[119] "Xi-Chu Meeting Consolidated Sino-Taiwanese Cooperation Framework," *Deutsche Welle* (May 4, 2015), accessible at: http://www.dw.de/xi-chu-meeting-consolidated-sino-taiwanese-cooperation-framework/a-18428392.

[120] "Opposition Party Raises Alarm over Chu-Xi Meeting," *Focus Taiwan News* (May 4, 2015), accessible at: http://focustaiwan.tw/news/aipl/201505040034.aspx.

[121] "Daily Press Briefing by Jeff Rathke," The US Department of State (May 4, 2015), accessible at: http://www.state.gov/r/pa/prs/dpb/2015/05/241844.htm#CHINA.

[122] "1992 Consensus Verified by History: Ma," *The China Post* (May 15, 2015), accessible at: http://www.chinapost.com.tw/taiwan/china-taiwan-relations/2015/05/15/436072/1992-Consensus.htm.

[123] "U.S. Takes No Stance on '1992 Consensus': AIT Spokesman," *The China Post* (May 16, 2015), accessible at: http://www.chinapost.com.tw/taiwan/china-taiwan-relations/2015/05/16/436153/US-takes.htm.

for the U.S. to either favor or disfavor."[124] On the same day, Assistant Secretary Russel made similar comments regarding the "1992 consensus," telling reporters that "the substance of where cross-strait relations go and the scope of the interactions between Taiwan and the mainland—those policy issues, number one, are for the people of Taiwan to decide what position they want to take; number two, for the candidates themselves to explain to the voters."[125] It is interesting to note as well that the Obama administration exhorted Beijing to demonstrate greater "flexibility and restraint" in managing peaceful and stable cross-strait relations with Taiwan.[126] This implied that Beijing should not impose the "1992 consensus" as the only and stringent precondition for deepening cross-strait ties, especially as the "one-China" rubric is not popularly accepted by all on the island.[127] In this author's interview with Robert Sutter, he observed that these are good indications that the United States may be taking a more reserved position on the "1992 consensus." There are other ways, aside from the "1992 consensus," that could be used to maintain cross-strait peace and stability even though Beijing would probably not like this.[128]

3   Tsai-Ing-wen's US Visit in 2015

Throughout her campaign, the DPP's Tsai Ing-wen asserted that her China policy would be predicated on "maintaining cross-strait status quo, preserving cross-strait peace, and continuing the current stable development of the cross-strait relations." To differentiate her platform from those of Chen Shui-bian and Ma Ying-jeou, the DPP leader specified that, if elected, her administration would not "provoke contradictions, conflict, or confrontation" while, at the same time, "safeguarding Taiwan's

---

[124] "Stable Cross-Strait Ties Key to Taiwan-U.S. Relations: U.S. Officials," *The China Post* (May 22, 2015), accessible at: http://www.chinapost.com.tw/taiwan/national/national-news/2015/05/22/436643/Stable-cross-strait.htm. On Thornton's full speech transcript, see "Taiwan: A Vital Partner in East Asia" The US Department of State (May 21, 2015), accessible at: http://www.state.gov/p/eap/rls/rm/2015/05/242705.htm.
[125] "Readout of Secretary Kerry's Travel to Beijing, Seoul, and Seattle, by Daniel Russel, Assistant Secretary, Bureau of East Asian and Far Eastern Affairs."
[126] Susan Thornton, "Taiwan: A Vital Partner in East Asia."
[127] Alan Romberg, "Squaring the Circle: Adhering to Principle, Embracing Ambiguity," p. 13.
[128] Interview with Robert Sutter.

democratic values and future autonomy."[129] Evan Medeiros, the then National Security Council senior director for Asian Affairs, said at the US Department of State Press Center Briefing on April 27, 2015, "I follow very closely what Dr. Tsai has to say about cross-strait issues. I thought her recent comments were quite interesting and quite constructive, and we look forward to hearing more from her about what her approach is about."[130] During Tsai's US visit in June 2015, she pledged to "broaden multifaceted cooperation with the U.S." while "enhancing principled cooperation with China."[131] Though maintaining that she would "push for the peaceful and stable cross-strait relations in accordance with the will of the Taiwanese people and the existing ROC constitutional order," Tsai did not accept the "1992 consensus."[132] Creating room for ambiguity, Tsai's remarks, according to Alan Romberg, intended to convey the message that even though the DPP would not "embrace the political foundation of 'one China,' as Beijing has insisted, it would also not act in a manner inconsistent with it."[133]

The United States gave Tsai VIP treatments, as she was the first Taiwanese presidential candidate to enter the Department of State and the White House to meet American officials there.[134] The State Department later reported that it "had constructive exchange on a wide range of issues

[129] "DPP China Affairs Committee: Maintaining Cross-Strait Status Quo," the Democratic Progressive Party International Site (April 10, 2015), accessible at: http://english.dpp.org.tw/dpp-china-affairs-committee/.

[130] "Foreign Press Center Briefing on Visit of Japan's Prime Minister," US Department of State Foreign Press Center Briefing with Special Assistant to the President and National Security Council (NSC) Senior Director for Asian Affairs Evan Medeiros (April 27, 2015), accessible at: http://iipdigital.usembassy.gov/st/english/texttrans/2015/04/20150428315048.html?CP.rss=true#axzz3ZB7fIsVI.

[131] Tsai Ing-wen, "Taiwan Can Build on U.S. Ties," *The Wall Street Journal* (June 1, 2015), accessible at: http://www.wsj.com/articles/taiwan-can-build-on-u-s-ties-1433176635.

[132] "Taiwan Meeting the Challenges Crating a Model of New Asian Value," Tsai's Speech at the CSIS (June 3, 2015), accessible at: http://csis.org/files/attachments/150603_Tsai_Ing_wen_transcript.pdf.

[133] Alan Romberg, "Squaring the Circle: Adhering to Principle, Embracing Ambiguity," pp. 2–3.

[134] Nadia Tsao, "DPP's Tsai Visits White House, U.S. State Department," *Taipei Times* (June 6, 2015), accessible at: http://www.taipeitimes.com/News/front/archives/2015/06/06/2003620029.

with her."[135] Apparently, Tsai's "status quo" policy vision has resonated with Washington's position on cross-strait relations. Chapter 6 will examine more deeply President Tsai's mainland policy and, particularly, her interpretations of the "1992 consensus."

REFERENCES

Bader, Jeffrey. 2012. *Obama and China's Rise*. Washington, DC: Brookings Institute.
Bendini, Roberto. 2015. *In-Depth Analysis: Japan Foreign and Security Policy at a Crossroads*. European Union: Directorate-General for External Policies Policy Department.
Benson, Brett, and Emerson Niou. 2005. Public Opinion, Foreign Policy, and the Security Balance in the Taiwan Strait. *Security Studies* 14(2): 274–289.
Bush, Richard. 2004. *At Cross Purposes*. Armonk: M.E. Sharpe.
———. 2014. U.S.-Taiwan Relations Since 2008. In *Political Changes in Taiwan under Ma Ying-jeou*, ed. Jean-Pierre Cabestan and Jacques deLisle, 217–231. New York: Routledge.
Chanlett-Avery, Emma, and Ian Rinehart. 2016. *The U.S.-Japan Alliance*. Washington, DC: Congressional Research Service.
Chen, Dean. 2016. U.S.-China Rivalry and the Weakening of the KMT's '1992 Consensus' Policy: Second-Image Reversed, Revisited. *Asian Survey* 56(4): 754–778.
Cheng, Tuan. 2013. Taiwan-U.S. Relations. *China Report* 49(4): 371–384.
Christensen, Thomas. 2002. The Contemporary Security Dilemma: Deterring a Taiwan Conflict. *The Washington Quarterly* 25(4): 7–21.
Chung, Chien-peng. 2004. *Domestic Politics, International Bargaining and China's Territorial Disputes*. New York: Routledge.
Dittmer, Lowell. 2014. Taiwan's Narrowing Strait: A Triangular Analysis of Taiwan's Security Since 2008. In *The U.S. Strategic Pivot to Asia and Cross-Strait Relations*, ed. Peter Chow, 15–29. New York: Palgrave Macmillan.
Friedberg, Aaron. 2012. *A Contest for Supremacy*. New York: W. W. Norton.
Gilley, Bruce. 2010. Not So Dire Straits. *Foreign Affairs* 89(1): 44–60.
Glaser, Charles. 2011. Will China's Rise Lead to War: Why Realism Does Not Mean Pessimism. *Foreign Affairs*: 80–91.
———. 2015. A U.S.-China Grand Bargain? *International Security* 39(4): 49–90.
Goldstein, Avery. 2013. U.S.-China Interactions in Asia. In *Tangled Titans*, ed. David Shambaugh, 263–291. Lanham: Rowman & Littlefield.

---

[135] Marie Harf, "Daily Press Briefing," The US Department of State (June 5, 2015), accessible at: http://www.state.gov/r/pa/prs/dpb/2015/06/243249.htm#CHINA.

———. 2013. First Thing First: The Pressing Danger of Crisis Instability in U.S.-China Relations. *International Security* 37(4): 49–89.

Hayton, Bill. 2014. *The South China Sea*. New Haven: Yale University Press.

Hickey, Dennis. 2015. Parallel Progress: U.S. Taiwan Relations During an Era of Rapprochement. *Journal of Chinese Political Science* 20(4): 369–384.

Hickey, Dennis, and Lu. Lilly Kelan. 2007. Japan's Military Modernization: The Chinese Perspective. In *China and Japan at Odds*, ed. James Hsiung, 95–112. New York: Palgrave Macmillan.

Hsu, Philip. 2010. Between Identity Quest and Risk Aversion: Lessons from the Chen Shui-bian Presidency for Maintaining Cross-Strait Stability. *Journal of Contemporary China* 19(66): 693–717.

Hu, Weixing, ed. 2013. *New Dynamics in Cross-Strait Relations: How Far can the Rapprochement Go?* New York: Routledge.

Hughes, Christopher. 2014. Revisiting Identity Politics under Ma Ying-jeou. In *Political Changes in Taiwan under Ma Ying-jeou*, ed. Jean-Pierre Cabestan and Jacques deLisle, 120–136. New York: Routledge.

Lee, Wei-chin. 2014. A Quartet in Disharmony: Taiwan, Japan, China, and the U.S. in the Diaoyu(Tai)/Senkaku Islands Disputes in the 2010s. *American Journal of Chinese Studies* Special Issue, 95–109.

Lin, Chong-pin. 2015. Behind Rising East Asian Maritime Tensions with China: Struggle without Breaking. *Asian Survey* 55(3): 478–501.

Manyin, M., et al. 2012. Pivot to the Pacific? The Obama Administration's 'Rebalancing' toward Asia. Congressional Research Service Report for Congress, pp. 1–29.

Mearsheimer, John. 2010. The Gathering Storm: China's Challenge to U.S. Power in Asia. *The Chinese Journal of International Politics* 3: 381–396.

Mearsheimer, John. 2014. Taiwan's Dire Strait. *National Interest* 130: 29–39.

Morgenthau, Hans. 1985. *Politics among Nations*. New York: McGraw-Hill.

Rigger, Shelley. 2011. *Why Taiwan Matters*. Lanham: Rowman & Littlefield.

Romberg, Alan. 2003. *Rein In at the Brink of the Precipice*. Washington, DC: The Henry L. Stimson Center.

———. 2015. Squaring the Circle: Adhering to Principle, Embracing Ambiguity. *China Leadership Monitor* 47: 1–23.

Ryo, Sahashi. 2014. Japan-Taiwan Relations Since 2008: An Evolving practical, Non-Strategic Partnership. In *Political Changes in Taiwan under Ma Ying-jeou*, ed. Jean-Pierre Cabestan and Jacques deLisle, 232–246. New York: Routledge.

Shambaugh, David. 2013. *China Goes Global*. New York: Oxford University Press.

Smith, Sheila. 2016. *Intimate Rivals: Japanese Domestic Politics and a Rising China*. New York: Columbia University Press.

Sutter, Robert. 2015. More American Attention to Taiwan amid Heightened Competition with China. *American Journal of Chinese Studies* 22(1): 1–16.

Sutter, Robert, et al. 2013. Balancing Acts: The U.S. Rebalance and Asian Pacific Stability. Sigur Center for Asian Studies, The George Washington University, 1–53.
Tellis, Ashley. 2013. U.S.-China Relations in a Realist World. In *Tangled Titans*, ed. David Shambaugh, 75–100. Lanham: Rowman & Littlefield.
———. 2013. Balancing without Containment: A U.S. Strategy for Confronting China's Rise. *The Washington Quarterly* 36(4): 109–124.
Tonnesson, Stein. 2015. The South China Sea: Law Trumps Power. *Asian Survey* 55(3): 455–477.
Tseng, Hui-Yi. 2015. New Challenges to the New Leadership: The Deterioration of the Diaoyu Island Dispute. In *China Entering the Xi Jinping Era*, ed. Yongnian Zheng and Lance Gore, 285–302. New York: Routledge.
Tucker, Nancy. 2002. If Taiwan Chooses Unification, Should the United States Care? *The Washington Quarterly* 25(3): 15–28.
———. 2009. *Strait Talk*. Cambridge, MA: Harvard University Press.
Tucker, Nancy, and Bonnie Glaser. 2011. Should the United States Abandon Taiwan? *The Washington Quarterly* 34(4): 23–37.
U.S. Department of State, Bureau of Oceans and International Environmental and Scientific Affairs. 2014. *Limits in the Sea No. 143, China: Maritime Claims in the South China Sea*. Washington, DC: The U.S. Department of State Report.
Waltz, Kenneth. 1979. *Theory of International Politics*. New York: McGraw-Hill.
Wang, Zheng. 2015. Chinese Discourse on the 'Nine-Dashed Line': Rights, Interests, and Nationalism. *Asian Survey* 55(3): 502–524.

Author's Interviews

Interview with an official from the DPP's Department of China Affairs, who requested to remain anonymous, July 22, 2014, Taipei, Taiwan.
Interview with an official in Taiwan's Mainland Affairs Council, who requested to remain anonymous, August 7, 2014, Taipei, Taiwan.
Interview with Robert Sutter, Professor of Practice of International Affairs at the Elliot School of International Affairs, George Washington University, February 24, 2016 at Washington DC, USA.
Interview with Richard Bush, Director for the Center for East Asia Policy Studies at the Brookings Institute, February 25, 2016 at Washington DC, USA. He was Chairman of the Board and Managing Director of the American Institute in Taiwan (AIT), from 1997 to 2002.

CHAPTER 6

Tsai Ing-wen and the Weakening of the "1992 Consensus"

The KMT and DPP, as discussed throughout this book, have vastly divergent and even polarized national visions for Taiwan and the island's relations with mainland China. Nowhere is that difference more prominently expressed than in these two parties' respective treatments of the "1992 consensus." While the Ma Ying-jeou administration had defined the "1992 consensus" in terms of "one China, respective interpretations" and that "one China" is the ROC, the DPP president Tsai Ing-wen has refrained from accepting that formulation. To be sure, Tsai has become more pragmatic and centrist in her mainland policy stances (especially when compared to her more independence-leaning remarks during her first bid for the presidency in 2012), and this probably explains her strong victory in the January 2016 presidential election, as well as receiving firmer support from the United States. On May 20, 2016, during her inauguration speech, the new Taiwanese leader proclaimed,

> I was elected president in accordance with the Constitution of the Republic of China, thus it is my responsibility to safeguard the sovereignty and territory of the Republic of China. Regarding problems arising in the East China Sea and South China Sea, we propose setting aside disputes so as to enable joint development. We will also work to maintain the existing mechanisms for dialogue and communication across the Taiwan Strait. In 1992, the two institutions representing each side across the Strait (SEF & ARATS), through communication and negotiations, arrived at various joint

acknowledgements and understandings. It was done in a spirit of mutual understanding and a political attitude of seeking common ground while setting aside differences. I respect this historical fact. Since 1992, over 20 years of interactions and negotiations across the strait have enabled and accumulated outcomes which both sides must collectively cherish and sustain; and it is based on such existing realities and political foundations that the stable and peaceful development of the cross-strait relationship must be continuously promoted. The new government will conduct cross-strait affairs in accordance with the Republic of China Constitution, the Act Governing Relations between the People of Taiwan Area and the Mainland Area, and other relevant legislation. The two governing parties across the strait must set aside the baggage of history, and engage in positive dialogue, for the benefit of the people on both sides. By existing political foundations, I refer to a number of key elements. The first element is the fact of the 1992 talks between the two institutions representing each side across the Strait (SEF & ARATS), when there was joint acknowledgement of setting aside differences to seek common ground. This is a historical fact. The second element is the existing Republic of China constitutional order. The third element pertains to the outcomes of over twenty years of negotiations and interactions across the strait. And the fourth relates to the democratic principle and prevalent will of the people of Taiwan.[1]

Recall from Chaps. 3 and 5 that Tsai already stated many of these points during her June 2015 visit to the United States and her interview with Taiwan's *Liberty Times* shortly after her electoral win in January 2016.

1   Interpreting Tsai's Mainland Policy

The elements contained in the new president's policy position sound very similar to Ma Ying-jeou's "1992 consensus" stances, but not quite the same if one examines them more deeply. In this author's interview with a high authority in the Tsai government responsible for managing cross-strait affairs, it was stated that "we seek to show greater flexibility than the previous Chen Shui-bian and Ma Ying-jeou administrations."[2] In a sense,

---

[1] "Inaugural Address of ROC 14th Term President Tsai Ing-wen," Office of the President, Republic of China (Taiwan), May 20, 2016, accessible at: http://english.president.gov.tw/Default.aspx?tabid=491&itemid=37,416&rmid=2355.

[2] This author's interview with a high authority in the Tsai administration responsible for handling cross-strait policy, July 26, 2016, Taipei, Taiwan. The interviewee requested to remain anonymous.

"President Tsai wants to avoid getting into the debates on whether Taiwan and mainland are regions under one China, as Ma had noted in his 'one ROC, two areas' characterization. While following the ROC Constitution, we can't say 'one China.' People can interpret our position freely in their own way."[3] Indeed, Tsai's centrist approach resonates well with America's strategic interests toward the Taiwan Strait, as she "respects" the "historical fact of various joint acknowledgments and understandings arrived in 1992" and "cherishes" the "over 20 years of interactions and negotiations across the strait" and "accumulated outcomes" on which cross-strait relations should be based and sustained. Such description is, to a great extent, a more qualitative way of expressing the "1992 consensus" while incorporating the history of Taiwan's democratization and the rise of the DPP in that narrative.

Furthermore, her mentioning of the "ROC constitutional order" and "Act Governing Relations between the People of Taiwan Area and the Mainland Area" echoes the point that mainland China and Taiwan are not international but cross-strait relations.[4] Nevertheless, using the notions of "other relevant legislation" and "constitutional order or framework" (which can be defined in terms of Taiwan's core values of freedom, democracy, human rights, and the rule of law) instead of strictly the ROC Constitution (which is in itself a "one-China" Constitution), Tsai has constituted a more expansive discourse that could include potential future referenda on drafting a Republic of Taiwan Constitution or deciding Taiwan's international and political status. Hence, the DPP leader has also insisted on following the "democratic principle and prevalent will of the people of Taiwan." During her interview with *The Washington Post*, Tsai firmly rejected that Taiwan will accept a Beijing-imposed deadline for conditions to agree to the "1992 consensus" because these are "against the will of the Taiwanese people."[5] This, however, does not mean the president is tossing out the possibility of accepting the "1992 consensus" in the future, but simply opposing any deadlines or preconditions forcibly demanded by the PRC in contradiction with the democratic preferences of the Taiwanese public.[6]

[3] Ibid.
[4] Ibid.
[5] Lally Weymouth, "Taiwanese President Tsai Ing-wen: Beijing Must Respect our Democratic Will," *The Washington Post* (July 21, 2016), accessible at: https://www.washingtonpost.com/opinions/2016/07/21/44b0a1a4-4e25-11e6-a422-83ab49ed5e6a_story.html?utm_term=.c2b44f19b3c6.
[6] Interview with a high authority.

Comparing the China Policy of Presidents Ma Ying-jeou and Tsai Ing-wen

Meanwhile, President Tsai has enjoyed strong public backing for her mainland policy stances. Table 6.1 shows that during President Ma's second term, when the MAC began to survey the public views on the KMT government's "1992 consensus" policy, the general reactions were only weakly supportive. In September 2011 and July 2015, about 49 percent endorsed "one China, respective interpretations," with "one China" being the ROC. With the exception of November 2015, when the fanfare surrounding the historic Xi–Ma summit led to a highly favorable rating of 62 percent, the overall average had been 54 percent for identifying with the OCRI. About a third of the population takes an opposing response. Nonetheless, according to Table 6.2, when the MAC used the term "ROC constitutional framework" in its questionnaires, the majority support had become overwhelming, with roughly 73.4 percent backing such assertion, whereas 14 percent registered a negative attitude. For Tables 6.3 and 6.4, about 75 percent has endorsed Tsai's mainland policy approach outlined in her May 20th inaugural address. Lastly, her references to the Taiwanese democratic will gave her a resounding 91 percent of public affirmation, as illustrated in Table 6.5.

Table 6.1 The Taiwanese people's public views on Ma Ying-jeou's definition of "1992 Consensus" based on "one China, respective interpretations" in which "one China" is the ROC

Year (Month)	Yes	No	No opinion/Don't know
2011 (Sept)	49.4%	34.7%	15.9%
2012 (Dec)	55.5%	31.5%	13.0%
2014 (Jan)	55.6%	28.6%	15.8%
2014 (July)	52.3%	33.2%	14.5%
2015 (July)	49.7%	32.7%	17.6%
2015 (After Xi–Ma Summit in November)	61.6%	23.3%	15.1%
Average	54.0%	30.1%	15.3%

Source: The Mainland Affairs Council, ROC, Taiwan; 2011–15

Table 6.2 The Taiwanese people's public views on the statement of handling cross-strait relations on the basis of the "ROC constitutional framework"

Year (Month)	Yes	No	No opinion/Don't know
2012 (May)	70.0%	16.8%	13.3%
2013 (Oct)	73.7%	12.2%	14.1%
2014 (July)	68.1%	17.1%	14.8%
2015 (July)	72.2%	17.7%	10.1%
2016 (March)	81.9%	9.9%	8.2%
2016 (June)	74.4%	9.6%	16.1%
Average	73.4%	13.9%	12.8%

Source: The Mainland Affairs Council, ROC, Taiwan; 2012–16

Table 6.3 The Taiwanese people's public views on President Tsai Ing-wen's inauguration address on May 20, 2016, emphasizing "respecting the historical fact of the 1992 talks"

Year (Month)	Yes	No	No opinion/Don't know
2016 (June)	74.6%	10.8%	14.5%

Source: The Mainland Affairs Council, ROC, Taiwan; June 2016

Table 6.4 The Taiwanese people's public views on President Tsai's inauguration address on May 20, 2016, stressing that she would handle cross-strait relations in "accordance to the Republic of China Constitution, Act Governing Relations Between the People of Taiwan Area and the Mainland Area, and other relevant legislation"

Year (Month)	Yes	No	No opinion/Don't know
2016 (June)	74.4%	9.6%	16.1%

Source: The Mainland Affairs Council. ROC, Taiwan; June 2016

Table 6.5 The Taiwanese people's public views on President Tsai's inauguration address on May 20, 2016, stressing that she would also manage cross-strait relations based on the "democratic principle and prevalent will of the people of Taiwan"

Year (Month)	Yes	No	No opinion/Don't know
2016 (June)	90.9%	3.9%	5.1%

Source: The Mainland Affairs Council, ROC, Taiwan; June 2016

2   US–CHINA RIVALRY AND THE ROLE OF TAIWAN

Chapter 5 has noted that the KMT's "1992 consensus" and common identification with the CCP on "one China" placed Taipei and Beijing in a close strategic union that undermined some of America's security interests across the Asia-Pacific, particularly in an age of rising Chinese power and influence.

Xi Jinping and a More Assertive China

Despite Beijing's declared emphasis on global peace, it is clear that Xi Jinping has inaugurated a more audacious foreign policy agenda in recent years—particularly toward the disputed territories in the South China Sea and East China Sea.[7] As we have learned, a series of incidents have led the United States and China's neighbors to voice concern. Washington has pushed for deeper strategic and economic ties with Japan, South Korea, Australia, India, and ASEAN in its rebalancing or "pivot" to Asia-Pacific. Moreover, in seeking to promote the "Chinese Dream" and "rejuvenation of the Chinese nation" (terms with highly nationalistic significance), Beijing has launched the new Silk Road project to deepen continental infrastructure development and maritime trade with South Asia, Central Asia, Africa, the Middle East, and Europe. To help finance these initiatives, the Xi administration has established the AIIB. Some observers perceive the new banking organization as a rival to the US-dominated World Bank and IMF.[8]

---

[7] Elizabeth Economy, "China's Imperial President," *Foreign Affairs* 93, no. 6 (2014), pp. 80–91.

[8] The United States has not agreed to join the AIIB despite some of Washington's key allies having already entered, such as Great Britain, Australia, France, Germany, Israel, and South Korea, to name just a few. Some have argued that to ensure the bank's proper functioning in

It is likely that the Xi Jinping government will continue to pursue the peaceful development strategy, but behave more belligerently and assertively on various peripheral and international issues that pertain to its "core interests." How China defines the notion "core interests" will certainly affect its relations with neighboring countries as well as the United States. Whereas traditionally "core interests" have encompassed the Chinese mainland, Tibet, and Taiwan, Beijing's tougher stances on the South and East China Seas' maritime and island territories seem to confirm that these contested regions will be included as well. This means Sino-American relations may become more antagonistic, especially in the aftermath of the judgment rendered by the PCA on July 12, 2016. The court decision was highly favorable to the Philippines (and by extension, the United States and its other Southeast Asian allies pertaining to the dispute) and essentially rebuffed the PRC's so-called Nine-Dashed Line and its accompanying "historical rights" claims over the South China Sea maritime territories. The PCA also ruled that land features in the Spratlys, including the Taiwan-occupied Itu Aba or Taiping, are not islands under the UNCLOS, and hence have no rights to the 200-nautical miles of EEZs.

For its part, Beijing has boycotted the proceedings, saying that the tribunal had no jurisdiction and that it would ignore its decision. Suggesting that the PCA is a "lackey of some outside forces" (implying the United States and Japan),[9] the Chinese also staged a series of air-patrol and naval exercises in the region. Though China's reactions have, for the most part, stayed restrained, it remains to be seen how it would charter its relations with Washington and other claimants.[10] Nevertheless, the Philippines, under its new president Rodrigo Duterte, has shifted its stance toward

---

accordance with international law, human rights, environmental protection, and liberal internationalism, the United States should join AIIB too rather than sitting out. See Stephen Olson, "Time for the U.S. to Join the Asian Infrastructure Investment Bank," *The Diplomat* (November 9, 2015), at http://thediplomat.com/2015/11/time-for-the-us-to-join-the-asian-infrastructure-investment-bank/.

[9] Jane Perlez, "Tribunal Rejects Beijing's Claims in South China Sea," *The New York Times* (July 12, 2016), at http://www.nytimes.com/2016/07/13/world/asia/south-china-sea-hague-ruling-philippines.html?action=click&contentCollection=Asia%20Pacific&module=RelatedCoverage&region=EndOfArticle&pgtype=article.

[10] "The South China Sea: Courting Trouble," *The Economist* (July 16, 2016), at http://www.economist.com/news/china/21702069-region-and-america-will-now-anxiously-await-chinas-response-un-appointed-tribunal.

greater accommodation with China by agreeing to shelve the PCA ruling, conduct bilateral negotiations to address the South China Sea contentions, and focus on joint economic cooperation. Proclaiming that his administration would charter a more "autonomous" foreign policy course of action (away from overreliance on the United States), Duterte has viewed the PRC's increasing economic clout as benefiting his country's infrastructure and economic development.[11] The seeming "defection" of the Philippines from the US Asia pivot may escalate competition between Washington and Beijing as each side seeks to drive away their respective allies and partners in the region.

The United States and China will also continue to quarrel over other issues including trade, foreign exchange rates, human rights, cybersecurity, and the protection of intellectual property rights, to name just a few. Yet, both Beijing and Washington have affirmed repeatedly that these contentions (while inevitable) must not derail their bilateral cooperation required to address a series of major global challenges.[12] A case in point is the firm shared commitment of President Barack Obama and President Xi Jinping to set stringent measures in their respective countries to reduce global warming gases and curb carbon dioxide emissions.[13] This intermix of cooperation and competition, also known as "coopetition," is likely to characterize Sino-American relations in the years to come. It will also characterize China's relations with many regional powers.

The DPP Administration's Position on the South China Sea

Consequently, Taiwan's role will also matter significantly in Washington's strategic calculations even though the United States has been very careful

---

[11] Jane Perlez, "Rodrigo Duterte Gets Closer to China, and the Neighbors Notice," *The New York Times* (October 24, 2016), accessible at: http://www.nytimes.com/2016/10/25/world/asia/rodrigo-duterte-philippines-china.html.

[12] "Remarks by President Obama and President Xi Jinping in Joint Press Conference," The White House Office of the Secretary (September 25, 2015), at https://www.whitehouse.gov/the-press-office/2015/09/25/remarks-president-obama-and-president-xi-peoples-republic-china-joint.

[13] "U.S.–China Joint Presidential Statement on Climate Change," The White House Office of the Press Secretary (March 31, 2016), at https://www.whitehouse.gov/the-press-office/2016/03/31/us-china-joint-presidential-statement-climate-change. See also Mark Landler and Jane Perlez, "Rare Harmony as China and U.S. Commit to Climate Deal," *The New York Times* (September 3, 2016), accessible at: http://www.nytimes.com/2016/09/04/world/asia/obama-xi-jinping-china-climate-accord.html?_r=0.

with its support of Taipei, fearing that any too obvious backing would strain its relations with the PRC. Unlike the KMT, which also makes similar claims to the South China Sea as Beijing, the DPP president Tsai Ing-wen has assumed a more reserved position following the July 12th PCA verdict. Though voicing strong protest against the ruling that denies Taiping's "island" status, the Tsai administration has not used the terms the "Eleven-Dashed Line" or "Nine-Dashed Line" in its policy statements. President Tsai has reaffirmed that her government would follow the UNCLOS and would focus on joint economic and scientific development of the South China Sea maritime territories with all relevant parties. The administration also rejected Taiwan being referred to by the PCA as "an authority of China."[14] When several Taiwanese fishing boats set out their own expedition to the Taiping Island to assert ROC sovereignty in late July, the Tsai government did not give its blessing and even threatened to punish these fishermen for their unilateral actions on the grounds of jeopardizing Taiwan's national security.[15] The KMT has been concerned that Tsai's behaviors are essentially "relinquishing China" and placing far more importance on Taiwan's alliance with the United States and Japan.[16]

But the government also wishes to maintain a certain degree of "ambiguity" to avoid being seen as taking up an blatant anti-China position.[17] Thus, according to the president's press releases, the "ROC government reiterates its firm position that the ROC has sovereignty over the South China Sea Islands and their relevant waters. The government will staunchly safeguard the country's territory and sovereignty, and ensure that national interests are not jeopardized."[18] In the statement issued by the MAC, it emphasizes that "in 1947, 'Location Map of the South China Sea Islands' published by the government clearly showed the scope of the territory and waters of the ROC. Since that time, the government has staunchly defended the ROC's territory and sovereignty over the South China Sea

---

[14] Lally Weymouth, "Taiwanese President Tsai Ing-wen: Beijing Must Respect our Democratic Will."

[15] "Taiwan Fishermen Excited to Set Foot on Taiping Island," *Focus Taiwan News* (July 26, 2016), accessible at: http://focustaiwan.tw/news/aipl/201607260005.aspx.

[16] Interview with Chou Chih-wei.

[17] Interview with a high authority.

[18] "ROC Government Position on the South China Sea Arbitration," The Office of the President, Republic of China (Taiwan), July 12, 2016, accessible at: http://english.president.gov.tw/Default.aspx?tabid=491&itemid=37,703&rmid=2355.

islands and their relevant maritime rights, and this will not change."[19] In a sense, therefore, Tsai has acquiesced to the ROC position tracing back to the Chiang Kai-shek era.

America's Attitude on the "1992 Consensus"

As we examined in Chap. 5, the US attitude toward the "1992 consensus" has become less forthcoming in recent years. Though there is no direct linkage indicating that growing reservation is due to the intensification of US–China competition, one also cannot entirely discount that China's growing aggressiveness, its more potent strategic challenges, and the defense of Taiwan's security and democracy are essential considerations for American policymakers. Several Obama administration officials stated that the United States should not be involved in asserting a position with respect to that policy formulation, and that this should be left to the people on both sides of the Taiwan Strait to decide. Moreover, the Obama government has indicated that Beijing should allow for greater latitude on Tsai Ing-wen's mainland policy. In this author's interview with Richard Bush, the former AIT chairman, he said that the United States is "very pragmatic," as it cares what "devices" would work and help to stabilize cross-strait relations. It could be the "1992 consensus" or something else. Washington "doesn't think it's productive to get into too much details on how the two sides should engage each other."[20] In my interview with Douglas Paal, the former AIT director, he mentioned that the "1992 consensus" was Su Chi's creation, and President Ma, being a Chinese nationalist, used the consensus to refer to the "ROC Constitution and the 'one China' concept." However, the United States believes it is "really an issue for the people of Taiwan and China to decide."[21] To some extent, Paal added, President Tsai was also beginning to "embrace the ROC," though not specified in the same manner as Ma Ying-jeou.[22]

In June 2016, Raymond Burghardt, the then AIT chairman, in an interview with Voice of America, remarked, "It's important to remember, I think everyone in China knows, the term '1992 consensus' was

---

[19] "MAC Issues Solemn Statement on the South China Sea Arbitration Case," the Mainland Affairs Council, ROC, Taiwan, July 12, 2016, accessible at: http://www.mac.gov.tw/ct.asp?xItem=115,090&ctNode=6337&mp=3.

[20] Interview with Richard Bush.

[21] Interview with Douglas Paal.

[22] Ibid.

not used by anyone until 2001, no, 2000. Su Chi, President Ma's first national security advisor was the first person to use that term, to describe the understanding that had been reached in 1992, before that, I mean, in all the times that I met with Wang Daohan or Koo Chen-fu, they never called it that, they never called it the 1992 consensus, because the name didn't exist. Koo Chen-fu would sometimes just call it 1992 understanding."[23] He felt that President Tsai already "showed a fair amount of flexibility in what she said." When asked about the differences between the KMT and DPP, Burghardt noted that "the KMT, particularly under Ma Ying-jeou, had a great interest in the Republic of China's history--ROC history, its contribution during the WWII, those kind of things. These are not things fundamentally important to our relationship, but there are things that we noticed these administrations are interested in, so that whole historical narrative is important for KMT. In the case of the DPP, it's the emergence of democracy on Taiwan, and the fight for democracy on Taiwan. That's their historical narrative, but those are more sort of the background painting of the relationship rather than the core of the relationship."[24]

The AIT chairman's responses, to some extent, reflected Washington's general reaction to cross-strait relations and the nationalistic/ideological division between the KMT and DPP. It seems obvious that the KMT represents a more Sino-centric political organization than the more Taiwan-based DPP. And, when balance of power in international politics is concerned, as the PRC gets stronger and more proactive in regional affairs, rivalry between Washington and Beijing will only escalate. Then, a Taiwan governed by an administration that is less China-friendly would definitely be more palatable and resonant with regard to American's national interests. As well, Washington's long-standing strategic ambiguity policy would also be better served if Taiwan could maintain a healthy balance with mainland China. A conciliatory Ma government had, in a sense, enhanced Beijing's perception (or emboldened its confidence) that Washington is no longer interested or relevant in deterring China from coercing unification with Taiwan. Therefore, the US encouragement of cross-strait rapprochement could be construed as Washington's acquies-

---

[23] "Interview with Raymond Burghardt, the AIT Chairman," *The Voice of America* (June 25, 2016), accessible at: http://www.voachinese.com/a/voa-interview-burghardt-20,160,624/3391730.html.
[24] Ibid.

cence to the PRC's sovereign claim over Taiwan. Thomas Christensen insightfully pointed out, "Cross-strait détente is generally welcomed in Washington. Ironically, however, the lack of tensions in relations across the Taiwan Strait deprived the Obama administration of the opportunities afforded to the Clinton and Bush administrations to reassure the PRC about U.S. strategic intentions without appearing overly weak or compromising in the process."[25]

In my interview with Chou Chih-wei, the former KMT chairperson of the Culture and Communications Committee, he suggested that the United States obviously has its "national interests in mind" when coping with mainland China and cross-strait affairs. This is natural for a superpower state. However, even after suffering from its worst electoral setbacks in 2014 and 2016, the KMT, he stressed, cannot renounce the "1992 consensus" because this is one of the key foundations of the party. Without it, the KMT may alienate more of its core supporters.[26]

3 Conclusion

It remains to be seen whether the Tsai administration and the PRC can reach some agreement on these thorny issues. Whether or not the "1992 consensus" or whatever formulations Tsai would call it, the essential point for Beijing is whether Taipei would accept that both Taiwan and the mainland are parts of "one China." If the DPP government would clearly define the ROC in the same manner as Ma Ying-jeou, then the Chinese elites would probably be more satisfied. If the ROC, however, is only used to instrumentally help the cause of Taiwan independence, then cross-strait relations may become more uncertain and even dangerous.

Indeed, in the months leading up to Tsai's inauguration, China has begun to take on the offensive in order to pressure the new administration into accepting the "1992 consensus." On the international front, Beijing backed away from the "diplomatic truce" that it implicitly agreed with the Ma government in 2008–16, in which both the PRC and Taiwan would stop using money or other inducements to get each other's diplomatic partners to switch allegiance. In March 2016, Beijing established ties with

---

[25] Thomas Christensen, *The China Challenge* (New York: W. W. Norton, 2015), p. 296.
[26] Interview with Chou Chih-wei.

Gambia, which used to be Taipei's ally.²⁷ Then, in May, the World Health Assembly, the executive arm of the World Health Organization, continued its tradition since 2009 to invite Taiwan to attend, as an observer and under the name "Chinese Taipei," its annual meeting in Geneva. Yet, under Beijing's influence, the invitation this time specifically mentioned that Taipei's participation is predicated upon the "one-China" principle.²⁸ At the same time, the Chinese authority had extradited Taiwanese suspects in alleged telephone fraud scams from Kenya and Malaysia. Moreover, China is tightening up its economic exchanges with Taiwan, in particular by reducing the flow of Chinese tourists to the island. The PRC made it clear that any crisis across the Taiwan Strait would be blamed on the Tsai government.²⁹ In late June 2016, Beijing also announced that it would suspend all contact and negotiations with Taipei, pending Tsai's acceptance of the "1992 consensus."³⁰ In addition, in the first few months after Tsai was inaugurated as president, a series of crises (though they were largely contained) erupted between Taiwan and China,³¹ such as Taiwan's naval forces mistakenly firing the Hsiung Feng III anti-ship missiles in the direction of mainland China (the missiles did not go far enough but hit a Taiwanese fishing boat off Penghu Island, killing one person) and the unfortunate and tragic Taiwan tourist bus fire that killed all 24 mainland tourists and the two Taiwanese tour guides and bus driver aboard. These instances also happened in the absence of direct communications between high officials from both sides, leading to resentments, suspicions, and misunderstandings. As cross-strait relations continued to deteriorate, the ICAO, under pressure from Beijing, did not invite Taiwan to attend its meeting in September 2016 (as it did last time in October 2013). In

---

²⁷ "Relations between China and Taiwan: The Gambia Gambit," *The Economist* (March 26, 2016), accessible at: http://www.economist.com/news/asia/21695563-china-resumes-old-diplomatic-game-gambia-gambit.
²⁸ "Taiwan Tells WHO It Will Attend the WHA Meeting," *Focus Taiwan News* (May 9, 2016), accessible at: http://focustaiwan.tw/news/aipl/201605090024.aspx.
²⁹ "Taiwan Readies for a New President: Sizing Tsai Up," *The Economist* (May 14, 2016), accessible at: http://www.economist.com/news/asia/21698707-tsai-ing-wen-has-delicate-balancing-act-both-home-and-china-sizing-tsai-up.
³⁰ "China Suspends Diplomatic Contact with Taiwan," *The New York Times* (June 25, 2016), accessible at: http://www.nytimes.com/2016/06/26/world/asia/china-suspends-diplomatic-contact-with-taiwan.html?_r=0.
³¹ "A Series of Unfortunate Events," *The Economist* (July 30, 2016), accessible at: http://www.economist.com/news/asia/21702808-new-president-faces-troubles-home-and-abroad-series-unfortunate-events.

response, Tsai affirmed that Taiwan would not "bow to the pressure from China."[32]

To be sure, the KMT–CCP rapprochement in the last eight years placed Washington at much greater ease with respect to the Taiwan Strait tensions. The situation was calm and allowed the United States and China to concentrate on other crucial issues in their relationship including climate change, cyber-security, North Korea's nuclear programs, and economics. Yet, as discussed, the KMT's pro-China platform also challenged Washington's security interests in the East and South China Seas, as well as its liberal interests in defending the democratic preferences of the Taiwanese people. The Ma government's attempt to reinvigorate a China-centric nationalism on Taiwan had met with strong domestic opposition and widened the gulf of political divisions and mistrust. This would not be beneficial to Taiwan's unity and security interests when facing a stronger and more assertive China. Thus, the United States have welcomed greater circumspection between the two sides if more and more Taiwanese people (particularly the younger generation) view closer relations as tools to simply advance Beijing's goal of political control.

In its 2016 report on the PRC's military power, the US Department of Defense reiterates America's "one-China" policy based on the three Joint Communiqués and the TRA, and stresses that it "opposes any unilateral change to the status quo in the Taiwan Strait by either side and does not support Taiwan independence."[33] Nevertheless, the analysis also cautions that, in spite of the positive cross-strait interactions such as the Xi–Ma meeting, there "have been no signs that China's military posture opposite Taiwan has changed significantly." The People's Liberation Army continues to "develop and deploy military capabilities intended to coerce Taiwan or to attempt an invasion if necessary."[34] Hence, while welcoming the improvement of cross-strait ties, Washington has refrained from endorsing the "1992 consensus."

---

[32] "China Can't Make Taiwan 'Bow to Pressure,' Island's Leader Says," *The Wall Street Journal* (October 4, 2016), accessible, http://www.wsj.com/articles/china-cant-make-taiwan-bow-to-pressure-islands-leader-says-1,475,616,782.

[33] The Office of the Secretary of Defense, "Annual Report to Congress: Military and Security Developments involving the People's Republic of China 2016," The U.S. Department of Defense (April 26, 2016), accessible at: http://www.defense.gov/Portals/1/Documents/pubs/2016%20China%20Military%20Power%20Report.pdf.

[34] Ibid.

Though reiterating her earlier pledges to manage cross-strait relations on the basis of the ROC constitutional order and acknowledging the "1992 talks" and the "20 years of negotiations that followed," President Tsai has acted cautiously to stop short of upholding the "one-China" principle underlying the "1992 consensus" that Beijing has so eagerly wanted her to accept. The PRC is certainly dismayed by this, criticizing Tsai's "vague attitude" and describing her remarks as "an incomplete examination paper."[35] Nonetheless, Bush stressed that Beijing should not "prejudge Tsai based solely on her past behaviors, policy stances, and remarks." These could be "very unreliable indicators" of her future intent and policy approach toward the mainland. After all, as the president, Tsai would have to be responsible for the consequences of her decisions, unlike when she was only the leader of the opposition.[36]

Tsai has strived to govern moderately. However, her party, the DPP, has many pro-independence stalwarts who are likely to push the new president to assume a more aggressive approach toward Beijing.[37] Their force would be great given the DPP's strong majority in the Legislative Yuan. Thus, in this author's interview with a high authority in the Tsai government, it is stressed that to exert a good balance upon these domestic pressures would certainly be a challenging task for the new administration.[38] If history is any guide, Washington is unlikely to tolerate Taiwan's unrestrained moves toward political separation and independence since doing so would compromise US–PRC relations and plunge the Taiwan Strait into grave danger and instability. Sutter, Bush, and Paal, in our conversations, all commented that the United States will be outspoken if Taiwan takes any reckless moves to destabilize cross-strait relations.[39] Wu Yu-shan correctly described America's interests as follows: "Even though Washington does not want to see an 'inter-Chinese alliance' in the territorial disputes in the East and South China Sea between China and Taiwan, it has even greater reason to worry about a conflict between the two caused by Taiwan flirting with independence. One of the primary reasons for the territorial disputes to flare up in those waters is the rising military power of the PRC. With

---

[35] Austin Ramzy, "Taiwan President Takes Cautious Line on China at Inauguration," *The New York Times*, May 20, 2016, http://www.nytimes.com/2016/05/21/world/asia/taiwan-president-tsai-ing-wen.html?_r=0.
[36] Interview with Richard Bush.
[37] Wu, "Heading towards Troubled Waters?" pp. 67–68.
[38] Interview with a high authority.
[39] Interviews with Robert Sutter, Richard Bush, and Douglass Paal.

the gap between the U.S. and Chinese militaries narrowing, it has become more and more difficult for Washington to defend Taiwan in waters adjacent to China ... Washington may not be intrinsically opposed to Tsai's stance on the 'one China' principle, but is quite aware of what Beijing's response will be if its red line is crossed, and thus wants to set limits to the DPP president's maneuvering space."[40]

Meanwhile, the DPP and its political partners (the New Power Party) in the Legislative Yuan are already floating around several de-Sinification proposals, including the possibility of removing Sun Yat-sen's (the ROC founding father) portraits from government, schools, and other public institutions, demolishing the Chiang Kai-shek memorial hall, and retaining Taiwanese history textbooks in line with a more separatist interpretation (see Chap. 4). Moreover, partisan strife between the DPP and the KMT is intensifying. On July 25, 2016, the DPP-dominated legislature voted to establish a government commission empowered to retrieve assets stolen by political parties since 1945—a move clearly targeted at the KMT, which the DPP has accused of having (long ago) pinched properties and other state-owned items that Japanese colonials gave back to Taiwan at the end of WWII. The KMT, as a much weaker minority party now, seems to have surrendered to the DPP's majority dominance, accusing the latter of attempting to "destroy the KMT once and for all," which would be detrimental to Taiwan's Constitution, liberal democracy, and pluralistic party system.[41] President Tsai must also handle rifts within her own party. At its recent congress some delegates said the DPP should drop its call for an independent Taiwan (which would please mainland China), while others called for Taiwan's official name, the ROC, to be abolished (which would infuriate it).

If pursued fully on these initiatives, the new DPP government may fall back to the similar nation-building projects that put Taiwan in a never-ending vicious political attrition. Indeed, Taiwan cannot afford another four years wasted on these sensational and divisive initiatives. While transitional justice is important for recognizing KMT's past wrongs and fostering political reconciliation, self-centered politicians may also maneuver these issues to gain partisan advantage, which, in turn, creates greater political ills. Taiwan, Robert Sutter posited, needs to behave more like a

---

[40] Wu, "Heading towards Troubled Waters"? p. 74.
[41] Interview with Chou Chih-wei.

mature and responsible democracy.[42] Accordingly, the United States could not bless Tsai Ing-wen's position without qualification because "that would create the possibility of 'blank check' dynamics that complicated the U.S.-Taiwan relations during the last six years of the Chen Shui-bian administration."[43]

Consequently, it seems that (see Fig. 2.2) neither the KMT nor DPP has been able to embrace a rational and centrist cross-strait policy approach because of each party's own ideational and nation-building proclivities. What, however, really constitutes a strategically sound policy for Taiwan? To be sure, there is no clear-cut answer to that question, as a state's security interests may alter from time to time, depending on the changes of the prevailing world political environment.[44] Indeed, Hans Morgenthau had long postulated that national interest is defined in terms of power, which, is an "objective category which is universally valid, but it does not endow that concept with a meaning that is fixed once and for all."[45] Nonetheless, he also stated that a rational foreign policy "minimizes risks and maximizes benefits and, hence, complies both with the moral precept of prudence and the political requirement of success."[46] Since Taiwan's interests are best served by having constructive and beneficiary ties with both the United States and the PRC, the island must strive to maximize its interests without alienating either party.

Thus, the ROC government should pursue a combination of two strategies: binding engagement and soft balancing. Schweller contended that a weaker state may sometimes employ binding engagement to bind its powerful rival to exert some measure of control or "voice opportunities," thereby "prevent[ing] or at least ameliorating [its] domination by stronger partner."[47] The gradual institutionalization of various cross-strait socioeconomic cooperative regimes could facilitate mutual expectations, build confidence, foster greater transparency of each other's decision-makings, and reduce misunderstanding and conflicts. More importantly,

---

[42] Author's interview with Robert Sutter.
[43] Richard Bush, "Taiwan's January 2016 Elections and Their Implications for Relations with China and the United States," p. 21.
[44] For more in-depth discussion, see Dean P. Chen, "Security, Domestic Divisions, and the KMT's Post-2008 'One China' Policy: A Neoclassical Realist Analysis," *International Relations of the Asia-Pacific* 15, no. 2 (2015), pp. 324–326.
[45] Hans Morgenthau, *Politics Among Nations* (New York: McGraw Hill, 1985), p. 10.
[46] Ibid.
[47] Randall Schweller, "Managing the Rise of Great Powers," p. 13.

Taiwan's engagement of Beijing may promote greater moderation of China's policy behavior and even liberalization of its domestic institutions. Robert Sutter has compared binding engagement to a "Gulliver strategy," designed to "tie down aggressive, assertive, or other negative policy tendencies of the other power through webs of interdependence in bilateral and multilateral relationships."[48] Taiwan's democratic experience has always been lauded as the "beacon of hope" for China's political change.[49]

At the same time, it is also prudent for Taipei to enact a soft-balancing approach, that is the use of diplomatic, economic, and other non-military initiatives to constrain the influence of a rising power.[50] By championing its long-standing security and economic ties with the United States and Japan, Taiwan is indirectly deterring the PRC from waging military offensives and economic strangulation to overpower the island. Taipei should focus more on the democratic dimension of the ROC. Unlike mainland China, according to Jacques deLisle, Taiwan shares and embodies "cosmopolitan (and, in particular, U.S.-supported) norms of democracy, human rights, and the rule of law—traits that, in the post-Cold War world, affect the international acceptance and stature of states and state-like entities and thus can augment Taiwan's ability to accomplish its goals (including enhanced security) through value-based appeals."[51] Though President Ma stressed democracy and human rights as great features of Taiwan which should serve as emulation for the PRC, he avoided voicing strong criticisms of Beijing's repressive governance. "Anniversaries of June 4 continue to be observed and repression in Tibet became an issue in the 2008 Taiwan presidential campaign, yet Ma drew criticism for what some saw as an indefensibly cautious approach to high-profile symbols of human rights-based oppositions to the PRC regime, including the Dalai Lama, Rebiya Kadeer, and Chen Guangcheng."[52] By focusing overly upon cross-strait détente and deepening the "one-China" nationalism,

---

[48] Sutter, *U.S.-Chinese Relations*, p. 154.

[49] Rigger, *Why Taiwan Matters*, pp. 189–191.

[50] Derek McDougall, "Responses to 'Rising China' in the East Asian Regions: Soft Balancing with Accommodation," *Journal of Contemporary China* 21, no. 73 (2012), pp. 1–17. See also Robert Pape, "Soft Balancing against the United States," *International Security* 30, no. 1 (Summer 2005), pp. 7–45.

[51] Jacques deLisle, "Taiwan and Soft Power," in Jean-Pierre Cabestan and Jacques deLisle eds., *Political Changes in Taiwan under Ma Ying-jeou*, pp. 280–281.

[52] Ibid., pp. 282–283.

the Ma administration failed to reassure Taiwan's allies, regional partners, as well as the international community that its vibrant democratic politics, civil society, and rule of law are Taiwan's assets and distinctive attributes separating the ROC from the PRC. The ROC government should continue cultivating these soft powers to gain greater international support and, in the words of Robert Pape, to "delay, frustrate, and undermine"[53] Beijing's assertive impulse. As for the Tsai government, it has indeed stepped up on the emphasis of Taiwan's liberal democratic system and values. Yet, by acquiescing the DPP legislators' promotion of anti-China domestic initiatives and unrelenting political struggle against the KMT and denying all of the latter's past contributions to Taiwan, President Tsai has dismissed the importance of pursuing binding engagement to reassure Beijing of her sincerity and commitment to defend the ROC Constitution and institutional order. In other words, while this author believes Beijing should give President Tsai more credit for her greater moderation (compared to Chen Shui-bian) and more inclusive cross-strait policy position, it would be unproductive if the DPP's Taiwan-first initiatives are carried out to a level of total negation of Taiwan's relations and history with China.

Meanwhile, the United States' balanced position (or strategic ambiguity) on the Taiwan Strait is facing some uncertainties as Washington commences the Donald Trump presidency in January 2017. A Hillary Clinton administration, as most observers had anticipated initially, would have continued to push for the US rebalancing policy to Asia to respond to and constrain China's assertiveness. A hardening of America's China approach could be expected on cyber-security, North Korea's nuclear ambitions, the East and South China Seas, human rights, and the PRC's unfair economic practices.[54] Yet, whereas Clinton did not say much about the Taiwan issue during her campaign, she is likely to maintain Washington's perennial policy stance. Jake Sullivan, a senior policy advisor to Clinton, noted in July 2016 that "(Former) Secretary Clinton supports the current [Obama] administration's policy on China and Taiwan, will continue to do so, and believes that peaceful development strengthening of cross-strait relations is important." He added that Clinton supports the TRA, as well as the "one

---

[53] Robert Pape, "Soft Balancing against the United States," p. 10.

[54] "Philippines 'Separation' from U.S. Jilts Hillary Clinton, Too," *The New York Times* (October 21, 2016), accessible at: http://www.nytimes.com/2016/10/22/us/politics/philippines-china-us-asia-pivot.html.

China" policy, and there will not be "surprises or significant departures" from her position on the relationship from the Obama administration.[55]

Nonetheless, in a stunning upset victory, Donald Trump is elected president of the United States on November 8, 2016. Although the Republican leader as well had not commented much about Taiwan during his campaign, his Asia policy advisor and director of the newly created US National Trade Council, Peter Navarro, suggested that America must not "dump Taiwan" and that Washington should continue to reassure the island and the world of the United States' commitment to both the Taiwan Relations Act and Reagan's Six Assurances. Noting Trump's "peace through strength" vision, Navarro criticized the Obama administration's neglect to strengthen Taiwan's military capabilities and advocated that the island should, possibly with America's and Japan's assistance, construct a fleet of diesel-electric submarines to repel Beijing's sea strangulation.[56] The Republican Party also included, for the first time, both the TRA and Six Assurances in its party platform adopted in July 2016.[57] It seems that the Trump administration would be more proactive in supporting and defending Taiwan's security and interests.

In an unprecedented move since the United States established diplomatic relations with the PRC in 1979, Trump, on December 2, 2016, spoke directly with President Tsai Ing-wen on the phone. In addition to accepting her congratulatory remarks about Trump's victory, both spoke about strengthening US–Taiwan economic and security ties. Though receiving Tsai's call in his president-elect capacity (still more than a month then before his inauguration on January 20, 2017), Trump shocked the world and particularly Beijing as speculations soon emerged over whether the new American president was merely inexperienced about foreign policy or was signaling a potential change in Washington's long-standing

---

[55] "Adviser Expects Clinton to Continue Obama's Taiwan Policy," *The China Post* (July 27, 2016), accessible at: http://www.chinapost.com.tw/taiwan/intl-community/2016/07/27/473524/Adviser-expects.htm.

[56] Peter Navarro, "America Can't Dump Taiwan," *The National Interest* (July 19, 2016), accessible at: http://nationalinterest.org/feature/america-cant-dump-taiwan-17040?page=2. See also Alexander Gray and Peter Navarro, "Donald Trump's Peace Through Strength Vision for the Asia-Pacific," *Foreign Policy* (November 7, 2016), http://foreignpolicy.com/2016/11/07/donald-trumps-peace-through-strength-vision-for-the-asia-pacific/.

[57] "Six Assurances to Taiwan Included in Republican Party Platform," *The Focus Taiwan News* (July 19, 2016), accessible at: http://focustaiwan.tw/news/aipl/201607190005.aspx.

Taiwan Strait policy because no president or president-elect had ever spoken directly (not to mention about publicizing it) with Taiwan's head of state since 1979. Mainland China, as expected, immediately protested and sternly warned Washington to adhere to its "one-China" policy. Although the outgoing Barack Obama administration reassured Beijing that America had not deviated away from its "one-China" policy based on the three Sino-American Joint Communiqués and the Taiwan Relations Act, Trump noted unyieldingly that it was "interesting how the U.S. sells Taiwan billions of dollars of military equipment but I should not accept a congratulatory call."[58] To be sure, there were instances of Republican presidents (i.e., Richard Nixon, Ronald Reagan, and George W. Bush) taking up initially very friendly approach toward Taipei though soon switching toward patching up with Beijing due to pragmatic considerations. However, none could compare with the historic 12-minute direct phone conversations made between Trump and Tsai.

In any event, it is too early to judge whether there will be any fundamental shifts in America's Taiwan Strait policy, especially when Trump's positions are not entirely in line with the Republican Party foreign policy establishment and he has sent many mixed or inconsistent signals on whether America would continue Obama's Asia pivot policy. He opposed the TPP (and, in fact, officially withdrew from it on January 23, 2017) and stressed that traditional US allies like Japan and South Korea should assume greater military and financial responsibilities in defending their own national security—even leaving open the option that these two countries should acquire nuclear weapons themselves.[59] (To be sure, a nuclearized Japan or South Korea would not be in the interests of America or other Asian countries and would certainly escalate tensions and exacerbate the security dilemma.) Nevertheless, Japan's Shinzo Abe was actually the first foreign leader Trump met shortly after his election victory.

---

[58] "Donald Trump Thrusts Taiwan back on the Table, Rattling a Region," *The New York Times* (December 3, 2016), http://www.nytimes.com/2016/12/03/us/politics/donald-trump-taiwan-china.html?hp&action=click&pgtype=Homepage&clickSource=story-heading&module=a-lede-package-region&region=top-news&WT.nav=top-news.

[59] "Donald Trump's Victory Promises to Upend the International Order," *The New York Times* (Nov 9, 2016), http://www.nytimes.com/2016/11/09/world/donald-trumps-victory-promises-to-upend-the-international-order.html?action=click&pgtype=Homepage&clickSource=story-heading&module=span-abc-region&region=span-abc-region&WT.nav=span-abc-region.

On China, the president has concentrated primarily on criticizing the latter's trade and currency policies and how he would retaliate economically by raising tariffs on Chinese imports to America.[60] His national security strategy has called for strengthening US naval power to counter Beijing's behaviors in the South China Sea. The Trump administration suggested it would not allow China access to islands it has built in the South China Sea, implying a potential military confrontation with the PRC since the latter is unlikely to renounce its claims and island control in these waters. Yet, the new government did not elaborate much detail on how such blockade would be implemented.[61] When stepping up criticisms of China and defended his call with Taiwan, Trump as well consulted frequently with Henry Kissinger (the key engineer who shaped, with President Nixon, America's current "one-China" policy) and selected Terry Branstad, the Iowa governor and a long-time friend of Chinese president Xi Jinping, as the administration's ambassador to the PRC.[62] Thus, it is difficult to assess how President Trump would exactly shore up support for Taiwan and combat the PRC while planning to alter America's economic and security relations with the Asia-Pacific and displaying both pro-China and anti-China behaviors and rhetoric.

President Donald Trump's unconventional policymaking style would probably let allies, partners, and adversaries to continue guessing how the United States would actually respond in foreign policy crises and contingencies. Moreover, Trump's foreign policy belief, rooted, to some extent, in the Jacksonian nationalism, sees defending and protecting America's national interests as the priority. Military interventions, alliance commitments, and economic agreements are necessary as long as they enhance US security and prosperity and repel external threats. The promotion of democratic governance abroad or nation-building, however, does not

[60] "What Donald Trump's 'America First' Vision of the World Looks Like," *CBSNEWS* (March 26, 2016), http://www.cbsnews.com/news/donald-trump-america-first-vision-world-election-2016/.

[61] "Is Trump Ready for War in the South China Sea, or Is His Team Just Not Being Clear?" *Washington Post* (January 24, 2017), https://www.washingtonpost.com/news/world-views/wp/2017/01/24/is-trump-ready-for-war-in-the-south-china-sea-or-is-his-team-just-not-being-clear/?utm_term=.c81a31b83ef5.

[62] "Kissinger Says Impressed by China's 'Calm' Reaction to Trump's Taiwan Call," *Reuters* (December 5, 2016), http://www.reuters.com/article/us-usa-trump-china-kissinger-idUSKBN13U2XU?il=0; "Terry Branstad, Iowa Governor, Is Trump's Pick as Chinese Ambassador," *The New York Times* (December 7, 2016), http://www.nytimes.com/2016/12/07/us/politics/terry-branstad-china-ambassador-trump.html.

resonate with such "America first" orientation.⁶³ Essentially, American democratic experience is unique and exceptional, but it is not particularly relevant to other countries. "We do not seek to impose our way of life on anyone," Trump posited, "but rather to let it shine as an example for everyone to follow."⁶⁴ For Jacksonians, then, the liberal international order that the Wilsonians want to build is a "moral impossibility, even a moral monstrosity."⁶⁵ Given this logic, the liberal rationale underpinning Washington's constructive engagement of mainland China may no longer stand. As a result, the US treatment of Taiwan may become less sensitive to or constrained by the normative need in preserving Chinese national unity, territorial integrity, and fostering its eventual open-door democratization (see discussion in Chap. 5).

This author believes, nonetheless, that the Trump administration would continue to follow America's long-standing Taiwan Strait policy, particularly strategic ambiguity, as described in Chap. 5, is an appropriate response to tackling the complex and delicate balance between Beijing and Taipei. America's national interests require peace and stability across the strait. Indeed, foreign policymaking is usually made with the national interests in mind. Having stable and constructive ties with China is certainly in Washington's national security and economic interests. Though personal inclinations and domestic lobbying interests may inevitably weigh in, national security considerations ultimately prevail in decision-making.⁶⁶

Of course, as this book suggests, with US–China security and economic rivalry heightening in the twenty-first century, Washington would step up pressure on Beijing to constrain the latter's growing assertiveness by using the Taiwan issue as leverage to that effect. Under such international political dynamics, the DPP government's more hostile China policy (as opposed to the more friendly ones of the KMT) would be more palatable

---

⁶³Walter R. Mead, "Donald Trump's Jacksonian Revolt," The Hudson Institute (November 13, 2016), http://www.hudson.org/research/13010-donald-trump-s-jacksonian-revolt. For more in-depth discussion on the Jacksonian foreign policy tradition, see Walter R. Mead, *Special Providence* (New York: Routledge, 2002), Ch. 7; Henry Nau, *Conservative Internationalism* (Princeton, NJ: Princeton University Press, 2015), pp. 42–46.

⁶⁴"With Echoes of the 30s, Trump Resurrects a Hard-Line Vision of 'America First'" *The New York Times* (January 20, 2017), https://www.nytimes.com/2017/01/20/us/politics/trump-resurrects-dark-definition-of-america-first-vision.html.

⁶⁵Mead, *Special Providence*, p. 245.

⁶⁶"Bob Dole Worked behind the Scenes on Trump-Taiwan Call," *The New York Times* (December 6, 2016), http://www.nytimes.com/2016/12/06/us/politics/bob-dole-taiwan-lobby-trump.html.

to American interests. In addition to having a less upbeat attitude about the "1992 consensus," taking President Tsai's call could be interpreted as America's calculated moves to raise Chinese hackles and to get the PRC's greater compliance with US interests. In an interview with the Fox News, Trump said, "I don't know why we have to be bound by a 'one-China' policy unless we make a deal with China having to do with other things, including trade." He also complained that China has been "building a massive fortress in the middle of the South China Sea, which they shouldn't be doing, and frankly with not helping us at all with North Korea's nuclear weapons."[67] Nonetheless, that does not mean the Trump administration would really revamp the "one-China" policy, which has been the cornerstone of Sino-American relations since 1979. The *Economist* opined that "there are lots of excellent reasons why America should deepen its relations with Taiwan, the raucous, friendly, and dynamic island of 25 million people that shows that democracy and Chinese can coexist." However, in light of China's growing power and the CCP's deeply indoctrinating nationalist education to insist on national territorial integrity, America's recognition of Taiwan as an independent sovereign state would mean war and "setting up Taiwan for a fall." The "one-China fiction" is, at the same time, a "life-saving one," because "there is no chance that, if forced to choose between peaceful relations with China and friendship with Taiwan, any American president would choose Taiwan."[68]

Thus, at his confirmation hearing before the Senate Foreign Relations Committee in early January 2017, the new Secretary of State Rex Tillerson said that he "doesn't know of any plans to alter the one-China policy." Navarro posited that while supporting Taiwan, the United States would not "unnecessarily poke" Beijing, meaning that "America should never refer to Taiwan as a 'nation' or 'country'—even as they should recognize it as a 'democracy' and 'political entity.'"[69] Mike Pence, Trump's vice president, stressed the phone conversation was merely a "courtesy call" and not "a discussion about policy." He likened the uproar about the call to a "tempest in a teapot" and suggested it was not intended to show a

---

[67] "Trump Says U.S. Not Necessarily Bound by 'One China' Policy," *Reuters* (December 11, 2016), http://www.reuters.com/article/us-usa-trump-china-idUSKBN1400TY?il=0.

[68] "How to Read Donald Trump's Call with Taiwan's President," *The Economist* (December 4, 2016), http://www.economist.com/blogs/democracyinamerica/2016/12/us-china-relations?spc=scode&spv=xm&ah=9d7f7ab945510a56fa6d37c30b6f1709.

[69] Navarro, "America Can't Dump Taiwan."

shift in US China policy.⁷⁰ Trump's transition team also noted that the "president-elect is fully aware of the 'one-China' policy" and "is not out there making policy or policy prescriptions."⁷¹ Still, short of impinging on the "one-China" policy framework, the American government is likely to make more pronounced adjustments to deepen economic and military exchanges⁷² with Taipei and emphasize on Taiwan's vibrant democratic status. The Trump team has been unapologetic about its referral of Tsai Ing-wen as "president of Taiwan"—a "reality that is obvious to average Americans, Taiwanese, and Chinese, but something diplomats like to pretend isn't so."⁷³ Pence contended that "it's striking to me that President Obama would reach out to a murderous dictator in Cuba and be hailed as a hero. And, President-Elect Donald Trump takes a courtesy call from the democratically elected president of Taiwan and it becomes something of a thing in the media."⁷⁴

More uncertainties, however, still abound. China's political transition will commence as well in late 2017 with the opening of the 19th CCP Party Congress. Although President Xi Jinping would stay on as the party general secretary for another five-year term, many of the Communist Party's all-powerful Politburo Standing Committee members will retire due to age requirements, leading to political struggle among the elitist and populist factions within the CCP.⁷⁵ Xi, who recently elevated as the CCP "core leader"⁷⁶—an unusual esteemed title accorded to only Mao Zedong, Deng Xiaoping, and Jiang Zemin—may be inclined to further

---

[70] "Pence Downplays Significance of Trump's Call with Taiwan President," *Reuters* (December 4, 2016), http://www.reuters.com/article/us-usa-trump-idUSKBN13T0SQ.

[71] "Conway: Trump's Talk with Taiwan Leader 'Just a Call,' Not a Policy Shift," *Fox News* (December 4, 2016), http://www.foxnews.com/politics/2016/12/04/conway-trumps-talk-with-taiwan-leader-just-call-not-sign-policy-shift.html.

[72] "Ministry Welcomes Bill for Taiwan-U.S. Military Exchanges," *The Taipei Times* (Dec 4, 2016), http://www.taipeitimes.com/News/taiwan/archives/2016/12/02/2003660417.

[73] Stephen Yates and Christian Whiton, "Why Trump Was Right to Talk with Taiwan's President," *Fox News* (December 4, 2016), http://www.foxnews.com/opinion/2016/12/04/why-trump-was-right-to-talk-with-taiwans-president.html.

[74] "Mike Pence Defends Trump's Controversial Chat with Taiwan's Leader," *Business Insider* (December 4, 2016), http://www.businessinsider.com/mike-pence-taiwan-china-trump-call-2016-12.

[75] Li Cheng, *Chinese Politics in the Xi Jinping Era* (Washington DC: Brookings Institute, 2016).

[76] "Xi Jinping May be 'Core Leader' of China, but He's Really Nervous," *The New York Times* (November 1, 2016), accessible at: http://www.nytimes.com/2016/11/02/world/asia/xi-jinping-core-leader-china.html.

consolidating his power by breaking from the institutionalized succession (term-limit) and collective leadership precedents established in the post-Mao era to serve beyond two terms after 2022.[77] Meanwhile, Beijing must confront various domestic problems and challenges, including managing economic slowdown, curbing financial debt problems, fighting official corruptions, reforming inefficient state-owned enterprises, and addressing social discontents and unrests, to name just a few. Internal vulnerabilities and political uncertainties could prompt Beijing to assume even harsher (and more nationalistic) position toward Taiwan, particularly when Tsai continues to reject the "1992 consensus." In his meeting with the KMT-chairwoman, Hung Hsiu-chu in November 2016, Xi Jinping maintained that the CCP would be "overthrown" by the 1.3 billion Chinese people if Taiwan's push for independence is left unrestrained, indicating how the unification issue is nonnegotiable and tied seriously to the regime stability and ruling legitimacy of the Communist Party.[78] Trump's suggestion that the "one-China" policy may serve as a quid pro quo in dealing with Beijing has added greater vagaries to the already fragile cross-strait equilibrium. The DPP administration has welcomed the new Republican president's supportive remarks on Taiwan even though Taipei has downplayed its elation to refrain from incurring Beijing's wrath. Nonetheless, emboldened, Taipei could take up more anti-China policy stances if it believes that Washington would ultimately back up Taiwan independence. Misperception and miscalculation due to such moral-hazard problem could plunge the Taiwan Strait into grave danger. Making Taiwan a transactional ploy, however, is not entirely good news for Taipei. It implies that if Washington and Beijing strike a favorable "deal" on other major economic and security issues, Taiwan could be sacrificed.

Adding to the unpleasant mix would be Beijing's interpretations of Trump's China policy. His dangling of the "one-China" policy as a bargaining chip could undermine the PRC's confidence in Washington's neutral arbiter role in the Taiwan Strait impasse. "Mixing trade with an issue seen by Beijing as involving sovereignty is likely to produce an angry

---

[77] "Xi Jinping May Delay Picking China's Next Leader, Stoking Speculation," *The New York Times* (October 4, 2016), accessible at: http://www.nytimes.com/2016/10/05/world/asia/china-president-xi-jinping-successor.html.

[78] "Xi Jinping Warns Communist Party Would be 'Overthrown' If Taiwan's Independence Push Left Unchecked." *South China Morning Post* (November 4, 2016), accessible at: http://www.scmp.com/news/china/policies-politics/article/2042784/xi-jinping-warns-communist-party-would-be-overthrown-if

Chinese backlash and worsen both issues," said Jeffrey Bader.[79] And, more importantly, if the CCP authority views that Trump would genuinely uproot the "one-China" policy and that the window of opportunity on resolving the Taiwan issue is closing, military actions could be initiated. Even if China may not prevail ultimately (as the US and Japanese forces intervene timely to assist Taiwanese military to effectively deny and repeal the Chinese offenses), enough damages would have been inflicted to harm Taiwan and destabilize regional peace and security. The costs for US national interests would be high. Christensen stated, "While responsible Chinese elites might view the Chinese military as weaker than the United States, and their strategic writings suggest that they almost universally do, they might still be emboldened by certain new coercive capabilities under development. This is particularly true if they believe that the issues at stake matter more to China than to the United States. Chinese leaders might believe they have greater resolve regarding sovereignty disputes, for example, even if their military is not as powerful as that of the United States."[80] The PRC has stepped up coercive diplomacy toward Taiwan shortly after Trump's controversial remarks on the "one-China" policy. Its military aircraft flew over the East China Sea and circled the international airspace around Taiwan.[81] As well, in late December, in what Beijing called routine exercises, China's first and only aircraft carrier and a fleet of warships sailed past Taiwan's south, prompting Taipei to deploy fighter jets to monitor the fleet.[82] Furthermore, the Chinese government has repeatedly warned the new Trump White House against reneging on the "one-China" policy, threatening serious repercussions would result to damage Sino-American relations.[83]

---

[79] "Trump Suggests Using Bedrock China Policy as Bargaining Chip," *The New York Times* (December 11, 2016), http://www.nytimes.com/2016/12/11/us/politics/trump-taiwan-one-china.html?hp&action=click&pgtype=Homepage&clickSource=story-heading&module=first-column-region&region=top-news&WT.nav=top-news&_r=0.

[80] Christensen, *The China Challenge*, pp. 96–97.

[81] "Chinese Aircraft Fly around Taiwan," *Taipei Times* (December 11, 2016), http://www.taipeitimes.com/News/front/archives/2016/12/11/2003660975.

[82] "Taiwan's President Heads to U.S., but Won't Meet with Trump," *Fox News* (January 7, 2017), http://www.foxnews.com/us/2017/01/07/taiwans-president-heads-to-us-but-wont-meet-with-trump.html.

[83] "Chinese State Tabloid Warns Trump, End One China Policy and China Will Take Revenge," *Reuters* (January 9, 2017), http://www.reuters.com/article/us-china-usa-taiwan-idUSKBN14T02Q.

In essence, an important tenet of America's strategic ambiguity policy is to reassure both Taipei and Beijing that Washington would not implement policies compromising either party's security position, but doing so without overly committing to either side's cause in order to discourage rash unilateralist behaviors. America is surely right to defend Taiwan's freedom and democracy from Beijing's authoritarianism and military coercion. Yet, it should do so neither by giving Taipei false hope nor implying that American support for Taiwan could be exchanged or traded away for another US interest. In December 2016, President Obama urged the incoming Trump administration to seriously "think through what the consequences are" for "upending" the "one-China" policy. "For China," he said, "the issue of Taiwan is as important as anything on their docket. ... The idea of one China is at the heart of their conception as a nation. ... The Chinese will not treat that the way they'll treat some other issues. They won't even treat it the way they treat issues around the South China Sea where we've had a lot of tensions." Moreover, "that [cross-strait] status quo, although not completely satisfactory to any of the parties involved, has kept the peace and allowed the Taiwanese to be a pretty successful…economy and a people who have a high degree of self-determination."[84]

On the eve of Trump's inauguration, Tsai Ing-wen embarked on a trip to reinforce diplomatic relations with Taiwan's allies in Central America. (Beijing just resumed ties with Sao Tome and Principe which broke relations with Taipei in late December 2016, and Taiwan's few remaining allies, mostly in Latin America and the Caribbean, may be tempted to switch to the PRC eventually.) Tsai made transit stops in the United States, in accordance with past protocols, but the Trump team official made it clear that neither Trump himself nor his transition officials would be meeting with the Taiwan leader while she stopped over in Houston and San Francisco. While this could be seen as Trump's returning to the "one-China" trajectory, Tsai still met with Republican heavyweights including Senator Ted Cruz and had a phone conversation with Senator John McCain. Despite Beijing's pressure, Cruz bluntly refused to allow Beijing to "set the terms of meetings between officials from the United States and

---

[84] "Obama Says Change in U.S. Policy toward Taiwan Would Have Consequences with China," *Reuters* (December 16, 2016), http://www.reuters.com/article/us-usa-obama-china-idUSKBN1452PL.

Taiwan."[85] In light of the Grand Old Party (GOP)'s total control of both the executive and legislative branches after the 2016 elections, the Tsai administration seized the opportunity to deepen ties with top echelon of the Republican Party. Such helped to raise Taiwan's international profile and harden relations between Taipei and Washington.

The Taiwan Strait is once again heading toward great quandary and, perhaps, turbulence, except this time, unlike the Chen Shui-bian years, Sino-American relations are becoming more competitive and volatile, Taiwan is drifting further away from mainland China, and that the PRC is more unyielding on many national security interests. All actors involved in this delicate balance must tread carefully.

REFERENCES

Chen, Dean. 2015. Security, Domestic Divisions, and the KMT's Post-2008 'One China' Policy: A Neoclassical Realist Analysis. *International Relations of the Asia-Pacific* 15(2): 319–365.

Christensen, Thomas. 2015. *The China Challenge*. New York: W. W. Norton.

deLisle, Jacques. 2014. Taiwan and Soft Power. In *Political Changes in Taiwan under Ma Ying-jeou*, ed. Jean-Pierre Cabestan and Jacques deLisle, 265–295. New York: Routledge.

Economy, Elizabeth. 2014. China's Imperial President. *Foreign Affairs* 93(6): 80–91.

Li, Cheng. 2016. *Chinese Politics in the Xi Jinping Era*. Washington, DC: Brookings Institute.

McDougall, Derek. 2012. Responses to 'Rising China' in the East Asian Regions: Soft Balancing with Accommodation. *Journal of Contemporary China* 21(73): 1–17.

Mead, Walter R. 2002. *Special Providence*. New York: Routledge.

Morgenthau, Hans. 1985. *Politics among Nations*. New York: McGraw Hill.

Nau, Henry. 2015. *Conservative Internationalism*. Princeton: Princeton University Press.

Pape, Robert. 2005. Soft Balancing against the United States. *International Security* 30(1): 7–45.

Rigger, Shelley. 2011. *Why Taiwan Matters*. Lanham: Rowman & Littlefield.

---

[85] "Taiwan's President Meets with Ted Cruz in the U.S., and China Objects," *The New York Times* (January 9, 2017), http://www.nytimes.com/2017/01/09/world/asia/taiwan-ted-cruz-china.html?ribbon-ad-idx=5&rref=world/asia&module=Ribbon&version=context&region=Header&action=click&contentCollection=Asia%20Pacific&pgtype=article.

Schweller, Randall. 1999. Managing the Rise of Great Powers: History and Theory. In *Engaging China*, ed. Alastair Iain Johnston and Robert Ross, 1–31. New York: Routledge.

Sutter, Robert. 2013. *U.S.-Chinese Relations*. Lanham: Rowman & Littlefield.

Wu, Yu-shan. 2016. Heading Towards Troubled Waters? The Impact of Taiwan's 2016 Elections on Cross-Strait Relations. *American Journal of Chinese Studies* 23(1): 59–76.

Author's Interviews

Interview with Robert Sutter, Professor of Practice of International Affairs at the Elliot School of International Affairs, George Washington University, February 24, 2016 at Washington DC, USA.

Interview with Richard Bush, Director for the Center for East Asia Policy Studies at the Brookings Institute, February 25, 2016 at Washington DC, USA. He was Chairman of the Board and Managing Director of theAIT, from 1997 to 2002.

Interview with Douglas Paal, Vice President for Studies and Director of the Asia Program at the Carnegie Endowment for International Peace, March 16, 2016 at Washington DC, USA. He previously served as the Director of the AIT, from 2002 to 2006.

Interview with a high authority from the Tsai Ing-wen administration responsible for handling cross-strait policy, July 26, 2016, Taipei, Taiwan. The interviewee requested to remain anonymous.

Interview with Chou Chih-wei, July 28, 2016, Taipei, Taiwan. Chou was the Chairperson of the KMT's Culture and Communications Committee from April 2016 to October 2016.

Index

A
Acheson, Dean, 28, 29n117
AIIB. *See* Asian Infrastructure Investment Bank (AIIB)
AIT. *See* American Institute in Taiwan (AIT)
American Institute in Taiwan (AIT), 4n9, 10n38, 11, 15, 148, 166, 166n123, 182, 183, 183n23
Anti-Secession Law, 74, 104, 105
ARATS. *See* Association for Relations across the Taiwan Strait (ARATS)
Asian Infrastructure Investment Bank (AIIB), 6, 165, 178, 178–9n8
Association for Relations across the Taiwan Strait (ARATS), 110n38, 139

B
Burghardt, Raymond, 183, 183n23
  interview with the Voice of America, 182
Bush, George. W, 46
  relations with Taiwan, 12, 85, 86, 104, 137, 148

C
Cairo Declaration, 118, 119, 119n78
Campbell, Kurt, 64n75, 75n18, 138, 139n5, 141n18
Carter, Ashton, 17, 17n67
CCP. *See* Chinese Communist Party (CCP)
Chen Shui-bian, vi, ix, 12, 14, 31, 32, 34, 36, 41, 48–51, 51n39, 52n44, 52n46, 53, 54, 56, 59, 62, 64, 70, 77, 82, 85, 105n15, 110, 111, 115, 139n6, 167, 174, 189, 191, 201
  relations with the United States, 48, 57, 104, 148
Chiang Ching-kuo, 36, 51, 60, 75, 78, 80, 108, 111, 115
Chiang Kai-shek, 1, 1n1, 28, 36, 60, 75, 78, 90, 108, 111, 115, 118, 119, 160, 182, 188
Chinese civil war, ix, 28, 36, 78, 116
Chinese Communist Party (CCP), viii, x, 1, 1n1, 2–10, 15, 16, 24, 32–6, 70–3, 75, 76, 78–80, 83, 85n49, 86, 89, 90, 93, 94, 97, 101, 103, 110, 110n41, 111, 119, 124,

131, 144, 146, 160, 162, 165, 166, 178, 186, 196–9
civic national identity, 24, 53, 101
Clinton, Bill, 74
three nos, 12
Clinton, Hillary, 158, 191, 191n54, 192n55
China policy, 192
Taiwan strait policy, 191, 198
U.S. presidential election 2016, 188
constructivism, 76–8
Cross-Straits Agreement on Trade in Services, 128, 128n114

D

Definition of One China Resolution, 80, 109
Democratic Progressive Party (DPP), vi, vii, ix, x, xi, 4–6, 7–8n27, 9, 10, 12, 14, 17, 18, 25, 26, 31, 32, 34–7, 41–3, 50, 51, 59–64, 70, 71, 73, 76, 77, 82, 85, 94, 96, 97, 101, 105n15, 106–11, 113, 114, 115n63, 116, 118, 121–31, 145, 146, 148, 149, 154n64, 163, 166–8, 173, 175, 180–4, 187–9, 191, 195, 198
Deng Xiaoping, 2, 71, 71n4, 79, 79n28, 80n29, 197
de-Sinification, ix, 12, 13, 35, 36, 51, 111, 116, 188
DPP. *See* Democratic Progressive Party (DPP)
Dulles, John Foster, 29, 29n118
Duterte, Rodrigo
relations with China, 179, 180

E

Economic Cooperation Framework Agreement (ECFA), 57, 112, 128n114, 129

EEZ. *See* exclusive economic zone (EEZ)
Eleven-Dashed Line, x, 15, 160, 161, 181
Eric Chu, 5, 7, 9, 145, 146n37, 164
meeting with Xi Jinping, 165, 165n114
Taiwan presidential election 2016, 4
exclusive economic zone (EEZ), 15, 16, 157, 179

F

freedom of navigation operations (FONOPS), 14

H

history textbook "fine-tuning" or reform, 145
Hong Kong
meeting of 1992, 82, 110
umbrella Movements 2014, 102
Hu Jintao
Hu-Lien meeting 2005, 32
peaceful development, 72, 72n9, 74, 85n49, 91, 93
relations with Taiwan, 32, 73, 85, 91, 93, 106, 111, 137
Hung Hsiu-chu, 5, 116, 145, 198

J

Jiang Zemin, 12, 73, 82, 83, 83n39, 85n48, 85n49, 197

K

Kissinger, Henry, 29, 30, 30n125, 194, 194n62
Koo Chen-fu, 81, 110, 183

Kuomintang, or Nationalist Party (KMT)
  authoritarianism and Taiwan, 26, 27, 75, 102, 116
  mainstream faction, 108
  nativists faction, 108
  relations with the CCP, 36, 50, 61, 113, 137, 146, 181

L

Lee Teng-hui, ix, 12, 32, 36, 48, 51, 53, 60, 70, 77, 81, 82, 108, 111, 114
Legislative Yuan, 4, 9, 31, 42, 88, 102, 108, 129, 131n122, 145, 187, 188
Liberal Democratic Party (LDP), 149
Lien Chan, 32, 52n46, 85n49, 91, 108, 110

M

Mainland Affairs Council (MAC)7, 7–8n28, 9n33, 73, 80, 80n31, 82, 92, 93, 93n78, 93n79, 96, 104n13, 106n23, 109n37, 110n40, 111n43, 111n46, 112n53, 123, 123n100, 124n101, 127, 127n108, 128n111, 129, 130, 130n119, 154n61, 176–8, 181, 181n19
Mao Zedong, 1, 1n1, 2n4, 78, 89, 197
Ma Ying-jeou, v, 1, 3n7, 6, 7n24, 9n33, 10, 14, 17, 18, 31, 34–6, 41, 42, 49, 54–63, 69, 71, 74, 87, 89, 101–21, 129, 131n122, 137, 140–2, 145, 145n31, 148, 153, 160, 162, 165, 167, 173, 174, 176–8, 182–4

N

name rectification, 52
naming China, 34, 36, 103
Nanjing, ROC capital City, 27, 92, 93, 93n79, 115, 116, 160
nationalism, x, 9, 13, 18, 21, 22, 24, 28, 60, 75, 101, 102, 107, 123, 131, 178–9n8, 186, 190, 194
nation-building, ix, 18, 22–6, 33, 34, 59–61, 71, 97, 101, 102, 113, 114, 132, 188, 189, 194
  mechanisms of nation-building, 24, 36
nativization, ix. *See also* Taiwanization
neoclassical realism, 33–5, 41–64, 76–8, 132
new one China syllogism, 73
New Power Party (NPP), 188
Nine-Dashed Line, x, 15, 16, 155–64, 179, 181
1992 consensus
  interpretations, viii, 6, 7, 32, 35, 55, 62, 64, 69, 73, 76, 85, 86, 91, 108, 110, 121, 169, 173, 176
  origins, ix, 6, 15, 35, 71
1992 Talks, ix, 174, 177, 187
Nixon, Richard, 29, 193, 194

O

Obama, Barack
  policy towards Taiwan, 95
  relations with China, 148, 165
  relations with Japan, 152
OCRI. *See* one China, respective interpretations (OCRI)
old one China syllogism, 73
one China policy, vii, xi, 62, 74, 84, 141, 147–67, 186, 193, 194, 196–200

one China principle, viii, ix, 3, 5, 6, 6n20, 7–8n27, 29, 35, 37, 70, 71, 73, 74, 76, 77, 80, 83, 83n42, 84, 85, 88, 90n69, 92, 93, 95, 97, 123, 131, 143, 143n27, 155, 185, 187, 188
one China, respective interpretations (OCRI), viii, 6, 7, 32, 55, 64, 69–71, 73, 76–8, 81, 82, 85, 86, 97, 108, 109n38, 110, 112, 121, 137n1, 166, 173, 176
one country, two systems, 2, 52, 71, 73, 77, 79, 82, 83, 111
one ROC, two areas, 88, 109, 111
   Ma Ying-jeou inauguration 2012, 55, 175

P
PCA. *See* Permanent Court of Arbitration (PCA)
People's First Party (PFP), 32, 52, 107
People's Republic of China (PRC), v–xi, 1–4, 6, 7–8n27, 9–18, 26–37, 50, 52n46, 54–8, 60, 62, 64, 69–73, 75–80, 80n31, 82–4, 86, 87, 89–91, 93, 95–7, 102, 104, 106, 109n37, 109n38, 110–12, 112n50, 113, 114, 119, 121–4, 127, 128, 128n111, 130–2, 137–9, 141, 142n20, 143, 144, 147, 150, 151, 153, 154n65, 155, 157, 160, 162, 164, 175, 179–81, 183–6, 186n33, 187, 189–92, 194, 196, 198–201
Permanent Court of Arbitration (PCA), 15, 16, 162, 179–81
PFP. *See* People's First Party (PFP)
PRC. *See* People's Republic of China (PRC)

Q
Qian Qichen, 73, 84, 85n48

R
Reagan, Ronald, vii, 143, 143n27, 163, 192, 193
   Six Assurances, vii, 143, 143n27, 163, 192
Republic of China (ROC), Taiwan, v, vii–x, 1, 6–9, 15, 16n65, 18, 24, 27, 31, 32, 34–6, 49, 51, 52, 52n46, 54, 55, 59, 60, 62–4, 69–71, 73–6, 78–82, 84–97, 101–32, 138, 144, 154, 154n61, 160, 162–4, 166, 168, 173–8, 181, 181n18, 182–4, 187–91
   ROC constitutional framework, 176, 177
Resolution on Taiwan's Future, 1999, 122
ROC. *See* Republic of China (ROC), Taiwan
Rusk, Dean, 29, 29n119
Russel, Daniel, 17, 147, 147n38, 164, 164n111, 167, 167n125

S
second image reversed, x, 18–22, 147, 147n39
SEF. *See* Strait Exchange Foundation (SEF)
Senkaku Islands or Diaoyu Islands, 151, 151n53, 153, 154, 154n65, 154n65, 155, 158n85, 161n99
Shanghai Communiqué, 29, 29n123
Shinzo Abe, 149–53, 155n69, 193
Sino–Japanese relations, 149–53
   War of Resistance against Japan, Second World War, 117–20
Soong, James, 32, 52–3n46, 107
South China Sea
   China's island reclamations, x
   contentions between China and Southeast Asian Nations, 156
Strait Exchange Foundation (SEF), 80, 80n31, 81, 82, 92, 96, 109,

109–10n38, 110, 112, 121, 128n114, 139, 173, 174
Strategic Ambiguity, viii, xi, 10–14, 36, 37, 56, 137–69, 183, 195, 200
U.S. policy towards the Taiwan Strait, 11, 55, 139, 143n27
Sunflower movements, 88, 129
Sun Yat-sen, 89, 90, 93, 93n79, 108, 118, 128n113, 188

T
Taiping (Itu Aba) island, 15, 15n61, 16, 16n62, 177, 181, 181n15
Taiwan Affairs Office (TAO), 3, 80, 84, 87, 88, 92, 93, 95, 96, 109n37
Taiwan Independence Clause, 1991, 122
Taiwanization, ix, 13, 36, 51, 53n47, 123, 127
Taiwan Relations Act (TRA), vii, viii, 104, 105, 141, 143, 143n27, 163, 186, 191–3
Taiwan Strait crisis, 1995–96, 12, 46, 82, 83, 85
TAO. *See* Taiwan Affairs Office (TAO)
Thornton, Susan, 142, 166, 167n126
three Sino–U.S. communiqués, 104, 141, 143, 143n27
TPP. *See* Trans-Pacific Partnership (TPP)
TRA. *See* Taiwan Relations Act (TRA)
Trans-Pacific Partnership (TPP), 151, 163, 193
Truman, Harry, 1, 28, 45
Tsai Ing-wen
  inauguration address, May 2016, 177, 178
  relations with China, 148
  Taiwan presidential election 2016, 4, 122, 146, 148, 173
two-states theory, 12, 52, 77, 82

U
UNCLOS. *See* United Nations Convention on the Law of the Seas (UNCLOS)
under-balancing, v, 18, 36, 56–61, 63
United Nations Convention on the Law of the Seas (UNCLOS), 15, 157–8, 160–2, 179, 181
U.S.–Japan Military Defense Guidelines (MDGs)
  Article 9 of Japan's constitution, reinterpretation under Abe, 150
  collective self-defense, 150–2
U.S.–Japan Security Treaty, Article 5, 151, 151n53
U.S. Pivot to Asia, vin3, 14n54, 178
U.S. rebalancing to Asia, 37, 64, 142

W
Wang Daohan, 73, 81, 84, 110, 183
Wang Jin-pyng, 108, 131n122
Wang Yu-chi, 92, 93n79, 109n37

X
Xi Jinping
  19th Party Congress, 197
  One Road, One Belt (New Silk Road), 6
  rejuvenation of Chinese dream, 8, 75, 178
  Xi-Ma Summit, November 2015, 1, 145, 176

Z
Zhang Zhijun, 3, 92, 94n81, 95, 109n37

GPSR Compliance

The European Union's (EU) General Product Safety Regulation (GPSR) is a set of rules that requires consumer products to be safe and our obligations to ensure this.

If you have any concerns about our products, you can contact us on

ProductSafety@springernature.com

In case Publisher is established outside the EU, the EU authorized representative is:

Springer Nature Customer Service Center GmbH
Europaplatz 3
69115 Heidelberg, Germany